First World War
and Army of Occupation
War Diary
France, Belgium and Germany

19 DIVISION
Divisional Troops
36 Sanitary Section
19 July 1915 - 31 March 1917

WO95/2073/3

The Naval & Military Press Ltd
www.nmarchive.com
Published in association with The National Archives

Published by

The Naval & Military Press Ltd

Unit 10 Ridgewood Industrial Park,
Uckfield, East Sussex,
TN22 5QE England
Tel: +44 (0) 1825 749494

www.naval-military-press.com
www.nmarchive.com

This diary has been reprinted in facsimile from the original. Any imperfections are inevitably reproduced and the quality may fall short of modern type and cartographic standards.

© Crown Copyright
Images reproduced by permission of The National Archives, London, England, 2015.

Contents

Document type	Place/Title	Date From	Date To
Heading	WO95/2073/3 19 Divn. 36 Sanitary Section 1915 July-1917 March		
Heading	19th Division No 36 19th Divl. Sanitary Section Jly 1915-1917 Mar		
Heading	19 Div 36 San Sect.		
Heading	19th Division 19th Divisional Sanitary Section No 36 Many Section Vol I		
Heading	War Diary of 19th Divisional Sanitary Section. from 19th July to 31st July 1915		
War Diary	Salisbury	19/07/1915	19/07/1915
War Diary	Havre	20/07/1915	21/07/1915
War Diary	Tilques Near Stomer	22/07/1915	22/07/1915
War Diary	Tilques	23/07/1915	27/07/1915
War Diary	Busnes	28/07/1915	29/07/1915
War Diary	Busnes And St Venant	30/07/1915	30/07/1915
War Diary	St Venant And Merville	31/07/1915	31/07/1915
Heading	19th Division 36th Sanitary Section 19th Divl Sanitary Section Vol II from 1-31.8.15 August 1915		
Heading	War Diary Of Sanitary Section 36 attached XIX Division from 1st August 1915 to 31st August 1915 Volume 2		
War Diary	Merville	01/08/1915	30/08/1915
War Diary	Merville and Lacon	31/08/1915	31/08/1915
Heading	19th Division 19th Div Sanitary Section Vol III Sept 1.15		
Heading	War Diary Of 19th Divisional Sanitary Section From September 1st To September 30th Volume 3		
War Diary	Locon	01/09/1915	30/09/1915
Heading	19th Divl Sanitary Section (No 36) Vol 4 Oct 15		
Heading	War Diary of Sanitary Section 36 attached XIX Division from October 1st 1915 to October 31st 1915 Volume 4		
War Diary	Locon	01/10/1915	02/10/1915
War Diary	Locon And Fosse	03/10/1915	03/10/1915
War Diary	Fosse	04/10/1915	20/10/1915
War Diary	Fosse and Locon	21/10/1915	21/10/1915
War Diary	Locon	22/10/1915	31/10/1915
Heading	19th Division Sanitary Section No. Sanitary Section No. 26 19th Division Vol: 5 Nov 15		
Heading	War Diary of Sanitary Section 36 from November 1st to November 30th 1915 (Volume 5)		
War Diary	Locon	01/11/1915	24/11/1915
War Diary	Locon St Venant	25/11/1915	25/11/1915
War Diary	St Venant	26/11/1915	30/11/1915
Heading	San Sect. 36 Vol 6 December 1915		
Heading	War Diary of Sanitary Section 36 from 1st December to 31st December 1915 (Volume 6)		
War Diary	St Venant	01/12/1915	03/12/1915
War Diary	Locon	04/12/1915	07/12/1915
War Diary	Locon Lestrem	08/12/1915	08/12/1915

War Diary	Lestrem	09/12/1915	31/12/1915
War Diary	19th Division 19th Div F/258/2 San Sect. 36 Vol 7 Jan 16		
War Diary	War Diary of Sanitary Section 36 from 1st January to 31st January 1916 (Volume 7)		
War Diary	Lestrem	01/01/1916	23/01/1916
War Diary	Lestrem Sivenant	24/01/1916	24/01/1916
War Diary	St Venant	25/01/1916	30/01/1916
Heading	19th Div 36th Sanitary Section Feb Mar 1916		
Heading	San Sect 36 Vol 8		
Heading	War Diary of Sanitary Section 36 from 1st February 1916 to 29th February 1916 (Volume 8)		
War Diary	St Venant	01/02/1916	16/02/1916
War Diary	Stvenant La Gorgue	17/02/1916	17/02/1916
War Diary	Lagorgue	18/02/1916	28/02/1916
Heading	War Diary of Sanitary Section 36 from 1st March to 31st March 1916 (Vol 9)		
War Diary	La Gorgue	01/03/1916	31/03/1916
Heading	War Diary of Sanitary Section 36 from 1st April to 30th April 1916 (Vol 10)		
War Diary	Lagorgue	01/04/1916	16/04/1916
War Diary	St Venant	17/04/1916	18/04/1916
War Diary	Norrent Fontes	19/04/1916	30/04/1916
Miscellaneous	First Army Training Area	24/04/1916	24/04/1916
Miscellaneous	First Army Training Area List Of Water Supplies In And Adjacent		
Miscellaneous	36th Sanitary Section. (19th Division)	00/04/1916	00/04/1916
Miscellaneous	To The Divin 3rd Echelon		
Heading	War Diary of Sanitary Section 36 from 1st May to 31st May 1916 (Vol 11)		
War Diary	Norrent Fontes	01/05/1916	07/05/1916
War Diary	Norrent Fontes Flesselles	08/05/1916	08/05/1916
War Diary	Flesselles	09/05/1916	31/05/1916
Miscellaneous	List Of Main Water Supplies In New Area Field District.	09/05/1916	09/05/1916
Miscellaneous	List Of Main Water Supplies In New Area Field Adjucent	30/05/1916	30/05/1916
Heading	No 36 Sanitary Section June 1916		
Miscellaneous	The War 3rd Echelon	01/07/1916	01/07/1916
Heading	War Diary of Sanitary Section 36 from 1st June to 30th June 1916 (Vol 12)		
War Diary	Flesselles	01/06/1916	15/06/1916
War Diary	St Gratien	16/06/1916	30/06/1916
Miscellaneous	List of main water supplies in the forward area.	20/06/1916	20/06/1916
Miscellaneous	List of main water supplies in New Area and District.	15/06/1916	15/06/1916
Miscellaneous	A New Chlorination A Metal Poison Test Case.		
Heading	19th Division 36th Sanitary Section July 1916		
Miscellaneous	To AA & QMG 19th Divn	05/08/1916	05/08/1916
Miscellaneous	To ADMS 19th Division	01/08/1916	01/08/1916
Heading	War Diary of Sanitary Section 36 from 1st July to 31st July 1916 (Vol 13)		
War Diary	Millencourt	01/07/1916	11/07/1916
War Diary	Millencourt Henencourt	12/07/1916	12/07/1916
War Diary	Henencourt	13/07/1916	19/07/1916
War Diary	Henencourt Albert	20/07/1916	20/07/1916
War Diary	Albert	21/07/1916	30/07/1916

War Diary	Albert Baizieux	31/07/1916	31/07/1916
Miscellaneous	List of main Water supplies Baizieux and District.	30/07/1916	30/07/1916
Heading	War Diary of 19th Divisional Sanitary Section No 36 from 1st August to 31st August 1916 Vol 14		
Miscellaneous	New Water Station	18/08/1916	18/08/1916
Miscellaneous	List Of Main Water System In 19th Divisional Area.	08/08/1916	08/08/1916
War Diary	Baizieux	01/08/1916	03/08/1916
War Diary	Long	04/08/1916	08/08/1916
War Diary	Westoutre	09/08/1916	31/08/1916
Heading	War Diary of No. 36 19th Divisional Sanitary Section from 1st To 30th September 1916 Vol 15		
Miscellaneous	List of main water supplies in 19th Divisional Area.	25/09/1916	25/09/1916
War Diary	Westoutre	01/09/1916	01/09/1916
War Diary	Westoutre Locre	02/09/1916	02/09/1916
War Diary	Locre	03/09/1916	05/09/1916
War Diary	Locre Pont D'achelles	06/09/1916	07/09/1916
War Diary	Pont D'Achelles	08/09/1916	21/09/1916
War Diary	Pont D'Achelles Merris	22/09/1916	22/09/1916
War Diary	Merris	23/09/1916	30/09/1916
Heading	19th Div No. 36. Sanitary Section Oct 1916		
Heading	19th Divisional Sanitary Sector 36th from 1st to 31st October 1916 Vol 16		
War Diary	Merris	01/10/1916	06/10/1916
War Diary	Marieux	06/10/1916	06/10/1916
War Diary	Marieux Authie	07/10/1916	07/10/1916
War Diary	Authie	08/10/1916	16/10/1916
War Diary	Authie Rubempre	17/10/1916	17/10/1916
War Diary	Rubempre	18/10/1916	20/10/1916
War Diary	Rubempre Warloy	21/10/1916	21/10/1916
War Diary	Warloy	22/10/1916	22/10/1916
War Diary	Warloy and W14b9.7 (Sheet 57)	23/10/1916	23/10/1916
War Diary	W14b9.7 (Sheet 57)	24/10/1916	31/10/1916
Miscellaneous	Supplementary List Of Water Supplies in 19th Divisional area.	31/10/1916	31/10/1916
Miscellaneous	List of water supplies in Rubempre and Neighbourhood.	17/10/1916	17/10/1916
Miscellaneous	List of Main Water Supplies in 19th Division Area.	18/10/1916	18/10/1916
Heading	War Diary of No. 36 Sanitary Section 19th Divisional Sanitary Section from 1st November to 30th Nov 1916 Vol 17		
War Diary	W14b9.7 (Sheet 57d) 1/40,000	01/11/1916	01/11/1916
War Diary	W14b9.7 (Sheet 57d)	02/11/1916	22/11/1916
War Diary	Contay	23/11/1916	23/11/1916
War Diary	Doullens	24/11/1916	24/11/1916
War Diary	Bernaville	25/11/1916	30/11/1916
Miscellaneous	List of main Water Supplies in the 19th Divisional area.	26/11/1916	26/11/1916
Miscellaneous	Supplementary List of main Water Supplies in 19th Divisional Area.	28/11/1916	28/11/1916
Heading	19th Div 36th Sanitary Section Dec 1916		
Heading	War Diary of 36th Sanitary Section R.A.M.C.T from 1st December to 31st December 1916 Vol 18		
War Diary	Bernaville	01/12/1916	31/12/1916
Heading	19th Div 36th Sanitary Section Jan. 1917		
Heading	War Diary of 36th Sanitary Section R.A.M.C. (T.F) from 1st to 31st January 1917 Vol 19		
War Diary	Bernaville	01/01/1917	21/01/1917
War Diary	Bernaville Couin	22/01/1917	22/01/1917

War Diary	Couin	23/01/1917	31/01/1917
Heading	19th Div. No. 36. Sanitary Section Feb 1917		
Miscellaneous	To D.D.M.S. V Corps	01/03/1917	01/03/1917
Heading	War Diary of 36th Sanitary Section from 1st to 28th February 1917 Vol 20		
War Diary	Couin	01/02/1917	28/02/1917
Heading	19th to 31st Div 5th Army 36th Sanitary Section Mar 1917		
Heading	War Diary of 36th Sanitary Section from 1st to 31st March 1917 Vol 21		
War Diary	Couin	01/03/1917	30/03/1917
War Diary	Couin Bucquoy	31/03/1917	31/03/1917

WO 95 2073/3

19 DIVN.
36 SANITORY SECTION
1915 JULY - 1917 MARCH

19TH DIVISION

No 36

19TH DIVL. SANITARY SECTION

JLY 1915-DEC 1916

19th MAR

To · 4 ARMY

19 DIV

36 SAN SECT.

~~Box 1796~~

TO 4 ARMY

& THEN TO ITALY NOV 1917.
with 15 Corps becoming
GHQ TROOPS

19th. Baracon

121/6300

Summarised, and not copied

12y/6300

19th — 31st July 15.

19th Divisional Sanitar Section — No 36 danglotin
Vol I.

7. Dec 16

Army Form C. 2118.

WAR DIARY
or
INTELLIGENCE SUMMARY

(Erase heading not required.)

Instructions regarding War Diaries and Intelligence Summaries are contained in F. S. Regs., Part II. and the Staff Manual respectively. Title pages will be prepared in manuscript.

Hour, Date, Place	Summary of Events and Information	Remarks and references to Appendices
	Confidential War Diary of 19th Divisional Sanitary Section From 19th July to 31st July 1915 Volume 1.	

Army Form C. 2118.

WAR DIARY
or
INTELLIGENCE SUMMARY
(Erase heading not required.)

Instructions regarding War Diaries and Intelligence Summaries are contained in F. S. Regs., Part II. and the Staff Manual respectively. Title pages will be prepared in manuscript.

Hour, Date, Place	Summary of Events and Information	Remarks and references to Appendices
1915		
July 19th SALISBURY	Motor Lorry with 1 Officer, 2 A.S.C. Drivers and 1 N.C.O. left Mary Camp, SALISBURY, at 7.50 pm for SOUTHAMPTON. Arrived 12 noon. Remainder of Section (26 N.C.O's and men) and 1 Horse entrained ANESBURY, SALISBURY 1.15 p.m. Arrived SOUTHAMPTON 3.30 p.m. Transshipped the whole to S.S. "CAYEBASSA" 4.30 pm. Left Port at 6 pm. Arrived HAVRE 2.30 am next morning. Disembarked the whole at 7 am. During the voyage magazine	
July 20th HAVRE	served out with Life Belts an next channel, the Section were commanded by the O.C. of the Ship to take charge of the sanitary arrangements and the Staff Sergeant of the Section was appointed Quarter Master Sergeant of the Ship. & deal with Rations &c. Men were marched into and arrived at Rest Camp No 5. HAVRE at 10 am.	OWP
July 21st HAVRE	Marched from Rest Camp and arrived at Station (Mechanica) HAVRE 7 am. Entrained and left 10.19 am with exception of Lorry with 1 Officer and 2 A.S.C. Drivers who left HAVRE 9.30 am and arrived at ABBEVILLE at 5.30 pm reporting to D.A.D.T. Iron rations drawn.	OWP
July 22nd TILQUES near ST OMER	Lorry left ABBEVILLE Rest Camp at 9 am in company with Convoy and arrived at TILQUES 5.30 pm. Section arrived at ST OMER 6 am and marched into Billets at Tilques. At the request of the M.O. of the 19th Divisional Train, an N.C.O and 1 man attended at the Bivouac Quarters of the Train at TILQUES and instructed him in detail as to Water Bottles.	OWP
July 23rd TILQUES	5 Squads were sent out in charge of N.C.O's to investigate sources to from which Units were drawing water supplies. Reports received showed excellent deep wells in neighborhood from which most water supplies were drawn.	OWP

WAR DIARY
or
INTELLIGENCE SUMMARY
(Erase heading not required.)

Army Form C. 2118.

Instructions regarding War Diaries and Intelligence Summaries are contained in F. S. Regs., Part II. and the Staff Manual respectively. Title pages will be prepared in manuscript.

Hour, Date, Place	Summary of Events and Information	Remarks and references to Appendices
July 24th TILQUES	Horrock's test applied and water was found extremely good. Practically the whole of the 19th Division marched off towards Houtcotmank. JHP	
July 25th TILQUES (Sunday)	Returns were received at the Railhead ST OMER after some difficulty as no staff of the 19th Division could be found remaining in the district and no ambulances were received during the day to report the Division. 3 Signals were taken on the road to ST OMER for the purpose of testing water but no other abnormal units of the 19th Division were found in the district. Iron rations consumed.	JHP
	Awaited instructions to rejoin Division but none received.	JHP
July 26th TILQUES	Section in squads were put through manipulation of Water Clarifier and Horrock's Test erected Incinerator and constructed latrine. O.C. of Section called at G.H.Q at ST OMER for information as to why no orders have been received to rejoin Division today being the fourth day without orders. The Division it was understood were over 20 miles away. There the D.G.M.S. Office a telegram was sent to the A.D.M.S of the 19th Division notifying that the Section was still at TILQUES awaiting orders	JHP
July 27th TILQUES	Telegram received 2:50 pm dated 26th July '15. To proceed to Bermen and report to A.D.M.S. B.H.Q. collector for arrangements as to proceeding to Bermen where instructions were then given for a return to be made 8 am 28/7/15 by Motor Bus.	JHP

Army Form C. 2118.

WAR DIARY
or
INTELLIGENCE SUMMARY
(Erase heading not required.)

Instructions regarding War Diaries and Intelligence Summaries are contained in F. S. Regs, Part II. and the Staff Manual respectively. Title pages will be prepared in manuscript.

Hour, Date, Place	Summary of Events and Information	Remarks and references to Appendices
July 28th BUSNES	Omnibus, Lorry & Horse ambulance column paraded at Section and proceeded from TILQUES 8 a.m. Arrived BUSNES 11.30 a.m. O C reported arrival to A.D.M.S.	
July 29th BUSNES	Instructions received to inspect billets at BUSNES. 5 officers & N.C.O's were detailed to carry out these instructions.	
July 30th BUSNES and ST VENANT	Billet inspection continued at BUSNES. Orders received from ADMS ST VENANT, to proceed there at 10 a.m. to proceed to the outskirts of ST VENANT and inspect billets en route where we were in camp for night.	
July 31st ST VENANT and MERVILLE	Billet inspection around outskirts of ST VENANT resumed. Orders received from A.D.M.S. to proceed to MERVILLE and occupy billets there. Arrived MERVILLE 7.30 p.m.	

131/6607

S 19th Division

Summarised but not copied.

36th Sanitary Section
19th Divl: Sanitary Section
Vol: II
From 1 - 31. 8. 15

August 1915

Army Form C. 2118.

WAR DIARY
or
INTELLIGENCE SUMMARY
(Erase heading not required.)

Instructions regarding War Diaries and Intelligence Summaries are contained in F. S. Regs., Part II. and the Staff Manual respectively. Title pages will be prepared in manuscript.

Confidential

War Diary
of
Sanitary Section 36
attached VII Division

From 1st August 1915 to 31st August 1915

(Volume 2.)

Army Form C. 2118.

WAR DIARY
or
INTELLIGENCE SUMMARY

(Erase heading not required.)

Instructions regarding War Diaries and Intelligence Summaries are contained in F. S. Regs., Part II. and the Staff Manual respectively. Title pages will be prepared in manuscript.

Hour, Date, Place	Summary of Events and Information	Remarks and references to Appendices
1915		
August 1st MERVILLE (Sunday)	Several squads inspected Billets in MERVILLE. General water supply of the Town tested	OHP
August 2nd MERVILLE	Billet inspection of MERVILLE and suburbs continued. Also camps in suburbs inspected	OHP
August 3rd MERVILLE	Billet and camp inspectors continued around suburbs of MERVILLE practically completing the first inspection of the whole area occupied by the XIV Division	OHP
August 4th MERVILLE	Squads sent out to ascertain whether depôts previously found to exist had been renewed and to carry out any necessary duties. Next visit to inspectors transports and arrangements made for cleansing troops.	OHP
August 5th MERVILLE	Squads sent to inspect new camps and billets required by Division who had moved up to nearer the firing line	OHP
August 6th MERVILLE	Inspector assumed LAHORE DIVISION area around ESTAIRES district. O.C. was located around for the purpose of studying the sanitary section of that Division for the purpose of studying the sanitary measures adopted there. Reserve trenches of firing line also inspected.	OHP
August 7th MERVILLE	Squads sent out in direction of Ville Chapelle and PONT DU HEM to carry out inspections. O.C. inspected the whole of the front line trenches held by LAHORE DIVISION.	OHP
August 8th MERVILLE (Sunday)	C.O. spent morning and afternoon inspecting 7th GLOUCESTER REGT. and enquired into trenches outside and German Mounds and treatment of Manure Heaps and Latrines.	OHP

Army Form C. 2118.

WAR DIARY
or
INTELLIGENCE SUMMARY

(Erase heading not required.)

Instructions regarding War Diaries and Intelligence Summaries are contained in F. S. Regs., Part II. and the Staff Manual respectively. Title pages will be prepared in manuscript.

Hour, Date, Place	Summary of Events and Information	Remarks and references to Appendices
August 9th MERVILLE	C.O. and 1 Squad inspected the THRESH Disinfector and Baths and examined the work carried on there. Squad left thus which day. Several squads resumed camp and billet inspection.	O.V.P.
August 10th MERVILLE	Camps & Billets inspected. One Squad superintended Baths and Disinfector	O.V.P.
August 11th MERVILLE	Camps & Billets inspected. One Squad superintended Baths and Disinfector. O.C. inspected Baths at neighbouring Divisions.	O.V.P.
August 12th MERVILLE	Camps & Billets inspected. One Squad at Baths and Disinfector. O.C. visited neighbouring Divisions to inspect Baths & Disinfector.	O.V.P.
August 13th MERVILLE	Camps and Billets inspected. One Squad at Baths and Disinfector.	O.V.P.
August 14th MERVILLE	– ditto –	O.V.P.
August 15th MERVILLE (Sunday)	Section instructed by C.O. as to carrying out tests for metallic poisons in water. The whole of week's work reviewed and criticised.	O.V.P.
August 16th MERVILLE	Camps and Billets inspected. One squad at Baths and Disinfector.	O.V.P.
August 17th MERVILLE	Camps and Billets inspected. One squad at Baths and Disinfector and one squad spraying and cleaning Billets	O.V.P.
August 18th MERVILLE	– ditto –	O.V.P.
August 19th MERVILLE	– ditto –	O.V.P.
August 20th MERVILLE	One & 1 Permanent Incinerator erected. Three Disinfector supplied and to be erected and controlled by the Section. Camps and Billets inspected. One squad at Baths and Disinfector.	O.V.P.

Army Form C. 2118.

WAR DIARY
or
INTELLIGENCE SUMMARY
(Erase heading not required.)

Instructions regarding War Diaries and Intelligence Summaries are contained in F. S. Regs., Part II. and the Staff Manual respectively. Title pages will be prepared in manuscript.

Hour, Date, Place	Summary of Events and Information	Remarks and references to Appendices
August 21st MERVILLE	Camps and Billets inspected. One Squad at Baths and Throat Swingheter and one squad spraying and cleansing Billets.	O.M.P.
August 22nd MERVILLE (Sunday)	Practical Demonstration by C.O. of Hy.Lift in Manure Heaps and experiments carried out as to destruction of special Latrines erected made out of Present Two with Urine and Faeces impregnated with the object of burning the Faeces in Incinerator. Kit inspection	O.M.P.
August 23rd MERVILLE	Camps and Billets inspected. One Squad at Baths and Throat Swingheter	O.M.P.
August 24th MERVILLE	— do —	O.M.P.
	and 1 Squad spraying and cleansing Billets	
August 25th MERVILLE	Camps and Billets inspected. One Squad at Baths and Throat Swingheter	O.M.P.
August 26th MERVILLE	Camps and Billets inspected. Two Squads at Baths and Throat Swingheter One Squad spraying and cleansing Billets	O.M.P.
August 27th MERVILLE	Camps and Billet inspected. One Squad at Baths and Throat Swingheter	O.M.P.
August 28th MERVILLE	Camps and Billets inspected. One Squad at Baths and Throat Swingheter	O.M.P.
August 29th MERVILLE (Sunday)	Pay Parade. Equipment, Stores checked and examined and packed as far as possible.	O.M.P.
August 30th MERVILLE	Equipment packed and Camps and Billets inspected	O.M.P.
August 31st MERVILLE and LACON	Section took up new Quarters at LACON	O.M.P.

1247 W 3299 200,000 (E) 8/14 J.B.C. & A. Form/C. 2118/11.

121/6971

19/11/15 invasion

Summarised but not copied

19th Div L's Sanitary Section
vol: III

Sept. 15

S
Sept '15

Army Form C 2118

WAR DIARY
INTELLIGENCE SUMMARY

(Erase heading not required)

Summary of Events and Information

Confidential

War Diary
of
19th Divisional Secunity Section

From September 1st to September 30th

Volume 3

(Secunity Section 3A)

WAR DIARY
or
INTELLIGENCE SUMMARY
(Erase heading not required.)

Army Form C. 2118.

Sanitary Section 36

Instructions regarding War Diaries and Intelligence Summaries are contained in F. S. Regs, Part II. and the Staff Manual respectively. Title pages will be prepared in manuscript.

Hour, Date, Place		Summary of Events and Information	Remarks and references to Appendices
September 1st	LOCON	Local Baths handed over to and to be worked by Section. Water service and supplies in Town (Locon) investigated and tested. Own Billet cleaned and sprayed. 3 men with special knowledge of Boilers attached to Section to work Boilers at Baths.	
September 2nd	LOCON	Billets and Camps inspected. One Squad water testing. One Squad at Baths. 9 B.X. men attached to Section for purpose of assisting at Baths.	O.N.P.
September 3rd	LOCON	Billets and Camps inspected. One Squad Water testing. One Squad at Baths. Typhoid cases amongst Civil population investigated.	O.N.P.
September 4th	LOCON	Billets and Camps inspected. One Squad Water testing. One Squad at Baths and Knock Disinfector. Typhoid cases amongst Civil population investigated.	O.N.P.
September 5th (Sunday)	LOCON	Billets and Camps Inspected. One Squad Water testing. One Squad at Baths and Knock Disinfector. Typhoid cases amongst Civil population investigated.	O.N.P.
September 6th	LOCON	Billets and Camps Inspected. One squad water testing. One Squad at Baths and Knock Disinfector. Typhoid cases amongst Civilian population investigated.	O.N.P.
September 7th	LOCON	Billets and Camps Inspected. One Squad at Baths and Knock Disinfector. Typhoid cases removed to Hospital. One Squad water testing.	O.N.P.
September 8th	LOCON	Billets and Camps inspected. One squad at Baths and Knock Disinfector. Typhoid cases removed to Hospital. One squad water testing. Instructions issued for discharging Faeces.	O.N.P.
September 9th	LOCON	Billets and Camps inspected. One Squad at Baths and Knock Disinfector. One Squad water testing.	O.N.P.
September 10th	LOCON	Billets and Camps inspected. One Squad at Baths and Knock Disinfector. One Squad Water testing.	O.N.P.

Army Form C. 2118.

WAR DIARY
or
INTELLIGENCE SUMMARY
(Erase heading not required.)

Instructions regarding War Diaries and Intelligence Summaries are contained in F. S. Regs., Part II. and the Staff Manual respectively. Title pages will be prepared in manuscript.

Hour, Date, Place	Summary of Events and Information	Remarks and references to Appendices
September 11th LOCON	Camps and Billets inspected. One Squad at Baths and Throat transports. One Squad water testing	O.N.Peters O.N.Peters
September 12th LOCON (Sunday)	One Squad at Bath and transport	
September 13th LOCON	Camps and Billets inspected. One Squad at Baths and Throat transports. One Squad water testing. 1% Cresol Bicarbonate Soda and Carbonate Soap, chloride and prepared for use in Trenches. Typhus cases investigated	O.N.Peters
September 14th LOCON	Camps and Billets inspected. One Squad at Baths and Throat transports. One Squad on Water duties	O.N.Peters
September 15th LOCON	Camps & Billets inspected. One Squad at Baths & Throat transport. One Squad on Water duties.	O.N.Peters
September 16th LOCON	Camps and Billets inspected. One Squad at Baths & Throat transport. One Squad on Water duties. Sanitary Survey of Locon and Lutenpte completed. Typhus cases investigated	O.N.Peters
September 17th LOCON	Camps and Billets inspected. One Squad at Baths & Throat transport. One Squad on Water duties. 2 Cwt Bicarbonate Soda and Carbonate Soap crushed and prepared for use in Trenches	O.N.Peters
September 18th LOCON	Camps and Billets inspected. One Squad at Baths & Throat transport. One Squad on Water duties. 1 Cwt Bicarbonate Soda and Carbonate Soap	O.N.Peters
September 19th LOCON (Sunday)	Camps and Billets inspected. One Squad at Baths & Throat transport. One Squad on Water duties	O.N.Peters

WAR DIARY
or
INTELLIGENCE SUMMARY

(Erase heading not required.)

Army Form C. 2118.

Instructions regarding War Diaries and Intelligence Summaries are contained in F. S. Regs., Part II. and the Staff Manual respectively. Title pages will be prepared in manuscript.

Hour, Date, Place		Summary of Events and Information	Remarks and references to Appendices
September 20th	LOCON	Billets and camps inspected. One Squad at Baths and Thresh Disinfecter. One Squad Water testing. 3 cwt. Phosphate Soda and Carbonate Soda crushed and prepared for use in Trenches.	
September 21st	LOCON	Billets and camps inspected. One Squad at Baths and Thresh Disinfecter. One Squad on Water duties. Dysentery case investigated.	
September 22nd	LOCON	Billets and camps inspected. One Squad at Baths and Thresh Disinfecter. One Squad on Water duties. Dysentery case removed to hospital.	
September 23rd	LOCON	Billets and camps inspected. One Squad at Baths and Thresh Disinfecter. One Squad on Water duties. 6 cwt of Phosphate Soda and Carbonate Soda crushed and prepared for use in Trenches.	
September 24th	LOCON	One Squad at Baths and Thresh Disinfecter. Kit inspection. Men instructed in the use of Field Dressings. 16 Cases of Scabies to attempt to Section for treatment.	
September 25th	LOCON	One Squad at Baths and Thresh Disinfecter. Wounded collected and taken to Lorry and Squad sent to collect wounded. Section's Billet cleaned and prepared to receive wounded. Nearly 50 cases would come in any Orderly Room transferred and new Billet occupied. One Squad at Baths and Thresh Disinfecter. One Squad and Lorry stood by for emergency call to collect wounded.	
September 26th (Sunday)	LOCON		
September 27th	LOCON	One Squad at Baths and Thresh Disinfecter. One Squad and Lorry standing by for emergency call to collect wounded. New Billet and adj. Room cleaned and disinfected.	
September 28th	LOCON	One Squad at Baths and Thresh Disinfecter. One Squad and Lorry standing by for emergency call to collect wounded.	

WAR DIARY
or
INTELLIGENCE SUMMARY

(Erase heading not required.)

Army Form C. 2118.

Hour, Date, Place	Summary of Events and Information	Remarks and references to Appendices
September 29th LOCON	One Squad at Baths and Thrush Strasifects. One Squad building special Latrinents to destroy Faeces re. Two men detailed to attend to Isolation Camp for Scabies patients attached to Section. 8 Act throughlists Sints and Carbonate Soda Crushed and prepared for use in Trenches. 2 men preparing Infection Disease Charts. O.H.Peters	
September 30th LOCON	One Squad at Baths and Thrush Strasifects. One Squad building special Trenerents to destroy Faeces re. Two men detailed to attend to Isolation Camp for Scabies patients attached to Section. 2 men preparing Infection Disease Charts. O.H.Peters	

Oct. 1915.

S

12/7593

Announced but not copied.

12/7593

19th Bir Li: Sanitary declin:
(No: 36)
Vol 4
Oct 15

Army Form C. 2118.

WAR DIARY
or
INTELLIGENCE SUMMARY.
(Erase heading not required.)

Instructions regarding War Diaries and Intelligence Summaries are contained in F. S. Regs., Part II. and the Staff Manual respectively. Title pages will be prepared in manuscript.

Hour, Date, Place	Summary of Events and Information	Remarks and references to Appendices
	Confidential War Diary of Sanitary Section 36 attached XIX Division From October 1st 1915 to October 31st 1915 Volume 4	

WAR DIARY
or
INTELLIGENCE SUMMARY

(Erase heading not required.)

Army Form C. 2118.

Instructions regarding War Diaries and Intelligence Summaries are contained in F. S. Regs., Part II. and the Staff Manual respectively. Title pages will be prepared in manuscript.

Hour, Date, Place		Summary of Events and Information	Remarks and references to Appendices
October 1st	Locon	One Squad at Baths and Throat Disinfector. 2 Men detailed to attend to Isolation Camp for Scabies & patients attached to Section. 2 men preparing Infectious Diseases Charts. One Squad testing sprayed disinfectants to destroy flies &c. Billets and Camps inspected. O.N. Peters	
October 2nd	Locon	One Squad at Baths and Throat Disinfector. 2 men detailed to attend to Isolation Camp for Scabies & patients attached to Section. 2 men preparing Infectious Disease Charts. Water test for Metallic and Organic Poison carried out. Fires and Equipment checked and prepared for moving. Cases of Diphtheria & Scarlet Fever and German Measles investigated. Disinfector carried out. O.N. Peters	
October 3rd	Locon and Fosse	Section 12 BX men and 21 Scabies Cases attached to Section, marched to Fosse to take up new Quarters. O.N. Peters	
October 4th	Fosse	Provision of Sanitary arrangement at Divisional HQrs superintended. New Billets cleaned and inspected. 2 men preparing Infectious Diseases Charts. Water tests carried out. 2 men detailed to attend to Isolation Camp for Scabies Patients &c. Sanitary Survey of Fosse made. O.N. Peters	
October 5th	Fosse	Billets and Camps inspected. 2 men detailed to attend to Isolation Camp for Scabies & patients attached to Section. 2 men preparing Infectious Diseases Charts. One Squad testing water. O.N. Peters	
October 6th	Fosse	Billets and Camps inspected. 2 men detailed to attend to Isolation Camp for Scabies or patients attached to Section. 2 men preparing Infectious Diseases Charts. One Squad testing water. C.O. and 1 men inspected trenches and water supply arrangements. O.N. Peters	
October 7th	Fosse	Camps and Billets inspected. 2 men attached to Isolation Camp for Scabies & patients attached to Section. C.O. delivered Lecture on Typhoid &c. 2 men on Throat Disinfector. O.N. Peters	

1247 W 3250 200,000 (E) 8/14 J.R.C.&A. Forms/C.2118/11

Army Form C. 2118.

WAR DIARY
or
INTELLIGENCE SUMMARY
(Erase heading not required.)

Instructions regarding War Diaries and Intelligence Summaries are contained in F. S. Regs., Part II. and the Staff Manual respectively. Title pages will be prepared in manuscript.

Hour, Date, Place	Summary of Events and Information	Remarks and references to Appendices
October 8th FOSSE	Camps and Billets inspected. 2 men attached to Isolation Camp for Scabies & patients attached to Section. 2 men on Road Transport. 2 men preparing Infectious Diseases charts. One Squad on Water Supplies. O.W.Peters	
October 9th FOSSE	Camps and Billets inspected. 2 men attached to Isolation Camp for Scabies & patients attached to Section. Urinoirs built. 2 men preparing Infectious Diseases Charts. One Squad on water supplies. 3 Bx men. Squad on underclothing at Baths. O.W.Peters	
October 10th FOSSE (Sunday)	2 men attached to Isolation Camp for Scabies & patients attached to Section. 2 men preparing Infectious Diseases Charts. One Squad on water supplies. 3 men on Road Transport. Camp and Billets inspected. 3 Bx men grooming underclothing at Baths. O.W.Peters	
October 11th FOSSE	Camps and Billets inspected. One Squad on water supplies. 2 men attached to Isolation Camp preparing Infectious Diseases Charts. 2 men attached to Section to patients. Underclothing at Baths. O.W.Peters	
October 12th FOSSE	3 Bx men grooming underclothing at Baths. Camps and Billets inspected. One Squad on Water Supplies. 2 men preparing Infectious Diseases Chart. 2 Men attached to Isolation Camp for Scabies to Patients attached to Section. One Urinoirs built. 2 men on Road Transport. 3 Bx men grooming underclothing at Baths. O.W.Peters	
October 13th FOSSE	Camps and Billets inspected. One Squad on Water Supplies. 2 men attached to Isolation Camp for Scabies & no change in Section. 2 men on Road Transport. 3 Bx men grooming underclothing at Baths. O.W.Peters	
October 14th FOSSE	Camps and Billets inspected. One Squad on Water supplies. 3 men attached to Isolation Camp for Scabies & Patients attached to Section. 2 men on Road Transport. 1 2nd on Infectious Diseases Charts. One Horse Manure Incinerator built. 2 X men engaged on H.Q cleaning Campsite. O.W.Peters	

Army Form C. 2118.

WAR DIARY
or
INTELLIGENCE SUMMARY
(Erase heading not required.)

Instructions regarding War Diaries and Intelligence Summaries are contained in F. S. Regs., Part II. and the Staff Manual respectively. Title pages will be prepared in manuscript.

Hour, Date, Place		Summary of Events and Information	Remarks and references to Appendices
October 15th	FOSSE	Camps and Billets inspected. One Squad on Water Supplies. 3 men detailed to Isolation Camp for Soldiers in charge of Section. 1 Man in Infection Diseases Chart. BX men supplied on Minimum Enamelite and belonging to H.Q. Camps. One man sick (one fractr). D.V. Peters	
October 16th	FOSSE	Camps and Billets inspected. One Squad on Water duties. 2 men detailed to Isolation Camp for Soldiers in charge of Section. One man in Infection Diseases Chart. C.O. and one man inspected Trenches and water supply servers thereto. Baths at VIEILLE CHAPPELLE handed over to Section to work. BX men and 1 Squad of the Section sent to these Baths as the Staff therefrom had ??? Thrust Disinfector. One man Sick (one fractr). D.V. Peters	
October 17th (Sunday)	FOSSE	Camps and Billets inspected. 2 men detailed to Isolation Camp for Soldiers in charge of Section. BX men and 1 Squad of Section employed Baths and Thrust Disinfector. One man sick (one fractr). D.V. Peters	
October 18th	FOSSE	Camps and Billets inspected. 2 men detailed to Isolation Camp for Soldiers in charge of Section. BX men and 1 Squad of Sanitary Section at Baths and Thrust Disinfector. One man in Infection Diseases Chart. one squad on Water duties. One man sick (one fractr). C.H. Peters	
October 19th	FOSSE	Camps and Billets inspected. 2 men detailed to Isolation Camp for Soldiers in charge of Section. BX men and 1 Squad of Sanitary Section at Baths and Thrust Disinfector. One man sick (one fractr). One man in Infection Diseases Chart. One Squad on Water duties. D.V. Peters	
October 20th	FOSSE	Camps and Billets inspected. 2 men detailed to Isolation Camp for Section in charge of Section. Camp empty and all latrines now evacuated. Vieille Chapelle Baths evacuated and BX such and 1 Squad of Section marched off and took possession of Locon Baths. One man sick (sole fractr), one man in Injection Diseases Chart. One Squad on Water duties. D.V. Peters	

Army Form C. 2118.

WAR DIARY
or
INTELLIGENCE SUMMARY
(Erase heading not required.)

Instructions regarding War Diaries and Intelligence Summaries are contained in F. S. Regs., Part II. and the Staff Manual respectively. Title pages will be prepared in manuscript.

Hour, Date, Place		Summary of Events and Information	Remarks and references to Appendices
21st October	FOSSE and LOCON	Section and equipment removed to LOCON. New Billet allotment to and Headquarters. Sanitary arrangements taken in hand. 12 B+ men and 1 Squad of Section at Baths and Thresh Disinfector. One man sick (Sanfectre) O.C. commenced LEAVE. D.A.D.M.S. has took over his duties	W3h
22nd October	LOCON	Camps and Billets inspected. One Squad on Water duty. 12 B+ men and 1 Squad of Section at Divisional Baths and Thresh Disinfector. One man sick (Sanfectre). One man on Infectious Storage Chart. Motor Lorry and 1 man dishinfected clean underclothing to various Baths from Laundry.	W3h
23rd October	LOCON	Camps and Billets inspected. One Squad on Water Duties. 12 B+ men and 1 Squad of Section at Divisional Baths and Thresh Disinfector. One man sick (Sanfectre). One man on Infectious Diseases to Chart. Motor Lorry and 1 man disinfected clean underclothing to various Baths from Laundry.	W3h
24th October LOCON (Sunday)		Camps and Billets inspected. One Squad on Water duties. 12 B+ men and one Squad of Section at Divisional Baths and Thresh Disinfecter. Motor Lorry under repair. H.Q. motor cart advance and repaired.	W3h
25th October	LOCON	Camps and Billets inspected. One Squad on Water Duties. 12 B+ men and one Squad of Section at Divisional Baths and Thresh Disinfector. Motor Lorry under repair. 5 cut of Thiosulphate Soda and Cartonate Soda received and prepared for use in Trenches. One man on Infectious Diseases Chart.	W3h
26th October	LOCON	Camps and Billets inspected. One Squad on Water duties. 12 men temporary attached and two Squads of Section at Divisional Baths and Thresh Disinfecter. Motor Lorry refixed and recommenced collecting dirty underclothing at various Baths for delivery to Laundry. 7 cut Thiosulphate Soda and Cartonate Soda received prepared for use in Trenches.	W3h

WAR DIARY
or
INTELLIGENCE SUMMARY

(Erase heading not required.)

Army Form C. 2118.

Instructions regarding War Diaries and Intelligence Summaries are contained in F. S. Regs., Part II. and the Staff Manual respectively. Title pages will be prepared in manuscript.

Hour, Date, Place		Summary of Events and Information	Remarks and references to Appendices
27th October	LOCON	Troops and Billets inspected. One squad on Water Duties. 12 men temporarily attached to Section and one squad of Section at Divisional Baths and three Disinfector Motor Lorry collected soiled underclothing at various Baths for delivery to Laundry.	WPk
28th October	LOCON.	Troops and Billets inspected. One squad on Water Duties. 12 men temporarily attached to Section and one squad of Section at Divisional Baths and three Disinfector Motor Lorry and one man collected soiled underclothing at various Baths for delivery to Laundry.	WPk
29th October	LOCON.	Camps and Billets inspected. One squad on Water Duties. 12 men temporarily attached and one squad of Section at Divisional Baths and three Disinfector Motor Lorry but no man collected soiled underclothing from various Baths for delivery to Laundry Co. W.H.Peters.	
30th October	LOCON	Camps and Billets inspected. One squad on Water Duties. 12 men temporarily attached and one squad of Section at Divisional Baths + Three Disinfector Motor Lorry and one man collected soiled underclothing from various Baths for delivery to Laundry. W.H.Peters	
31st October	LOCON	Camps and Billets inspected. One squad on Water Duties. 12 men temporarily attached and one squad of section at Divisional Baths and Three Disinfector Motor Lorry and one man collected soiled underclothing from various Baths for delivery to Laundry. W.H.Peters Lieut Sandy Section 36.	

Sanitäts Section No: 36
19ᵗʰ Division
Vol: 5

121/7678

S
19ᵗʰ Division
Sanitary Section No 36.
Summarised but not coded

Nov 1915

Nov 15.

Army Form C. 2118.

WAR DIARY
or
INTELLIGENCE SUMMARY

(Erase heading not required.)

Instructions regarding War Diaries and Intelligence Summaries are contained in F. S. Regs., Part II. and the Staff Manual respectively. Title pages will be prepared in manuscript.

Hour, Date, Place	Summary of Events and Information	Remarks and references to Appendices
	Confidential War Diary of Sanitary Section 36. from November 1st to November 30th 1915 (Volume 5)	

WAR DIARY or INTELLIGENCE SUMMARY

Army Form C. 2118.

(Erase heading not required.)

Instructions regarding War Diaries and Intelligence Summaries are contained in F. S. Regs., Part II. and the Staff Manual respectively. Title pages will be prepared in manuscript.

Hour, Date, Place		Summary of Events and Information	Remarks and references to Appendices
November 1st 1915	LOCON	Camps and billets inspected. One squad at Baths and through Disinfector. One squad on water. Baths, canal, people.	
November 2nd "	LOCON	Camps and billets inspected. One squad at Baths and through Disinfector. One squad on water. Pontzis. Arranged with French Bourgmestre to alter Pontzis Bergues Canal.	
November 3rd "	LOCON.	Camps and billets inspected. One squad at Baths and through Disinfector. One squad inspected water supplies in town area and trenches O.C. + 1 man arranged alterations to circle of Baths Canal with French Territorials. Major Boultounth Lieut Helewi of Hans et Ander Duff [illegible] in trenches.	O.M.Helewi.
November 4th "	LOCON.	Camps and billets inspected. One squad at Divisional Baths and through Disinfector. O.C. + 1 man inspected water supply arrangements in trenches. Superused French Territorial Officers Battle Canal.	
November 5th "	LOCON	Camps and billets inspected. O.C. in Funken re Water. O.M.Helewi One man with O.C. Engineers Dyke outpost. Through Disinfector. One squad at Divisional Baths put up at Divisional One squad on working order. O.M.Helewi.	
November 6th "	LOCON.	Camps and billets inspected & put into working order. O.M.Helewi Through Disinfector. One squad at Divisional Baths and supplied + guarded Divisional laths etc. One squad at Defaltering Caves. Motor lorry collected clean underclothing from laundry and returned to various Batts. One squad at Divisional Baths etc.	
November 7th " (Sunday)	LOCON.	Camps and billets inspected. One squad in water duties. Motor lorry collected clean underclothing from laundry and returned to various Batts. Through Disinfector. O.Burtebas AA.QMG arranging drying depots, + put mayor re cleaning waterways	

1247 W.3290 200,000 (E) 8/14 J.B.C. & C.

Army Form C. 2118.

WAR DIARY
or
INTELLIGENCE SUMMARY
(Erase heading not required.)

Instructions regarding War Diaries and Intelligence Summaries are contained in F. S. Regs., Part II. and the Staff Manual respectively. Title pages will be prepared in manuscript.

Hour, Date, Place		Summary of Events and Information	Remarks and references to Appendices
November 8th	LOCON	Camps and Billets inspected. 12 men temporarily attached to Section and one Squad of Section at Divisional Baths and Thresh Disinfector. One Squad on Water duties. 1 man with Motor Lorry collecting clean underclothing from Laundry for distribution to various Corps Baths. Visit of Col. Bevan Jr. and Army Commissioner on Sanitation — whole district inspected. Commencement made with Drying Room at Rue DE L'EPINETTE. Section Surveyor put on to obstructions in Canal System and arrangement for him to supervise these in future, the Mayor of Locon assisting. JNP
November 9th	LOCON	Camps and Billets inspected. 12 men temporarily attached to Section and one Squad of Section at Divisional Baths and Thresh Disinfector. One Squad on Water duties. 1 man with Motor Lorry collecting clean underclothing from Laundry for delivery to various Corps Baths. Work of constructing Drying Room at Rue DE L'EPINETTE proceeded with and 1 Sergeant and 3 men temporarily attached to Section for this purpose. JNP
November 10th	LOCON	Camps and Billets inspected. 12 men temporarily attached to Section and one Squad of Section at Divisional Baths and Thresh Disinfector. One Squad on Water duties. 1 man with Motor Lorry collecting clean underclothing from Laundry for delivery to various Corps Baths. Division of Drying Room at RUE DE L'EPINETTE proceeded with. Instructions re Canal System, sewers and Drainage Water supplied for this purpose. OC visited West Billets at Hamel. Part of Cupboards supplied for Drying Room at Baths & before drawing water going in Canal. JNP
November 11th	LOCON	Camps and Billets inspected. 12 men temporarily attached to Section and one Squad of Section at Divisional Baths and Thresh Disinfector. One Squad on Water duties. 1 man with Motor Lorry collecting clean underclothing from Laundry for delivery to various Corps Baths. Division of Drying Room at Rue DE L'EPINETTE proceeded with. JNP

WAR DIARY
INTELLIGENCE SUMMARY

Army Form C. 2118.

Hour, Date, Place	Summary of Events and Information	Remarks and references to Appendices
November 12th LOCON	Camps and Billets inspected. 12 men temporarily attached to Section and one Squad of Section at Divisional Baths and Thread Transports. One Squad on Water duties. One man with Motor Lorry collecting clean underclothing from laundry for delivery to various Drying Rooms. Mothedo purchased for establishing Drying Rooms. OMP	
November 13th LOCON	Camps and Billets inspected. 12 men temporarily attached to Section and one Squad of Section at Divisional Baths and Thread Transports. One Squad on Water duties. One man with Motor Lorry collecting clean underclothing from laundry for delivery to various Cape Baths. Drying Room at RUE DE L'EPINETTE completed and used by troops immediately upon completion. Further materials purchased for establishing Drying Rooms. Government improvements suggested and Divisional Bath Licor and put in hand by R.E's. OMP	
November 14th LOCON (Sunday)	12 men temporarily attached to Section and one Squad of Section at Divisional Baths and Thread Transports. One Squad on Water duties. Two men with Motor Lorry collecting clean underclothing from laundry, for delivery to various Cape Baths and also collecting material of Drying Rooms. Material for Drying Rooms proposed. One man on Infectious sickness Baths. Work of providing Drying Room at Divisional Baths, LOCON, proceeded with. OMP	
November 15th LOCON	12 men temporarily attached to Section and one Squad of Section at Divisional Baths and Thread Transports. One Squad on Water duties. One man with Motor Lorry collecting dirty underclothing from laundry for delivery to various Cape Baths. One Van to Laundry. Material for Drying Room purchased. Drying Room at Rue de L'EPINETTE inspected and additions made. Drying Room at Gorrenhall Maths, LOCON completed. Camps and Billets inspected. Arrangements made for drying room at Basine Battalion completed. Arrangements made for drying room at Basine Battalion. OMP	

Army Form C. 2118.

WAR DIARY
—or—
INTELLIGENCE SUMMARY

(Erase heading not required.)

Instructions regarding War Diaries and Intelligence Summaries are contained in F. S. Regs., Part II. and the Staff Manual respectively. Title pages will be prepared in manuscript.

Hour, Date, Place		Summary of Events and Information	Remarks and references to Appendices
November 16th	LOCON	12 men temporarily attached to Section and one Squad of Section at Divisional Baths and Thrust Disinfector. Camps and Billets inspected. The remainder on Water duties. One man with Motor Lorry collecting dirty underclothing from various Corps Baths, for delivery to Laundry. Drying Room at Rouen Battalion Wonacle Regt. inspected and additions made. Drying Room at Pres de L'EPINETTE inspected. One man on Infectious Canals waste wagon. Medicine purchased for Drying Room. OC. visited checked Canals with major.	CAP
November 17th	LOCON	Billets and Camps inspected. One Squad on Water duties. One man with Motor Lorry collecting dirty underclothing from various Corps Baths for delivery to Laundry. 12 men temporarily attached to Section and one Squad of Section at Divisional Baths and Thrust Disinfects. Drying room at Rouen Battalion Worcester Regt completed. One man on Infectious diseases charts.	CAP
November 18th	LOCON	Billets and Camps inspected. One Squad on Water duties. One man with Lorry collecting dirty underclothing from various Corps Baths for delivery to Laundry and Thrust Disinfects. 12 men temporarily attached to Section and one Squad of Section at Divisional Baths and Thrust Disinfects. Materials prepared for Drying Rooms. One man on Infectious diseases charts.	CAP
November 19th	LOCON	Billets and Camps inspected. One Squad on Water duties. One man with Lorry collecting dirty underclothing from various Corps Baths for delivery to Laundry. 12 men temporarily attached to Section and one Squad of Section at Divisional Baths and Thrust Disinfects. Materials prepared for Drying Rooms. One man on Infectious diseases charts.	CAP
November 20th	LOCON	Billets and Camps inspected. One Squad on Water duties. One man with Lorry collecting dirty underclothing from various Corps Baths for delivery to Laundry. 12 Men temporarily attached to Section and one Squad of Section at Divisional Baths and Thrust Disinfects. Improvement (Structure) carried out at Divisional Baths. C.O. and Staff Sgt. visited St VENANT and arranged Billeting accommodation for Section also Made enquiries to available buildings for new Baths in ST VENANT. re BELLI Parapet.	CAP

WAR DIARY or INTELLIGENCE SUMMARY

Army Form C. 2118.

Hour, Date, Place	Summary of Events and Information	Remarks and references to Appendices
1915 21st November (Sunday) LOCON	One Squad on Water Duties. One man in Infectious Diseases Chalets. 12 men (temporary) attached to Section and one Squad of Section at Divisional Baths and Street Disinfectors. Divisional improvements carried out at Divisional Baths. Fry Parade. One man and lorry collecting dirty underclothing of various Corps Billets for delivery to Laundry. M.O.	
22nd November LOCON	One Squad on Water Supplies. Camps and Billets inspected. 12 men (temporary) attached to Section and one Squad of Section at Divisional Baths and Street Disinfectors. One man in Infectious Diseases Chalets. Special inspection made throughout of vacated Billet Camps etc of Units who had recently moved off to new areas. Billets & of 7th South Lancs Regt found to be in very unsanitary condition. M.O.'s of Division considered gurney cattle off the best route asphalt/ obtainable in the new area. There was disagreement as to if billets in Supp 5 in. Billets & of 7th South Lancs Regt and 6th P.W.R One Squad on Water duties. Camps and Billets inspected. 12 men temporary attached to Section and One Squad of Section at Divisional Baths and Divisional disinfector. One Sergeant from 7th Staff Lancs Regt temporary attached to Section as a B.I. man. Special inspection made of Billets Camps & to Units who have moved off or who are about to move off to new area. C.O. together with the AA+QMG visited the Billets Camps & recently occupied by the 7th South Lancs Regt.	O.L.P.
23rd November LOCON		O.L.P.
24th November LOCON	One Squad on Water duties. 12 men temporary attached to Section and one Squad of Section and one Squad of Section at Divisional Baths - 4 of these temporary attached men were sent to rejoin their Regiments. Two M/o's Drivers and Foot Ambulance belonging to 5th & 6th FIELD AMBULANCE temporary attached to Section for a few days. Special inspection made of Billets Camps etc of Units who have moved off or who are about to move off to new area. Billets & of 5th SOUTH WALES BORDERERS Regt who had recently moved off & were once found in a very insanitary condition and report thereon made to D.H.Q. Cart & Kitchens Sink and department together with 7 men transported to ST VENANT to prepare new quarters of Section.	O.L.P.

WAR DIARY
or
INTELLIGENCE SUMMARY

(Erase heading not required.)

Army Form C. 2118.

Instructions regarding War Diaries and Intelligence Summaries are contained in F. S. Regs., Part II. and the Staff Manual respectively. Title pages will be prepared in manuscript.

Hour, Date, Place	Summary of Events and Information	Remarks and references to Appendices
25th November — LOCON — ST VENANT	One Squad on Water duties. 2 men temporarily attached to section and one Squad of Section at Divisional Baths LOCON. General inspection made of Billet Area in recently vacated by Units several of which were found in insanitary condition. Reports thereon forwarded to D.H.Q. Part of Section's Equipment and Stores removed to new billet at ST VENANT also 10 men.	O.W. Peters
26th November ST VENANT	2 men on Water duties. Remainder of Section's Equipment Stores & and men removed to new billet at ST VENANT. Part of D.H.Q. sanitary arrangement superintended. Further efforts forwarded to D.H.Q. in insanitary billets recently left by units in late divisional area.	O.W. Peters
27th November ST VENANT	C.O. delivered Lecture on Sanitation to School of Officers at LOCON. One Squad on Water duties. One man in Infantry disposed to Clerk. S.H.Q. sanitary arrangements superintended. Latrine Billets to Cleaned out and totally [illegible] middle to arrangement made with A.D.S.Q.M.S. for section to entire & administer new Divisional Baths at ST VENANT and ROBECQ. Case of MBAILEY (civilian) investigated.	O.W. Peters
28th November ST VENANT (Sunday)	One Squad on Water duties. Improvements (functionary at Isolation Mess carried out. D.H.Q sanitary arrangements superintended, also civil Refuse Disposal	O.W. Peters
29th November ST VENANT	Troops and Baths inspected. One Squad on Bath duties. Sanitary arrangements at D.H.Q. organization and one Squad engaged on such work. One man on Infantry Lectures at School. Two men on special treatment for 57th FIELD AMBULANCE. Divisional alteration at ROBECQ Bank superintended.	O.W. Peters

WAR DIARY
INTELLIGENCE SUMMARY
(Erase heading not required.)

Army Form C. 2118.

Instructions regarding War Diaries and Intelligence Summaries are contained in F. S. Regs., Part II. and the Staff Manual respectively. Title pages will be prepared in manuscript.

Hour, Date, Place	Summary of Events and Information	Remarks and references to Appendices
30th November - St VENANT.	Bns depart to Vieille station. Temporary arrangement appointments at D.H.Q. and one Officer engaged in out post, transport and Billet inspection. 8 men (Temporarily attached) and 1 Sergeant engaged in forming up and arranging Baths at St VENANT. Alteration at REBECQ Baths superintended. O.M.Peters.	

5

December 1915

F/258/1

19/1/08

Summarised but not copied
San: Sect: 36
Pol: 6

131/7936

Army Form C. 2118.

WAR DIARY
or
INTELLIGENCE SUMMARY
(Erase heading not required.)

Instructions regarding War Diaries and Intelligence Summaries are contained in F. S. Regs., Part II. and the Staff Manual respectively. Title pages will be prepared in manuscript.

Hour, Date, Place	Summary of Events and Information	Remarks and references to Appendices
	Confidential	
	War Diary	
	Sanitary Section 36	
	from 1st December to 31st December 1915	
	(Volume 6)	

WAR DIARY or INTELLIGENCE SUMMARY

Army Form C. 2118.

(Erase heading not required.)

Instructions regarding War Diaries and Intelligence Summaries are contained in F. S. Regs., Part II. and the Staff Manual respectively. Title pages will be prepared in manuscript.

Hour, Date, Place	Summary of Events and Information	Remarks and references to Appendices

1915

1st December – ST VENANT. Camps and Billets inspected. One officer in from Lewis & Sanitary arrangements examined at D.H.Q. and no great improvement is well not. Establishment of Baths at ST VENANT provided with. Glanton at ROBECQ Park approved. Arrangement made for Sanitary Inspector of each Infantry Battalion to be attached to Section for a few days sanitation course. O.M.P.

2nd December – ST VENANT. One officer in from Lewis. Camps and Billets inspected. Sanitary arrangements at D.H.Q. examined and no special improvements in work. Provisional site purchased for ROBECQ ST VENANT Baths. Which Detachment from No 2 Section, leaving Matin proceed in charge of Section. Eight men temporarily attached to Section and one again of Section at ROBECQ Park. O.M.P.

3rd December – ST VENANT. Camps and Billets inspected. One officer in from Lewis. Eight men Sanitary attached to Section and one officer 1 platoon at ROBECQ Park. Part 1 Section's equipment and stores removed to new billet at LUTON also sice men. The Sanitary Corporal from Infantry Battalion 1 Division attached to Section for three days sanitation course. Orders received that Division goes into the line, also Sanitary Inspector attached to 67th Infantry Brigade. O.M.P.

Army Form C. 2118.

WAR DIARY
or
INTELLIGENCE SUMMARY
(Erase heading not required.)

Instructions regarding War Diaries and Intelligence Summaries are contained in F. S. Regs., Part II. and the Staff Manual respectively. Title pages will be prepared in manuscript.

Hour, Date, Place	Summary of Events and Information	Remarks and references to Appendices
4th December - LOCON.	One squad on Water Duties. Two Sanitary Corporals returned to 56th Infantry Brigade and two to the 58th Infantry Brigade. Snobs part of Section equipment and other remainder now drawn in LOCON. OMP	
5th December - LOCON. (Sunday)	One squad on Water Duties. List of the chief water supplies of the new area prepared and forwarded to R.M.O's. Remainder of Section equipment and stores arrived at LOCON. Four men temporarily attached and one man 1 Section engaged in preparing brazier for Drying Room. O.C. inspected the Drying Rooms of the Division. OMP	
6th December - LOCON.	One squad on Water Duties. Motor lorry transport placed in charge of Section. Sanitary arrangements at D.H.Q. superintended and one squad engaged in such work. O.C. upon on Divisional Drying Rooms at D.H.Q. O.A. engaged in supervising for Braces for Section Dug-Baths. One squad 1 Section and Bx men (temporarily attached) engaged in cleaning Section Braces and opening drain armour Billet. OMP	
7th December - LOCON.	One squad on Water Duties. Camps and Billets inspected. Sanitary arrangements superintended at D.H.Q. and one squad engaged in such work. Billets etc. are arranged for Section	

WAR DIARY
or
INTELLIGENCE SUMMARY
(Erase heading not required.)

Army Form C. 2118.

Hour, Date, Place	Summary of Events and Information	Remarks and references to Appendices
8th December LOCON / LESTREM	at LESTREM. Part of Section Equipment and stores removed to LESTREM. The signal on water tank. Bambara Billets inspected. Base of Lathum investigated. Removal of equipment from the to LESTREM completed. Six men temporarily attached and three men of Section to Divisional Baths, LOCON. Armoury arrangements at D.H.Q. superintended and in spare engaged on such work. O.H.P.	
9th December LESTREM	Camps and Billets inspected. On again on water tank. One man on Injection disease. Class. Six men temporarily attached and three men of Section at Divisional Baths, LOCON. Salvos Billets cleaned. B.O. in company with the D.A.C.M.G. of Division and Capt. Johnson of 58 Field Ambulance, inspected Divisional Draping Room preparatory to handing the washing of the Forms over to the Field Ambulance. Camps and Divisional Baths Divisional Baths at LOCON, LESTREM and VIEILLE CHAPELLE in charge of Section. Staff Sergeant visited Divisional Baths and arranged as to supplies etc. Armoury arrangements at D.H.Q. superintended and one again of Section engaged on such work. O.H.P.	

Army Form C. 2118.

WAR DIARY
or
INTELLIGENCE SUMMARY
(Erase heading not required)

Instructions regarding War Diaries and Intelligence Summaries are contained in F. S. Regs., Part II. and the Staff Manual respectively. Title pages will be prepared in manuscript.

Hour, Date, Place	Summary of Events and Information	Remarks and references to Appendices
10th December - LESTREM	Camps and Billets inspected. One squad on Motor Bikes. Absentees improperly attired men three men of Lestrem Posts under LOCON. 3 cases of Typhoid investigated. Sanitary arrangements at D.H.Q. superintended and one squad of section engaged on such work. One man of section engaged on Garden party Disinfected at VIEILLE CHAPELLE Baths. OHP.	
11th December - LESTREM	One squad on Motor Bikes. Camps and Billets inspected. Three cases of civilian Typhoid further investigated as to contacts etc and the houses concerned disinfected and places Out of Bounds. One man of section assisting with Garden Party Disinfection at VIEILLE CHAPELLE Baths. C.O. in company with H.Q. and Visitor inspected LOCON Posts. Batt. Johnson of 58th Field Ambulance reported to C.O. as to his action in regard to unsound Angora Rices. C.O. arranged for supply of straw etc for new Wash House disinfector and Wash house of section at Divisional Baths LOCON. OHP.	
12th December - LESTREM (Sunday)	Camps and Billets inspected. One squad on Motor Bikes. Lestrem Baths suffered any trying floods. C.O. accompanied Lt Col by Thomas around the Gas Carts. Gas and Equipment attached one three men of section at Divisional Baths LOCON. B13 Margines ? to Bn. He range (Newport 1095) ammunitioned. OHP.	

Army Form C. 2118.

WAR DIARY
or
INTELLIGENCE SUMMARY
(Erase heading not required.)

Instructions regarding War Diaries and Intelligence Summaries are contained in F. S. Regs., Part II, and the Staff Manual respectively. Title pages will be prepared in manuscript.

Hour, Date, Place	Summary of Events and Information	Remarks and references to Appendices
13th December – LESTREM.	Telephone Battn inspected. One squad on Field Duties, two men at pump, attached and three men of duties as Divisional Bath, LOCON. Bathing parties LESTREM Baths inspected, rooms & forms. 400 Blankets at Lt-Bde HQrs (Liverpool Regt) disinfected by steam bag Disinfectors at LOCON Baths. C.O. attended Sanitation meeting at LOCON. OMP
14th December – LESTREM.	One squad on Field Duties. Camps and Billets inspected. Two men temporarily attached and three men of Section as Divisional Bath, LOCON. C.O. attended Lecture on Sanitation in Poland by Officer at LOCON. 400 Blankets of 1/4th Bn The Kings (Liverpool) Regt disinfected by steam bag Disinfectors, also 150 Blankets for the 57th Field Ambulance. Supplies of linen 15 hand petroleum & refined petroleum. One N.C.O. and one man from Hindu of various duties for the purpose and one man of Section superintending. LESTREM Baths attended. OMP
15th December – LESTREM.	One squad on Field Duties. Camps and Billets inspected. Two men temporarily attached and three men of Section as Divisional Bath, LOCON. Horses to have collection of refuse superintended in various areas. 4 O.R. intelligence sorted East of various divisions area working at 98th Bde R.F.A. OMP

WAR DIARY
or
INTELLIGENCE SUMMARY
(Erase heading not required.)

Army Form C. 2118.

Instructions regarding War Diaries and Intelligence Summaries are contained in F. S. Regs., Part II. and the Staff Manual respectively. Title pages will be prepared in manuscript.

Hour, Date, Place	Summary of Events and Information	Remarks and references to Appendices
16 December - LESTREM	B.H. opened on Wadi India. Camps and Billets inspected. Two men temporarily attached and three men of Section at LOCON Baths. C.O. investigated outbreak of Scabies amongst Units of Division. Four men of Mont of Dinard ordered also on horse and cart for the collection of horse refuse at LESTREM. One man of Section superintending. OHP	
17 December - LESTREM	Camps and Billets inspected. B.H. opened on Wadi India. Six men temporarily attached and three men of Section at LOCON Baths. Owing to coal supply being exhausted and materials to ensure fuel supply the three Divisional Baths closed. O.C. inspected Drying Room at Divisional Drying Rooms. OHP	
18 December - LESTREM	Camps and Billets inspected. B.H. opened on Wadi India. Six men temporarily attached and three men of Section on Divisional Baths LOCON. Divisional Baths at LOCON and LESTREM closed down owing to coal supply being exhausted. Bathing at VIEILLE CHAPELLE Baths carried on with usual, as full. Three men of Mont of Division ordered on horse & cart detailed for collection of horse & house refuse at LESTREM and such work superintended by one man of Section. OHP	

Army Form C. 2118.

WAR DIARY
or
INTELLIGENCE SUMMARY
(Erase heading not required.)

Instructions regarding War Diaries and Intelligence Summaries are contained in F. S. Regs., Part II. and the Staff Manual respectively. Title pages will be prepared in manuscript.

Hour, Date, Place	Summary of Events and Information	Remarks and references to Appendices
19th December – LESTREM (Sunday)	One Squadron Watr Duties. Sanops and Bellin inspected. Also an Hospitals attacked and Work man of Section at Devannes Baths LOCON. C.O. investigated outbreak of Diarrhoea in Division. During it no was being ambulance Divisional Baths at LOCON pm LESTREM storeyed down. Winnows and no have ans saw detention for outside of horse refuse and with superintended by one man of Section. OHP	
20th December – LESTREM	Sanops and Bellin inspected. One squadron Watr Duties. Storer of Section at Devannes Baths LOCON. Baths at LESTREM and LOCON closed down owing to coal supply being exhausted. C.O. inspected Refilling Points of Section of Divisions in Division. C.O. inspected Refilling Points of Divisions. OHP	
21st December – LESTREM	Sanops and Bellin inspected. One squadron on Watr Duties. Divisional Refilling Point opened permanenm at A.D.M.S of Division. Storer of Section at LOCON Baths. Divisional Baths at LOCON and LESTREM closed down owing to coal supply being exhausted. Three of Men of Division and one horse sent awaited for outside of horse refuse at LESTREM and one man of Section engaged in superintending such work. C.O. investigated case of horses thrown out LESTRE. OHP	

1247 W 3299 200,000 (E) 8/14 J.B.C.&A. Forms/C.2118/11.

WAR DIARY or INTELLIGENCE SUMMARY

Army Form C. 2118.

Hour, Date, Place	Summary of Events and Information	Remarks and references to Appendices
22nd December - LESTREM	Camps and Billets inspected. One agreed on Hors Serie. Three men of Section at Divisional Baths LOCON. LESTREM Divisional Baths closed down owing to coal supply being exhausted. Baths at LOCON and VIEILLE CHAPELLE carried on with return as fuel. Three men of Hut to B Section sent on horse and cart erection for collection of horse refuse at LESTREM and one man of Section superintending. Billets of Scowen Section parties at 187th R.E. sprayed and disinfected. Billets of men suffering from Influenza at MERVILLE sprayed and disinfected. OHP	
23rd December - LESTREM	One agreed on Hors Serie. Camps and Billets inspected. Three men of Section at Divisional Baths LOCON. LESTREM baths closed owing to coal being exhausted and Baths at LOCON and VIEILLE CHAPELLE carried on with wood as fuel. Collection of horse refuse at LESTREM superintended. One man on Inspection Sewage Ch'k in Vieille Chapelle - Glean Batts B.D.V. Rgn Str - Engr Insp L Bn of Baths - Divy Sewn Wks - by Col'l Latimer - District Merville. He same OO. OHP	
24th December - LESTREM	One agreed on Hors Serie. Camps and Billets inspected. Three men of Section at Divisional Baths LOCON. LESTREM Baths closed owing to coal being unavailable. Collection of horse refuse at LESTREM superintended. OHP	

WAR DIARY
or
INTELLIGENCE SUMMARY

(Erase heading not required.)

Army Form C. 2118.

Hour, Date, Place	Summary of Events and Information	Remarks and references to Appendices
25th December – LESTREM	Three men at Divisional Baths LOCON. Divisional Rendez-vous issued that Sanitary personnel of Battalion have three days instruction in Sanitation under O.C. I Section. Baths at LESTREM closed down owing to supply of fuel being exhausted. OMP	
26th December – LESTREM	Lamps and Billets inspected. In opinion of M.O. three men of Section at Divisional Baths at LOCON. Divisional Baths at LESTREM closed down owing to supply of coal not being available. Houses & huts inspection of refugees at LESTREM circumstances. E.O. investigation case of Diphtheria. OMP	
27 December – LESTREM	Lamps and Billets inspected. In opinion of M.O. three men of Section at Divisional Baths LOCON. Baths at LOCON and LESTREM closed down owing to supply of fuel not being available. House to house collection of refuse at LESTREM circumstances. Arrangements made as to custom of Sanitary Museum for instruction of Sanitary Corporal detailed for instruction. Two men on Inspection Drainage Cleaning. OMP	

Army Form C. 2118.

WAR DIARY
or
INTELLIGENCE SUMMARY
(Erase heading not required.)

Instructions regarding War Diaries and Intelligence Summaries are contained in F. S. Regs., Part II. and the Staff Manual respectively. Title pages will be prepared in manuscript.

Hour, Date, Place	Summary of Events and Information	Remarks and references to Appendices
28th December LESTREM	The squad in Water Duties, Baths and Billets inspected. The squad of section at LOCON Baths, Divisional Baths at LOCON closed for repair and Baths at LESTREM closed during day & full use being available. Horse to horse collecting officer at LESTREM superintended and horse and cart and three men from 1st Division ordered for such work. Broken Sanitary Corporals attached to section and given course of instruction in Sanitation.	OJP
29th December LESTREM	Baths and Billets inspected. The squad in Water Duties. The squad of section at Divisional Bath LOCON. Baths at LOCON closed for repair and LESTREM Baths closed owing to full use being available. Horse to horse collecting officer at LESTREM superintended horse and cart and three men of 1st Division ordered for such work. Sixteen Sanitary Corporals further instructed in Sanitation. 6.0 ordered Section to Sebourg & Officers, LOCON.	OJP
30th December LESTREM	Baths and Billets inspected. The squad in Water Duties. The squad of Section at Divisional Baths LOCON. Baths at LOCON and LESTREM	

WAR DIARY
or
INTELLIGENCE SUMMARY
(Erase heading not required.)

Army Form C. 2118.

Instructions regarding War Diaries and Intelligence Summaries are contained in F. S. Regs., Part II. and the Staff Manual respectively. Title pages will be prepared in manuscript.

Hour, Date, Place	Summary of Events and Information	Remarks and references to Appendices
	closer army to find no been available. Have num[be]r of Dwr[?] and have not been advised for election. Have appn. at LESTREM and such arms. requisitioned. Sudden flooding hampers further movement in connection with customary stand-to such trenches to remain with from 4th an additional deep reconnaissance. C.O. inspected trenches A & M 4.4 between Rue Biache & the 8th Bn. R.F.A. on the Zouave - Marine chapelle Road and approved as to ordinary shelter for infantry. OMP	
3rd December LESTREM.	Weather misty in morn. Drier. Camps and Billets inspected. The escort of section of Divisional Bath Loans, Baths at LESTREM and LOCON closed owing to supply of fuel being exhausted. Three men of those of A. comm. now have and and arranged for exercise of horses upon at LESTREM 12.14 and such work superintended. Further Sanitary improvements further investment in transportation under the direction of the C.O. C.O. attended to Member a Coursy of Enquiry at 5th Infantry Brigade HQ(during Print as to the supply of Supplies. OMP	

19th Division

18th Div
F/258/2.

San: Seef: 36
Vol: 7
Jan '16

Jan. 1916

Army Form C. 2118.

WAR DIARY
or
INTELLIGENCE SUMMARY

(Erase heading not required.)

Instructions regarding War Diaries and Intelligence Summaries are contained in F. S. Regs., Part II. and the Staff Manual respectively. Title pages will be prepared in manuscript.

Hour, Date, Place	Summary of Events and Information	Remarks and references to Appendices
	Confidential War Diary Sanitary Section 36 from 1st January to 31st January 1916. (Volume 7)	

WAR DIARY
INTELLIGENCE SUMMARY

(Erase heading not required.)

Army Form C. 2118.

Instructions regarding War Diaries and Intelligence Summaries are contained in F. S. Regs., Part II. and the Staff Manual respectively. Title pages will be prepared in manuscript.

Hour, Date, Place	Summary of Events and Information	Remarks and references to Appendices
1916		
1st January - LESTREM	Camps and Billets inspected. One squad in North India. One squad of Divisional Baths LOCON. Divisional Baths at LESTREM and LOCON closed down owing to no fuel being available. Hence to time utilised of squad at LESTREM entrainment & horse care and a demr ordered from HQrs of Division for each unit. Active training proposed approved. Much offices from about instruction in trenches. Lectr. Noted transport in and out of D.I.M.S. II Corps, proceeded to IBERGUES to inspect Remount in charge of the Remount C.O. inspected Army troops Workshops at BORRE. OUP
2nd January - LESTREM	Camps and Billets inspected. One squad in North India. One squad of Divisional Baths LOCON. Divisional Baths at LESTREM and LOCON closed down owing to lack of fuel. Horse exercise entrainment & repose at LESTREM entrainment and horse care and arms attention for each unit from HQrs of Division. Two men engaged in trenches. Inspection at Sanitary Institution established at LESTREM. Part of Sanitary equipment moved to new billet at LESTREM. One man in Hospital. Divisional Chart set. OUP
3rd January - LESTREM	One squad in North India. Camps and Billets inspected. One squad of Section at Divisional Baths LOCON. Divisional Baths at LOCON and LESTREM closed owing to want of fuel being unavailable. Horse & horse exertion & refuse at LESTREM superintended and one man sent

WAR DIARY or INTELLIGENCE SUMMARY

Army Form C. 2118.

(Erase heading not required.)

Instructions regarding War Diaries and Intelligence Summaries are contained in F. S. Regs., Part II. and the Staff Manual respectively. Title pages will be prepared in manuscript.

Hour, Date, Place	Summary of Events and Information	Remarks and references to Appendices
	Firmes awaited from Hurst of Donnison for such work. A.O. conferred with Major Johnson of 5th Field Ambulance as to Bryon Farms etc. C.O. made recce of 10th Royal Warwick Regt at VIEILLE CHAPELLE where one of miners tap received. OWP	
4 January – LESTREM	Camps and Billets inspected. Men squad – Water Duties. Three men of section at LOCON Baths. LOCON and LESTREM Baths there being a no. of post troop available. Firmes were sent detailed from Hurst of Donnison for several of hours refuse at LESTREM and the gun experimental sanitary arrangement improvement carried on at section near Billets at LESTREM. Two carpenters temporarily attached engaged in alteration to stew at LESTREM Baths. Case of carpenter Lintons Kisner or Burbles of 8th Hants. Staff R at EPINETTE investigated and report supply taken. OWP	
5th January. LESTREM.	Camps and Billets inspected. One squad on trade duties. Three men of section on Sanitary Baths LOCON. Sanitary Baths at LESTREM close owing to no post being available. One man and horse and carrier from Hurst of Donnison for collection of house refuse at LESTREM and work experimental. A.O. conferred with and accompanied Capt. Williams of 77 Howitzer Section on tour of Sanitary Baths Farm carpenter temporarily attached engaged in alteration of stew at LESTREM Baths. OWP	

WAR DIARY or INTELLIGENCE SUMMARY

Army Form C. 2118.

Hour, Date, Place	Summary of Events and Information	Remarks and references to Appendices
6th January 1916 – LESTREM	Camps and Billets inspected. One Squad on Water duties. Three men of section at Divisional Baths, LOCON. Divisional Police stating in future all clean underclothing to be applied for at Divisional Baths and not Corps Laundry. One man at VIEILLE CHAPELLE Baths and Drying Room to deal with this order. Divisional Baths LESTREM closed on account of no fuel being available and 4 Carpenters (temporary) attached engaged on alterations and improvements to these Baths. Two men and horse and cart detailed from Unit of Division for collection of house refuse at LESTREM and such work superintended. One case of suspected TYPHOID investigated. One man on Infectious Disease Escort. JWP	
7th January – LESTREM	One case of suspected TYPHOID and 1 case of MUMPS investigated and disinfection carried out. Camps and Billets inspected. One Squad on Water duties. Three men of section at Divisional Baths, LOCON. One man at VIEILLE CHAPELLE Baths and New Drying Room superintending team & then underclothing to Units. Divisional Baths, LESTREM closed on account of no fuel being available and 4 Carpenters (temporary) attached engaged on alterations and improvements at these Baths. Two men and horse and cart detailed from Unit of Division for collection of house refuse at LESTREM and work superintended. One man on Refuse of Disease Escort. JWP	
8th January – LESTREM	OC. attended HQ Supply Refilling Point as member of a Board to report on a consignment of Soling Rations. Camps and Billet inspected. One Squad on Water duties. Three men of section at Divisional Baths, LOCON. One man at VIEILLE CHAPELLE Baths and New Drying Room superintending issue of clean underclothing to Units. Divisional Baths LESTREM closed on account of no fuel being available and 4 Carpenters (temporary) attached engaged on alterations and improvements at these Baths. Two men, horse and cart detailed from Unit of Division for collection of house refuse at LESTREM and such work superintended. One man on Infectious Disease Escort. JWP	

WAR DIARY
INTELLIGENCE SUMMARY

(Erase heading not required.)

Army Form C. 2118.

Instructions regarding War Diaries and Intelligence Summaries are contained in F. S. Regs, Part II. and the Staff Manual respectively. Title pages will be prepared in manuscript.

Hour, Date, Place	Summary of Events and Information	Remarks and references to Appendices
9th January — LESTREM (Sunday)	Camps and Billets inspected. One Squad on Water duties. Three men at Divisional Baths, LOCON. One man at VIEILLE CHAPELLE Baths and New Drying Room superintending issue of clean underclothing to Units. Divisional Baths, LESTREM closed on account of no coal being available and 4 Carpenters temporarily attached engaged on alterations and improvements to these Baths. Two men, horse and cart detailed from Unit of Divisional for collection of horse refuse at LESTREM and such work superintended. C.O. together with the C.O. of Sanitary Section of the 38th Division visited this Section's Water Cart unit affiliated NEUVE CHAPELLE Trenches enroute to 10th Warwick Regt. also Drying Room No 4, 5 and 15. One man on Disinfection process there.	OYP
10th January — LESTREM	Camps and Billets inspected. One Squad on Water duties. Three men at Divisional Baths, LOCON. One man at VIEILLE CHAPELLE Baths and New Drying Room superintending issue of clean underclothing to Units. Divisional Baths, LESTREM closed on account of no coal being available and 4 Carpenters temporarily attached engaged on alterations and improvements to these Baths. Two men, horse and cart detailed from Unit of Division for collection of horse refuse at LESTREM and work superintended. C.O. attended weekly meeting of Quartermasters at LOCON and afterwards proceeded supplies of Coal, Water, supplies & Latrines. Baths and transport arrangements, and prognosis discussed in future, the needs of the Division investigated at LESTREM and POSIE.	OYP
11th January — LESTREM	Camps and Billets inspected. One squad on Water duties. Three men at Divisional Baths, LOCON. One man at VIEILLE CHAPELLE Baths and New Drying Room superintending issue of clean underclothing to Units. Divisional Baths, LESTREM closed in consequence of coal being available and 4 Carpenters temporarily attached engaged on alterations and improvements to those Baths. Two men, horse and cart detailed from Unit of Division for collection of horse refuse at LESTREM and such work superintended. 18 Sanitary Corporals John Unit of Division temporarily attached to Section in Course of instruction in Sanitation and Sanitary Measures asked to well further duties. Water supplies Disinfection &c. Protozoical investigation at VIEILLE CHAPELLE. One man on Disinfection process there.	OYP

WAR DIARY
INTELLIGENCE SUMMARY

(Erase heading not required.)

Army Form C. 2118.

Instructions regarding War Diaries and Intelligence Summaries are contained in F. S. Regs., Part II. and the Staff Manual respectively. Title pages will be prepared in manuscript.

Hour, Date, Place	Summary of Events and Information	Remarks and references to Appendices
12th January – LESTREM	Camps and Billets inspected. One squad on Water duties. Three men at Divisional Baths, LOCON. One man at VIEILLE CHAPELLE Baths and New Drying Room superintending issue of clean underclothing to units. Divisional Baths, LESTREM closed on account of no fuel being available and a Carpenter temporarily attached engaged on alterations and improvements to these Baths. Two men, three cart and cart detailed from Unit of Division for collection of house refuse at LESTREM and and work superintended. 1 P Sanitary Corporal from Unit of Division temporarily attached to Section for instruction in sanitation and Sanitary Measures. Routes to and from Billets, Water supplies & latrines at PARADIS and LEPINETTE investigated. One man on Infection Diseases duties. C.O. together with the M.S. & M.O. inspected Field Bren of Units of Lahore Division at LA GORGUE.	OP.
13th January – LESTREM	Camps and Billets inspected. One squad on Water duties. Three men at Divisional Baths, LOCON. One man at VIEILLE CHAPELLE Baths and New Drying Room superintending issue of clean underclothing to units. Divisional Baths, LESTREM closed on account of no fuel being available and a Carpenter temporarily attached engaged on alterations and improvements to these Baths, also arrangements made for R.E's to build a cold channel to carry away waste water. Officers and N.C.Os of Divisional Amusements. Two men, horse and cart detailed from Unit of Division for collection of house refuse at LESTREM and and work superintended. 1 P Sanitary Corporal from Unit of Division temporarily attached to Section for instruction in sanitation and Sanitary Measures exhibited and work further exhibits for Water supplies of Estaminets & LOCON investigated. Ten men on Infectious Diseases duties.	ONP
14th January – LESTREM	Camps and Billets inspected. One squad on Water duties. Three men at Divisional Baths, LOCON. One man at VIEILLE CHAPELLE Baths and New Drying Room superintending issue of clean underclothing to units. Divisional Baths, LESTREM closed on account of no fuel being available and a Carpenter temporarily attached engaged on alterations and improvements to these Baths, also further improvements carried out by R.E's &c, cold channel to carry away waste water Officers. Ten men on Infectious diseases duties. Water supplies & Latrines at LES LOBES and ZELOBES investigated. O.C. Medical Sanitary Officer of 3rd Division and inspected their Divisional Baths.	ONP

WAR DIARY
or
INTELLIGENCE SUMMARY
(Erase heading not required.)

Army Form C. 2118

Instructions regarding War Diaries and Intelligence Summaries are contained in F. S. Regs., Part II. and the Staff Manual respectively. Title Pages will be prepared in manuscript.

Place	Date	Hour	Summary of Events and Information	Remarks and references to Appendices
LESTREM	19th Jan 15		Camps and Billets inspected. One opened on Water Dutie. Three men at Divisional Baths, LOCON. One man at VIEILLE CHAPELLE Baths and New Drying Room superintending same & clean underclothing to Units. Divisional Baths, LESTREM closed on account of no full being available and & Carpenter & Handyman attached engaged on alteration and improvements to third Baths. Two men, three and cart detailed from Unit of Division for collection of house refuse at LESTREM and such such superintended. One man on Infectious Sickness Duty.	OHP
LESTREM	Jan 16		One opened on Water Dutie. Camps and Billets inspected. Three men at Divisional Baths LOCON. One man at VIEILLE CHAPELLE Baths and new Drying Room superintending same & clean underclothing to Units. LESTREM Divisional Bath closed owing to no fuel being available. Two Carpenter Handymans attached engaged on alteration and improvement to LESTREM Baths. Three and cart and two men from Units of Division attached for collection of house refuse at LESTREM and such such superintended.	OHP
LESTREM	Jan 17th		Camps and Billets inspected. One opened on Water Dutie. Three men at Divisional Baths LOCON. One man at VIEILLE CHAPELLE Baths and new Drying Room superintending same & clean underclothing to Units. Carpenter Handyman attached engaged on carrying out alteration and improvements at LESTREM Baths. LESTREM Baths reopened. Two men horse and cart detailed from Units of Division for collection of house refuse at LESTREM and such such superintended.	OHP
LESTREM	Jan 18th		One opened on Water Dutie. Camps and Billets inspected. Three men & 1 locon at Divisional Baths LOCON. One man at VIEILLE CHAPELLE Baths and new Drying Room superintending same & clean underclothing to	

1875 Wt. W593/826 1,000,000 4/15 J.B.C. & A. A.D.S.S./Forms/C. 2118.

WAR DIARY

INTELLIGENCE SUMMARY

(Erase heading not required.)

Army Form C. 2118

Instructions regarding War Diaries and Intelligence Summaries are contained in F.S. Regs., Part II. and the Staff Manual respectively. Title Pages will be prepared in manuscript.

Place	Date	Hour	Summary of Events and Information	Remarks and references to Appendices
LESTREM	Jany 19th		Units from Capuzon Regiment attached engaged in carrying out improvements and alteration at LESTREM Baths. Six men have been sent detailed from Unit of Division for collection of times refuse at LESTREM and such improvement. C.O. investigated case of suspected Enteric Group happening at Divisional Signal Coy. Six men engaged in running Thust Disinfector at VIEILLE CHAPELLE. Installation of the Thorpicol Biercom at VIEILLE CHAPELLE completed and 60 k remoulds impermanent has arriving of Division.	OMP.
			Kamps and Billets inspected. One squad on trailer duties. Three men of section at LOCON Baths. Six men of section at VIEILLE CHAPELLE Baths and new Drying Room superintending name of steam manuevching of Units of Division. Six men have and cart detailed from Unit of Division for collection of times refuse at LESTREM and such improvement. Carputic Desinfecant attached engaged in carrying out improvement and alteration to LESTREM Baths. Six men engaged in working Thust Disinfector at VIEILLE CHAPELLE Baths. C.O. conferred with CO 77c Sanitary Section as to the taking over of Billets Baths and Rear Horses. A.D. investigates outbreak of measles on the civil population at LESTREM.	OMP
LESTREM	Jany 20th		Camps and Billets inspected. One squad on trailer duties. Three men of section at LOCON Baths. Six men at VIEILLE CHAPELLE Baths and new Drying Room superintending name of steam enswaching of Units of Division. Two men engaged in running Thust Disinfector at VIEILLE CHAPELLE Baths. Two men have and cart detailed from Unit of Division for collection of times refuse at LESTREM. From Carputic Desinfecant attached engaged in carrying out alteration at LESTREM Baths. C.O. made STOMMT and arrangers as to taking over Billet. C.O. further investigates outbreak of measles amongst civil population of LESTREM. Two men also engaged in	OMP

Army Form C. 2118

WAR DIARY
or
INTELLIGENCE SUMMARY
(Erase heading not required.)

Instructions regarding War Diaries and Intelligence Summaries are contained in F. S. Regs., Part II. and the Staff Manual respectively. Title Pages will be prepared in manuscript.

Place	Date	Hour	Summary of Events and Information	Remarks and references to Appendices
LESTREM	Jany 21st		Camps and Billets inspected. Sir agreed on Water Duties. Three men of section at Divisional Baths LOCON. One man at VIEILLE CHAPELLE Baths and new Drying Room nearing steam manufacturing to Minch of Divisom. Two men engaged in working Wood Disinfector at VIEILLE CHAPELLE Baths. Two men have one cart actualis from Minch of Divisom for the purpose of collecting lines refuse and supplies to new Walk Walls Erysmat proceeded to ST VENANT to enquire in to further supplies and arrange in LESTREM and vicinity where intentes had resumed places. One of Guard to North Personal of RAMC (M.O.T Divisom) and 77 (sanitary) Section installed in Divisional Baths and Rest Homes and such men instruction in the running of the Baths etc.	OMP
LESTREM	Jany 22nd		Camps and Billets inspected. Sir agreed on Water Duties. Three men of section at Divisional Baths LOCON. One man at VIEILLE CHAPELLE Baths and new Drying Room nearing steam manufacturing to Minch of Divisom. Two men have one cart actualis from Minch of Divisom for collection of lines refuse at LESTREM and ROC Minch. Fatigue party furnished to Camp Commandant for cleaning Nobins etc of HQ White Roof work experiment. O.C. visited ST VENANT and ROBECQ and arranged as to Baths to be taken over in the new areas.	OMP
LESTREM	Jany 23rd		Camps and Billets inspected. Sir agreed on Water Duties. LOCON Baths agreed upon three men of section together with Back Stove installed at ROBECQ Baths. One man at VIEILLE CHAPELLE Baths and arrived to new Builder at ST VENANT. Two men have one cart actualis from three of Divisom for Part of lectual equipment collection of horse refuse at LESTREM and such work experiment. Two men from 2/N Staffs Regt	OMP

1575 W: W593/826 1,000,000 4/15 J.B.C. & A. A.D.S.S./Forms/C. 2118.

Army Form C. 2118.

WAR DIARY
or
INTELLIGENCE SUMMARY
(Erase heading not required.)

Instructions regarding War Diaries and Intelligence Summaries are contained in F. S. Regs., Part II. and the Staff Manual respectively. Title pages will be prepared in manuscript.

Hour, Date, Place	Summary of Events and Information	Remarks and references to Appendices
	Medical Section. Fatigue party of 20 men provided by Divisional Cyclist Co. for the purpose of cleansing billeting area of LESTREM. C.O. visited troops at LESTREM and saw that the sanitary arrangements were satisfactory before troops moved to new area. *OMP*	
LESTREM - January 24th STVENANT	Camps and Billets inspected. One squad on Main Road. Three men of Section at Divisional Baths. ROBECQ. The remainder 12 men detailed from Units of Division for collection of horse refuse at LESTREM, and also work superintended. Remainder of Section by regiment and sines removed to new Billets at ST VENANT. Billets & latrines cleaned etc. *OMP*	
ST VENANT - January 25th	Camps and Billets inspected. One squad withdrew batrine. Three men of Section at Divisional Baths ROBECQ. C.O. visited HAVERSKERQUE and enquired as to charge for use of Brewery as a Divisional Bath. Section Billets & latrines cleaned etc. One squad preparing Divisional Baths at ST VENANT. *OMP*	
ST VENANT January 26th	Camps and Billets inspected. One squad on Main Drain. Three men of Section at ROBECQ Baths. One man with main lorry collected clean underclothing from Laundry at La GORGUE. C.O. visited HAVERSKERQUE and endeavoured to arrange suitable terms for hiring of one of Breweries as Brewery. One squad 7 men engaged in preparing Baths at ST VENANT. *OMP*	

Army Form C. 2118.

WAR DIARY
INTELLIGENCE SUMMARY
(Erase heading not required.)

Instructions regarding War Diaries and Intelligence Summaries are contained in F. S. Regs., Part II. and the Staff Manual respectively. Title pages will be prepared in manuscript.

Hour, Date, Place	Summary of Events and Information	Remarks and references to Appendices
ST VENANT – Jan'y 27	Camps and Billets inspected. One squad on Water Duties. One squad at Divisional Baths ROBECQ. One squad preparing Baths at ST VENANT. One man and boy collected clean underclothing from Coy's Ranniers at LA GORGUE. ONP	
ST VENANT – Jan'y 28	Camps and Billets inspected. One squad on Water Duties. One squad at Divisional Baths ROBECQ. Divisional Baths at ST VENANT opened and one squad engaged at said Baths. One man and boy collected clean underclothing from Coys Ranniers at LA GORGUE. Arrangements made for the washing of soiled underclothing by civilian labour and two guards handed not for said purpose. Billets where case of Mumps occurred sprayed and disinfected. ONP	
ST VENANT – Jan'y 29th	Camps and Billets inspected. One squad on Water Duties. One squad at Divisional Baths ROBECQ. One squad at Divisional Baths ST VENANT. One man and boy collected clean underclothing from Coys Ranniers at LA GORGUE. Further guards of most underclothing handed to Civilians for washing. C.O. makes an enquiry with C.O. Divisional Divisional Sanitary Section Baths in Divisional Divisional Area. Billets where case of Mumps had occurred sprayed and disinfected (Next train) ONP	

WAR DIARY
or
INTELLIGENCE SUMMARY
(Erase heading not required.)

Army Form C. 2118.

Instructions regarding War Diaries and Intelligence Summaries are contained in F. S. Regs., Part II. and the Staff Manual respectively. Title pages will be prepared in manuscript.

Hour, Date, Place	Summary of Events and Information	Remarks and references to Appendices
St VENANT. Jany 30th	Kemp and Butler inspected the squad at Walz Butler. On squad at ROBECQ Bath. One squad at ST VENANT Baths. One man and lorry engaged in extracting clean underclothing from LA GORGUE Laundry. Two men on thresh disinfector at ST VENANT Baths. Wagon, horse and men detached from Hinges for execution of repairs at ST VENANT and such work subsequent. Four men temporarily attached engaged in cleaning areas of St VENANT. Butler of 8th N Staff Regt. near ROBECQ when cover of (?) German trenches occurred. Arranged relief in form and R.M.O. also as to methods of concert. AP Peters	
St VENANT January 31st	Kemp and Butler inspected. One squad on Walz Butler. One squad at ROBECQ Bath. One squad at ST VENANT Baths. One man and lorry engaged in extracting clean underclothing from Laundry at LA GORGUE. Horse, wagon & men from Hinges Division and four men temporarily attached to learn engaged in cleaning streets of St VENANT, and such work subsequent. C.O. inspected Divisional Supply Column at CALONNE and the town generally and returned to A.D.M.S. as to Sanitary arrangements. CNP.	

19th Div.

36th Savvy Section

Feb ⎫ 1916
Mar ⎭

San: Sect: 36
Vol: 8

Army Form C. 2118.

WAR DIARY
INTELLIGENCE SUMMARY
(Erase heading not required.)

Hour, Date, Place	Summary of Events and Information	Remarks and references to Appendices
	Confidential War Diary of Sanitary Section 36 from 1st February 1916 to 29th February 1916 (Volume 8)	

Instructions regarding War Diaries and Intelligence Summaries are contained in F. S. Regs., Part II. and the Staff Manual respectively. Title pages will be prepared in manuscript.

Army Form C. 2118.

WAR DIARY
INTELLIGENCE SUMMARY

(Erase heading not required.)

Instructions regarding War Diaries and Intelligence Summaries are contained in F. S. Regs., Part II. and the Staff Manual respectively. Title pages will be prepared in manuscript.

Hour, Date, Place	Summary of Events and Information	Remarks and references to Appendices
ST VENANT – February 1st 1916	Camps and Billets inspected. One squad in Water Duties. One squad engaged at ROSECQ Baths. One man and boy engaged in collecting clean underclothing from laundry at LA GORGUE. One man on Wheel Drainpipes at ST VENANT Baths. Two men temporarily attached to Section engaged in cleaning. Four of ST VENANT and each work superintended. One squad at ST VENANT Baths. JJP	
ST VENANT – February 2nd	Camps and Billets inspected. One squad in Water Duties. One squad at ST VENANT Baths. One man on Wheel Drainpipes at ST VENANT Baths. Two men temporarily attached to Section engaged in cleaning Four of ST VENANT and each work superintended. Car of Para System at 37th Brigade R.F.A. investigated. L.O. winter 87th Brigade R.F.A. JJP	
ST VENANT – February 3rd	Camps and Billets inspected. One squad in Water Duties. One squad at ST VENANT Baths. One man on Wheel Drainpipes at ST VENANT Baths. One man and hose man engaged from Hurs of Barrows and Mess temporary attached Mess engaged in cleaning Mess Four of ST VENANT and each work superintended. One man and boy engaged in collecting clean underclothing from laundry at LA GORGUE. JJP	
ST VENANT – February 4th	Camps and Billets inspected. One squad in Water Duties. Two men engaged in Wheel Drainpipes at ST VENANT Baths. One squad as before at ST VENANT Baths. One man engaged in Wheel Drainpipes during thirty and further two men engaged during night. One man, hour one	

1247 W 3299 200,000 (E) 8,14 J.B.C.&A. Forms/C.2118/11.

WAR DIARY or INTELLIGENCE SUMMARY

Army Form C. 2118.

(Erase heading not required.)

Instructions regarding War Diaries and Intelligence Summaries are contained in F. S. Regs., Part II. and the Staff Manual respectively. Title pages will be prepared in manuscript.

Hour, Date, Place	Summary of Events and Information	Remarks and references to Appendices
ST VENANT - February 1st	Camps and Billets inspected. One opened in main Drain. One opened at ST VENANT Baths. One opened at FOSSE Q Bath. The horse men and wagon from Hind of Divsn ordered for collection of offal refuse at ST VENANT - two men temporarily attached engaged on work experimental. Rotary Pan Switzer cleaners which of town - fatigue party engaged and work experience. The men and lorry collection steam incinerators.	D.W.P.
ST VENANT - February 5th	Camps and Billets inspected. One opened in main Drain. One opened in ST VENANT Switzer cleaners etc. One opened at ST VENANT Baths. Two horses men wagon from Hind of Divsn ordered for collection of offal refuse etc at ST VENANT - two men temporarily attached also engaged in work experimental. Rotary Pan Switzer employed in cleaning streets of ST VENANT and the work of a fatigue party supervised. One horse and lorry collection steam incinerators from farming area of Gorgue. Two men in front Divsicion. CO further conferred with C.R.E. of Divsn as to new front here being extreme ST VENANT. Wagon collection from Hind of Divsn for refuse at ST VENANT, and sent experimental. Rotary Pan Switzer employed in cleaning streets of ST VENANT and sent experimental - fatigue party attached men employed in this work. One man and lorry collected steam incinerators from farming. CO conferred with C.R.E. of Divsn as to erection of new Bath here at ST VENANT.	D.W.P.

WAR DIARY or INTELLIGENCE SUMMARY

Army Form C. 2118.

(Erase heading not required.)

Hour, Date, Place	Summary of Events and Information	Remarks and references to Appendices
ST VENANT - February 7th	Farm Camp at La Gorgue. Two men on Thirst Draingtion at St Venant Baths. One agment of carpenters Workmen attached engaged in structural alteration to building proposed to be used as Divisional Laundry.	R.P.
ST VENANT - February 8th	Camps and Billets inspected. One agment in trade Baths. One man knot and wagon extricated from Thirst of Dannow for collection of refuse of Town - this Workpment attached men also employed on work experimented. Rotary Road Sweeper employed in cleaning streets of Town - fatigue party also engaged on work experimented. One man and lorry collected clean ammunition from Laundry at LA GORGUE. Two men on Thirst Draingtion. Fatigue parties from Units stationed at CALONNE engaged in putting the Town in sanitary condition under superintendent. C.O arranged purchase of tongue for purposes Laundry at St VENANT and conferred with C.R.E. as to erection of new Horse Baths at ST VENANT.	R.P.
ST VENANT - February 8th	Camps and Billets inspected. One agment in trade Baths. One man have and wagon collected from Town of Dannow was fatigue against from Units billeted at CALONNE engaged in cleaning town and work experimented. Rotary Road Sweeper employed on cleaning streets of ST VENANT refuse of fatigue parties ensuing. Sanitary men of Artillery units attached	

WAR DIARY
or
INTELLIGENCE SUMMARY
(Erase heading not required.)

Army Form C. 2118.

Instructions regarding War Diaries and Intelligence Summaries are contained in F. S. Regs., Part II. and the Staff Manual respectively. Title pages will be prepared in manuscript.

Hour, Date, Place	Summary of Events and Information	Remarks and references to Appendices
	Inspection for scabies in Laundry work. One man was down with articulus clean undercothing from Laundry at LA GORGUE. New Spray Baths at ST VENANT opened and one opened by five men engaged. Heat Baths are erected by Divisional R.E. from it 65 occupy men in two shifts with 970 men. Capacity of Bath 120 men each hour = 1070 men per day. can be bathed in the maximum of two days and. Two men engaged in Thread Disinfector. O.J. Peters	
ST VENANT – 9" February 1916	Camps and Billets inspected. One agreed in trade Rubin One opened at new Spray Bath ST VENANT. One man has arms and upper extricia from thirst of Derman and foreign parties from their billets at CALONNE engaged in cleansing that town and made experiment. Two men in Thread Disinfecta. Includes men of Divisional Artillery. Trade inspected in termination. The men are being collected clean undercothing from LANNOY, LA GORGUE and ALLOUAGNES and returning to the proposed Laundry. C.O. informed with C.R.E. of Division as to proposed Laundry to be erected at ST VENANT. O.J. Peters	
ST VENANT February 10"	Camps and Billets inspected. One opened in Male Rubin. One opened at Spray Bath ST VENANT. Two men in Thread Disinfector at ST VENANT. One man and one man collected clean undercothing from Civic Laundry. C.O. conferred with C.R.E. as to proposed laundry at ST VENANT and visited CALONNE Bath and for proposed allocation.	

1247 W 3299 200,000 (E) 8/14 J.B.C.&A. Form C. 2118/11.

WAR DIARY
INTELLIGENCE SUMMARY

(Erase heading not required.)

Army Form C. 2118.

Instructions regarding War Diaries and Intelligence Summaries are contained in F. S. Regs., Part II. and the Staff Manual respectively. Title pages will be prepared in manuscript.

Hour, Date, Place	Summary of Events and Information	Remarks and references to Appendices
ST VENANT - February 11th	Recruits and Billets inspected. One squad in Nouie Buissie. Two men in Thiel Brainfeta. One squad at Spray Baths ST VENANT, the men own lorry collected clean underclothing from laundry at LAGORGUE. Two men transport attached one man, lime and wagon cleaning the stable of ST VENANT. Attention autocratic at ST VENANT Baths. Four carpenters, shoe men, & leather companies, not attached at CALONNE Baths. C.O. conferred with CREE as to transport laundry at ST VENANT.	N. Peters
ST VENANT - February 12th	Recruits and Billets inspected. One squad in Nouie Buissie. Two men in Thiel Brainfeta. One squad at Spray Baths ST VENANT. One man and lorry collected clean underclothing from Corps Laundry. Two men transport attached and one man, lime and wagon engaged in collecting refuse from billets + ST VENANT. Four carpenters, transport attached to leather engaged in carrying out attention at CALONNE Baths. Two men & leather also engaged C.O. visited CALONNE Baths and inspected transport workshops & Ypres capital.	Od Peters
ST VENANT - February 13th	Recruits and Billets inspected. One squad in Nouie Buissie. One squad at Spray Baths ST VENANT. Two men in Thiel Brainfeta. One man and lorry collected clean underclothing from Corps Laundry. One man, lime and wagon from front of Barracks and two transport attached men engaged	O.H.P.

Army Form C. 2118.

WAR DIARY
INTELLIGENCE SUMMARY
(Erase heading not required.)

Instructions regarding War Diaries and Intelligence Summaries are contained in F. S. Regs., Part II. and the Staff Manual respectively. Title pages will be prepared in manuscript.

Hour, Date, Place	Summary of Events and Information	Remarks and references to Appendices
ST VENANT - 14th February	On collecting report from sketch of ST VENANT Form confirmed and two men/ section engaged in carrying out alteration at CALONNE Baths. CO inspected the work. OVP Kampa and Billet inspected. One squad in Water Works. One squad at Spray Baths ST VENANT. Two men temporarily attached and one man, know and wagon engaged in cleaning street of ST VENANT. Two carpenter craftsmen attached and two men of section engaged installing the steam system at CALONNE Baths. CO conferred with CRE as to proposed journey to the new area ex ST VENANT. OVP	
ST VENANT - 15th February	Kampa and Billets inspected. One squad on Water works. One squad at Spray Baths ST VENANT. Two men temporarily attached and one man, horse and wagon engaged in cleaning street of ST VENANT. CO visited area to be occupied by Division and arranged as to Baths, Laundry etc. M. O. & / Maur. / Duncan examined with list of work required in new area. Party of Advance Storm and one man arranged to new billets as now KL GORGUE. OVP	

WAR DIARY
~~or~~ INTELLIGENCE SUMMARY

Army Form C. 2118.

Instructions regarding War Diaries and Intelligence Summaries are contained in F. S. Regs., Part II, and the Staff Manual respectively. Title pages will be prepared in manuscript.

(Erase heading not required.)

Hour, Date, Place	Summary of Events and Information	Remarks and references to Appendices
ST VENANT 16 February	Kemps and Butler inspected the squad on train Butler Camps Brances of clothing Parts of section clean and equipment and spare men inspected to men billets at LA GORGUE. Two motor transports attached and one man. Four men sent from 2nd Division engaged in cleaning shoes of ST VENANT. OAP	
ST VENANT } 17" N LA GORGUE }	Kemps and Butler inspected the squad in Vala Butler. The squad at present Baths PONT DU HEM. One squad at Baths, CROIX BARBEE. Remainder of section equipment, chins etc removed to new billets at LA GORGUE. Sanitary arrangement made and billets four in men. Bath, Laundry attendants etc. 35" Divisional Sanitary Section. OAP	
LA GORGUE – 18" S	Kemps and Butler inspection. One squad on train Butler. One squad at PONT DU HEM Bath and one squad at CROIX BARBEE Bath. One man in charge of Laundry Laundry LA GORGUE. Spoken from Divisional placed in charge of Section. Stephens Butler arranged and sanitary arrangement completed from contractors engaged on Divisional attention at present Baths. PONT DU HEM and CROIX BARBEE. OAP	

WAR DIARY
INTELLIGENCE SUMMARY
(Erase heading not required.)

Army Form C. 2118

Instructions regarding War Diaries and Intelligence Summaries are contained in F. S. Regs., Part II. and the Staff Manual respectively. Title Pages will be prepared in manuscript.

Place	Date	Hour	Summary of Events and Information	Remarks and references to Appendices
LA GORGUE	19th Feb.		Camps and Billets inspected. One squad in Nath Rufus. One squad at PONT DU HEM Baths and one squad at CROIX BARBEE Baths. Four carpenters engaged in alterations to forward Bath House. One man at Divisional Laundry LA GORGUE. Sanitary arrangements at D.H.Q. superintended. One man and party engaged in delivering clean and collecting soiled underclothing from various baths. Report [illegible] engaged in erection of Steam supply pipe Guards. Sanitair report 1DIHQ on erection of Steam supply pipe Guards. CROIX BARBEE Bath.	OMP
LA GORGUE	20th	Do	Camps and Billets inspected. One squad in Nath Rufus. One squad at PONT DU HEM Baths and one squad at CROIX BARBEE Baths. Four carpenters Henrymans attached engaged in alterations to forward Baths – PONT DU HEM and CROIX BARBEE. One man at Divisional Laundry LA GORGUE. Two men and thirty engaged in delivering clean underclothing to forward Baths. Sanitary work of LA GORGUE superintended. Sapper & Phelan engaged in fitting steam pipes at CROIX BARBEE Bath.	OMP
LA GORGUE	21st	Do	One squad in Nath Rufus Camps and Billets inspected. One squad at PONT DU HEM Baths and one squad at CROIX BARBEE Baths. The lorry from Div. Park engaged in allowing clean underclothing to Baths in forward area. Divisional Baths and Laundry at LA GORGUE superintended. Four carpenters Henrymans attached engaged in carrying out alteration at forward Baths.	OMP
LA GORGUE	22nd	Do	Camps and Billets inspected. One squad in Nath Rufus. One squad at PONT DU HEM Baths and one squad at CROIX BARBEE Baths. The lorry from Div. Park attached for delivery of clean underclothing to Baths in forward area. Divisional Baths and Laundry at LA GORGUE superintended. Case 1 German invalids at MERVILLE investigated and Active etc. changed and cleaned.	OMP

Army Form C. 2118

WAR DIARY
INTELLIGENCE SUMMARY
(Erase heading not required.)

Instructions regarding War Diaries and Intelligence Summaries are contained in F. S. Regs., Part II. and the Staff Manual respectively. Title Pages will be prepared in manuscript.

Place	Date	Hour	Summary of Events and Information	Remarks and references to Appendices
LA GORGUE	23rd February		Camps and Billets inspected. One squad in Water Duties. One squad at PONT DU HEM Baths and one squad at CROIX BARBÉE Baths. One lorry detailed from dis-Park and one man / section engaged in delivering and collecting underclothing, at baths in forward area. LA GORGUE Baths and outside employed in cleaning sheds. Laundry arrangements of LA GORGUE superintended.	OMP
LA GORGUE	24th	Do	Camps and Billets inspected. One squad in Water Duties. One squad at PONT DU HEM Baths and one squad at CROIX BARBÉE Baths. One lorry detailed from dis-Park and one man / section engaged in delivering and collecting underclothing from laundry to forward Baths. Baths and Laundry at LA GORGUE superintended. Rotary Press Freezer employed in cleaning sheds. C.O. visited No. 1 LA GORGUE and was informed that no infection arose had occurred in the 4 weeks and a case scarcely not specimen would be sent A.C.O. Engineers enhancing PONT DU HEM Baths. Rest Houses attendance and arrangements made with DADMS for removal of clothes etc.	OMP
LA GORGUE	25	Do	Camps and Billets inspected. One squad in Water Duties. One squad at PONT DU HEM Baths and one squad at CROIX BARBÉE Baths. One lorry detailed from dis-Park and one man / section engaged in collection and delivery of underclothing at forward Baths. Baths and Laundry at LA GORGUE superintended and the distribution of all shirts / drawers / clean men underclothing undertaken. Fatigue party attached and engaged in repairing roadways near Sections Billets. Engineers extending PONT DU HEM Baths.	OMP
LA GORGUE	26th	Do	Camps and Billets inspected. One squad in Water Duties. One squad at PONT DU HEM Baths and one squad at CROIX BARBÉE Baths. One lorry detailed from dis-Park and one man / section engaged in collection and delivery of underclothing at forward baths. Baths and Laundry at LA GORGUE superintended and the distribution of all shirts / drawers / clean men underclothing carried out. One squad of temporary attached engaged in making kits etc for Divisional Laundry. Report forwarded to D.H.Q. on arrival of Field Affects Persons in Rest Area.	OMP

WAR DIARY or INTELLIGENCE SUMMARY

Army Form C. 2118

(Erase heading not required.)

Place	Date	Hour	Summary of Events and Information	Remarks and references to Appendices
LA GORGUE	27 February		Camps and Billets inspected. One squad on Water duties. Three carpenters temporarily attached making racks etc for laundry. One squad at PONT DU HEM Baths and one squad at CROIX BARBÉE Baths. One lorry diverted from Lub Park and men engaged in collection and attery of material to forward baths. Baths and Laundry at LA GORGUE superintended and the distribution of new and clean underclothing to Units of Division carried out. REB. erecting PONTDUHEM Baths.	OMP
LA GORGUE	28th	Do.	Camps and Billets inspected. One squad on Water duties. One squad in forward area. Three carpenters temporarily attached engaged on making racks etc for Divisional Laundry. One squad at PONT DU HEM Baths and one squad at CROIX BARBÉE Baths. One lorry from Lub Park and one man from Lub Park and one man of section engaged in collection and delivery of material to forward Baths. Divisional Baths and Laundry superintended and the distribution of clean and new underclothing to Units of Division carried out. Bowsery and Section Bulls further made up. C.O. makes agreement to new PONT RIQUEUL Bath. & 7 frames a week so that Baths can be reconstructed with Brick-work.	OMP
LA GORGUE	29th	D	Camps and Billets inspected. One squad on Water duties. One squad at PONT DU HEM Baths and one squad at CROIX BARBÉE Baths. One lorry from Lub Park and one man of Section engaged in collection and delivery of underclothing to forward Baths. Divisional Baths and Laundry at LA GORGUE superintended and the distribution of clean and new underclothing to Units of Division carried out. Bowsery near Section Billet refilled. Engineers engaged in extending PONT DU HEM Baths. VIEILLE CHAPELLE Bath taken over. Case of measles at LA GORGUE investigated rooms sprayed and cleansed.	OMP

Army Form C. 2118

WAR DIARY
or
INTELLIGENCE SUMMARY

(Erase heading not required.)

Confidential

War Diary
of
Sanitary Section 36
from 1st March to 31st March 1916
(Vol. 9)

Remarks and references to Appendices: 36 San Sec Vol 9

WAR DIARY
or
INTELLIGENCE SUMMARY

(Erase heading not required.)

Army Form C. 2118

Instructions regarding War Diaries and Intelligence Summaries are contained in F. S. Regs., Part II. and the Staff Manual respectively. Title Pages will be prepared in manuscript.

Place	Date	Hour	Summary of Events and Information	Remarks and references to Appendices
LA GORGUE	1st March 1916		Camps and Billets inspected. Two men engaged in investigating water supplies in the trenches and sample of water obtained with a view for testing for poison. Two men of section on Frozen Lorry Disinfector. One agreed at PONT DU HEM Baths and one agreed at CROIX BARBEE Baths. Engineer engaged in restoring PONT DU HEM Bath. One man of section and lorry attended from Sub-Park collected and delivered soiled and clean underclothes to Divisional Baths. Divisional Bath and Laundry at LA GORGUE superintended and the distribution of clean and new underclothing to all units of Division carried out. Report of case of measles (military) at LA GORGUE forwarded to A.D.M.S. of Division. Readings near section Billets made up by men Stringrud, marked station and work superintended. Inventory of the camp F.P. (28?) on file for Henrow 1/7 1/7/556, 1st Highland Light Inf. promulgated.	O.H.P
LA GORGUE	2nd March		Camps and Billets inspected. One agreed in Nalle Butte. Two men of section on Frozen Lorry Disinfector. One agreed at PONT DU HEM Baths and one agreed at CROIX BARBEE Baths. Engineer engaged in restoring PONT DU HEM Baths. One man of section and lorry attended from Sub Park collected and delivered soiled and clean underclothing to Divisional Baths. Divisional Baths and Laundry at LA GORGUE superintended and the distribution of clean and new underclothing to all units of Division carried out. C.C. orders LAVENTIE and inspected billets of 82nd Fields Co. R.E. North Wales Brothers, 57th Infantry, Brigade H.Q. Kt Royal Warwicks, 7th East Lancs Regt and 7th Loyal North Lancs Regt.	O.H.P
LA GORGUE	3rd March		Camps and Billets inspected. One agreed on Nalle Butte. Clothing and equipment of certain persons disinfected by Frozen Lorry Disinfector. One agreed at PONT DU HEM Baths and one agreed at CROIX BARBEE Baths. Engineer engaged in restoring PONT DU HEM Baths. Two men of section and lorry attended from Sub Park for collection and delivery of soiled and clean underclothing to Divisional Baths. Divisional Baths and Laundry at LA GORGUE superintended and the distribution of clean and new underclothing to North of Division carried out. C.C. and 157/6 A.S.C. investigated and Billets to sprayed. General sanitation of LA GORGUE superintended and cases of measles arose of temporary attached men engaged.	O.H.P

WAR DIARY
or
INTELLIGENCE SUMMARY
(Erase heading not required.)

Army Form C. 2118

Place	Date	Hour	Summary of Events and Information	Remarks and references to Appendices
LA GORGUE	4th March		Champ and Billet inspected. One squad on Motor Buses. Sample of water taken from it the fire Avenue. Statement of hired water supplies forwarded to D.H.Q. and A.D.M.S. One squad at PONT DU HEM Baths and one squad at CROIX BARBEE Baths. One man sent away from Rest Park extensive for collection and delivery of soiled and clean underclothes to forward Baths. Sanitary arrangements at LA GORGUE superintended and squads of Company attached are engaged in cleaning up. General Baths and Laundry LA GORGUE superintended and the distribution of clean and new underclothing to units of Division supervised. Most York Regt as & outgoing clothes and clean stamps. N.C.O. crossed MERVILLE and return N.E. and S. of the town (New Branch Baths) on sanitary condition. Case of Measles at General from Billet near MERVILLE investigated Base Billet of Gd. Welsh Regt visited on Sanitation. Billet House Bath, LA TOUR at forward Baths inspected and been laundry visited.	OAP
LA GORGUE	5th March		Camps and Billet inspected. One squad on train duties. One squad at PONT DU HEM Baths and one squad at CROIX BARBEE Baths. Divisional Laundry at LA GORGUE superintended and distribution of new and clean underclothing to Units of Division superintended. Baths at LA GORGUE closed during & cleaning of Noxies. One man sent away extensive from Rest Park for collection and delivery of soiled and clean underclothing to forward baths. Sanitation of LA GORGUE supervised. C.O. visited forward area on making Billet weather-proof with Major of Engineers. Drying Room to be arranged at CROIX BARBEE Baths. 1 Lance Cpl promoted to clerk at CROIX BARBEE Billet.	OAP

WAR DIARY
or
INTELLIGENCE SUMMARY
(Erase heading not required.)

Army Form C. 2118

Instructions regarding War Diaries and Intelligence Summaries are contained in F.S. Regs., Part II. and the Staff Manual respectively. Title Pages will be prepared in manuscript.

Place	Date	Hour	Summary of Events and Information	Remarks and references to Appendices
LA GORGUE	6th March		Camps and Billets inspected. One squad in Field Duties. One squad at PONT DU HEM Baths and one squad at CROIX BARBEE Baths. Personnel laundry and Baths superintended and the distribution of clean and new underclothing to Units of Division carried out. One man sent temy from Ext. Park detailed for collection and delivery of clean and soiled underclothing to Divisional Baths. Engineers engaged in extending PONT DU HEM Baths. One squad of Carpenters engaged in fitting up Divisional system on PONT RIQUEUL Baths. Sanitary arrangements of LA GORGUE superintended and fatigue squad engaged in cleaning up. A.D. visited Billets of Yorkshire Dragoons about were found to have been satisfactorily cleaned up after having been left in insanitary condition by French Dragoons.	O.B.Peters
LA GORGUE	7th March		Camps and Billets inspected. One squad on Field Duties. One squad at PONT DU HEM Baths and one squad at CROIX BARBEE Baths. Personnel Baths and laundry superintended and the distribution of clean and new clothing to Units of Division carried out. One man and lorry from Ext. Park detailed for collection and delivery of clean and soiled underclothing to Divisional Baths. The squad of Carpenters temporarily attached to Section engaged at PONT RIQUEUL Baths. Case of cholera outbreak at MERVILLE investigated. Sanitary arrangements of LA GORGUE superintended and fatigue party engaged in cleaning up.	O.P.
LA GORGUE	8th March		Camps and Billets inspected. One squad in Field Duties. One squad at PONT DU HEM Baths and one squad at CROIX BARBEE Baths. Personnel Baths and laundry at LA GORGUE superintended and the distribution of clean and new clothing to Units of Division carried out. One man and lorry from Ext. Park detailed for collection and distributed clean and soiled underclothing to Divisional Baths. Carpenters engaged in carrying out alterations at PONT RIQUEUL Baths. Sanitary arrangements at LA GORGUE superintended.	O.B.P

1875 W. W593/825 1,000,000 4/15 J.B.C.&A. A.D.S.S./Forms/C.2118.

WAR DIARY
or
INTELLIGENCE SUMMARY
(Erase heading not required.)

Army Form C. 2118

Instructions regarding War Diaries and Intelligence Summaries are contained in F. S. Regs., Part II. and the Staff Manual respectively. Title Pages will be prepared in manuscript.

Place	Date	Hour	Summary of Events and Information	Remarks and references to Appendices
LA GORGUE	9th March		Lamps and Billets inspected. One squad on Water Duties. One squad at PONT DU HEM Baths and one squad at CROIX BARBEE Baths. One man and limber collected and delivered clean and soiled underclothing to Divisional Baths. Divisional Baths and Laundry at LA GORGUE superintended and the distribution of clean and new underclothing to Units of Division carried out. Two carpenters engaged on carrying out alterations and improvements at PONT RIQUEUL Baths. Sanitary arrangements at LA GORGUE superintended and fatigue party engaged on cleaning up. C.O. in company with A.D.M.S. inspected PONT DU HEM Baths and CROIX BARBEE Baths and Billets of 7th L.N. Lancs Regt at CROIX BARBEE and 7th E. Lancs at RUE DU PUITZ. C.O. made visit of LA GORGUE Laundry. C.O. gave lecture on Field Sanitation at School of Instruction, MERVILLE.	O.A.P.
LA GORGUE	10th March		Lamps and Billets inspected. One squad on Water Duties. One squad at PONT DU HEM Baths and one squad at CROIX BARBEE Baths. One man and limber collected and delivered clean and soiled underclothing to Divisional Baths. Divisional Baths and Laundry at LA GORGUE superintended and the distribution of clean and new underclothing to Units of Division carried out. Two carpenters engaged on carrying out improvements at PONT RIQUEUL Baths. 60 inspected with 4 fatigue men on collection of linen of LA GORGUE. 60 visited Billets of 1st Hampshire Regt 22nd July 1st RE 35th Brit Sanitary and S.H. Staff Regt.	O.A.P.
LA GORGUE	11th March		Lamps and Billets inspected. One squad on Water Duties. One squad at PONT DU HEM Baths and one squad at CROIX BARBEE Baths. One man and limber collected clean and soiled underclothing at Divisional Baths. Divisional Baths and Laundry at LA GORGUE superintended and the distribution of clean and new underclothing to Units of Division carried out. Two carpenters carrying out	

WAR DIARY
or
INTELLIGENCE SUMMARY

(Erase heading not required.)

Army Form C. 2118

Place	Date	Hour	Summary of Events and Information	Remarks and references to Appendices
LA GORGUE	12th March		Alterations at PONT RIQUEUL Baths. Sanitary arrangements at LA GORGUE Superintended and fatigue squad engaged. M.O. inspected Room and Billets of 1st Hertfords Regt and M. staff along with A.D.M.S.	OMP
LA GORGUE	12th March		One squad in Water Duties. Carpenter and Butler inspected the squad at PONT DU HEM Baths and on squad at CROIX BARBEE Baths. Two carpenters engaged in structural alteration at PONT RIQUEUL Baths. One man and boy engaged in collecting and delivering clean and soiled underclothing to forward Baths. Divisional Baths and Laundry at LA GORGUE Superintended over the distribution of clean and new underclothing. A all Ranks ? Division carried out Sanitary arrangements at LA GORGUE Superintended and fatigue Party cleaning system.	OMP
LA GORGUE	13th March		Carpenter and Butler inspected the squad in Water Duties. One squad at PONT DU HEM Baths and one squad at CROIX BARBEE Baths. Squad of Carpenter engaged on structural alteration at PONT RIQUEUL Baths. One man and boy engaged in collecting and delivering clean and soiled underclothing to forward Baths. Divisional Baths and Laundry at LA GORGUE Superintended over the distribution of clean and new underclothing. A all Ranks of Division bathed and Sanitary arrangements of LA GORGUE Superintended and Fatigue Party engaged in cleaning of town. M.O. inspected Refitting Rooms ? H.C. Mess, 56th 57th and 58th Brigades. 60 men in Aryn Laundry and found that 38th Division were receiving 2800 sets of clean underclothing per day and that the Laundry was Turning out more than 2,900 sets per day for the 35th and 38th Division whereas the 116 Division troops have a average only 500 sets per day only from the Divisional Laundry. This matter was referred to D.M.S. and suggest means that the 116 Division obtain Linen or the increased output of the Corps Laundry. Lists of Civilian hospital (?) arrived at LA GORGUE.	OMP

WAR DIARY
or
INTELLIGENCE SUMMARY
(Erase heading not required.)

Army Form C. 2118

Instructions regarding War Diaries and Intelligence Summaries are contained in F.S. Regs., Part II. and the Staff Manual respectively. Title Pages will be prepared in manuscript.

Place	Date	Hour	Summary of Events and Information	Remarks and references to Appendices
LA GORGUE	14th March		Camps and Billets inspected. One squad on Water Duties. One squad at PONT DU HEM Baths and one squad at CROIX BARBEE. One man and lorry delivered clean and collected soiled underclothing on previous baths. Divisional Baths and Laundry at LA GORGUE superintended and the distribution of clean and new underclothing to Units of Division carried out. Two companies engaged in making alterations at PONT RIQUEUL Baths. Case of measles investigated at PONT DU HEM and billets sprayed. (Sobers Light Infantry) – Means of LA GORGUE inspected. Sanitary arrangements at LA GORGUE superintended and fatigue parties engaged on cleaning up town. C.O. rode to D.A.C. Lieut. BX now installed at Hospital Destruction at LA GORGUE.	OVP
LA GORGUE	15th March		Camps and Billets inspected. One squad on Water Duties. One squad at PONT OU HEM Baths and one squad at CROIX BARBEE Baths. One man and lorry delivered clean and collected soiled underclothing to and from previous baths. Divisional Baths and Laundry at LA GORGUE superintended and the distribution of clean and new underclothing to Units of Division carried out. Squad of sanitaries engaged in making structural alterations at PONT RIQUEUL Baths. Sanitary arrangements at LA GORGUE superintended and fatigue parties engaged on cleaning up town. Case of measles at LA GORGUE (35th Divisional Train) investigated and billet sprayed. One case of Diptheria(?) amongst civil population at LA GORGUE investigated. C.O. inspected CROIX BARBEE - Billets superintended and autocut carried. Also visited Baths at CROIX BARBEE, PONT DU HEM and PONT RIQUEUL and Hospital Destructors (2) at LA GORGUE.	OVP
LA GORGUE	16th March		Camps and Billets inspected. One squad on Water Duties. One squad at PONT DU HEM Baths and one squad at CROIX BARBEE Baths. One man and lorry delivered clean and collected soiled underclothing to and from previous baths. Divisional Baths and Laundry at LA GORGUE superintended and the distribution of clean and new underclothing to Units of Division carried out. One companies engaged on making repairs for collection of Water at LA GORGUE. Sanitary arrangements at LA GORGUE superintended and fatigue parties engaged in cleaning up town. Lieut. R. J. Batty RAMC attached to Section for training under Major J.	OVP

1375 Wt. W393/826 1,000,000 4/15 J.B.C. & A. A.D.S.S./Forms/C. 2118.

WAR DIARY or **INTELLIGENCE SUMMARY**
(Erase heading not required.)

Army Form C. 2118

Instructions regarding War Diaries and Intelligence Summaries are contained in F.S. Regs, Part II. and the Staff Manual respectively. Title Pages will be prepared in manuscript.

Place	Date	Hour	Summary of Events and Information	Remarks and references to Appendices
LA GORGUE	17th March		A.D.M.S. C Onsoles Sgt Tuda Ambulance and cost of Searce Form. CO inspected 89th Bde R.F.A. A Cam D Battery Wagon line. C.O inspected RIEZ BAILLEUL Billet and one of Searce Zone one. Inspection of Syphon Chas LA GORGUE morid. One squad on trade Braties. Camp and Billets inspected. One squad at PONT DU HEM Baths and one squad at CROIX BARBEE Baths. One man and lorry engaged in collection and return of dirty and clean washing previous to forward baths. Divisional Baths and Laundry at LA GORGUE superintended. The distribution of clean and new underclothing to Units of Division supervised. One captain engaged in arranging trip for collection of refuse at LA GORGUE. Sanitary arrangements at LA GORGUE and fatigue party engaged in cleaning up Town. C.O. inspected two battalions in LA GORGUE and made arrangements as to filter mending and erecting of Hospice Bedrooms. C.O. review Ammunition Column and Depots 1 A.B.C. and D Battersea of 88th Brigade R.F.A.	OMP
LA GORGUE	18th March		Camps and Billets inspected. One squad on trade Braties. One squad at BNT DU HEM Baths and one squad at CROIX BARBEE Baths. One man and lorry engaged in collection and return of dirty + clean underclothing to forward Baths. Divisional Baths and Laundry at LA GORGUE superintended and the distribution of clean and new underclothing to Units of Division experienced. Sanitary Arrangements at LA GORGUE superintended and fatigue party engaged in cleaning up Town. C.O. inspected Ammunition Column and wagon line of H.Q. and A.B.C and D Batteries of 87th Brigade R.F.A. and Battery in forward area at EPINETTE farm re manure endowment. Hospice Bedroom at LA GORGUE inspected. Ten men classified as "T.B." attached Lecture for light duty.	OMP

1875 Wt. W593/826 1,000,000 4/15 J.B.C. & A. A.D.S.S./Forms/C. 2118. -

WAR DIARY or INTELLIGENCE SUMMARY

Army Form C. 2118

Place	Date	Hour	Summary of Events and Information	Remarks and references to Appendices
LA GORGUE	1st March		Camps and Billets inspected. One squad on Water Duties. One squad at PONT DU HEM Baths and one squad at CROIX BARBEE Baths. The men and boys collected soiled underclothes and clean underclothing from same to Divisional Baths. Divisional Baths and Laundry at LA GORGUE superintended and the distribution of clean and new underclothing to Units of Division carried out. On instruction of A.D.M.S. Latter Lorry Disinfector provided to 11th Corps Laundry for five days disinfection of clothing and on Julius the Disinfector was to be placed at the disposal of the Corps Laundry for seven days weekly. Sanitary arrangements at LA GORGUE superintended and fatigue squad engaged in cleaning up town.	OMP
LA GORGUE	2nd March		Camps and Billets inspected. One squad on Water Duties. One squad at PONT DU HEM Baths and one squad at CROIX BARBEE Baths. One man and boy collected clean and collected soiled underclothing to and from Divisional Baths. Divisional Baths and Laundry at LA GORGUE superintended and the distribution of clean and new underclothing to Units of Division carried out. Two carpenters engaged in constructing oven for cleaning. Case of Measles at 10th Manchester investigated and dugouts in trenches cleansed. Trace of future investigation at 7th/8th Lancashire Regt. Enteric case of Measles investigated at CROIX MARMUSE. Arrangements made for fatigue squad of 50 men to clean up LA GORGUE and CROIX BARBEE. C.O. attended Charles. Mission meeting.	OMP
LA GORGUE	3rd March		Camps and Billets inspected. One squad on Water Duties. One squad at PONT DU HEM Baths and one squad at CROIX BARBEE Baths. The men and boys collected clean and collected soiled underclothing from same to Divisional Baths and Laundry at LA GORGUE superintended and the distribution of clean and new underclothing to Units of Division carried out. Two carpenters engaged in construction alterations at LA GORGUE Laundry and a man to increasing the output of washing. Sanitary arrangements at LA GORGUE	

WAR DIARY
or
INTELLIGENCE SUMMARY
(Erase heading not required.)

Army Form C. 2118

Instructions regarding War Diaries and Intelligence Summaries are contained in F. S. Regs., Part II. and the Staff Manual respectively. Title Pages will be prepared in manuscript.

Place	Date	Hour	Summary of Events and Information	Remarks and references to Appendices
			Superintended and fatigue party engaged in cleaning up town. Part 1 fatigue squad cleaning up CROIX BARBEE as Personnel. One of 3 Musicians at 3rd WELCH Regiment interviewed and billets arranged. Other personnel at DIVISIONAL BATHS as to system of Sanitary Inspection etc.	OTP
LA GORGUE	22nd March		Camps and Billets inspected. One squad in Rue Duchés. One squad at PONT DU HEM Baths and one squad at CROIX BARBEE Baths. The men and lorry attended clean underclothing to personnel Bath and attested own underclothing. Divisional Baths and Laundry at LA GORGUE superintended and the distribution of clean and new underclothing to Units & Divisional service ran. Three carpenters, temporarily attached Kitchen engaged in structural alteration at Divisional Laundry LA GORGUE. Sanitary arrangements at LA GORGUE superintended and fatigue party from Divisional Ambulance engaged in cleaning up town. Fatigue party from Divisional Ambulance also cleaned up in that ch. about PONT RIQUEUL and such work superintended. Arrangements made with D.W.O. for further Bath of 50 men for fatigue duty to attend on 23rd inst. O/C proceeded on leave & handed taking over to Lieut. Batty R.A.M.C. Work even and over during absence.	ILB
LA GORGUE	23rd March		Camps and Billets inspected. One squad in Rue Duchés. One squad at PONT DU HEM Baths and one squad at CROIX BARBEE Baths. The men and lorry attended clean underclothing to personnel Baths and collected soiled underclothing. Divisional Baths and Laundry at LA GORGUE superintended and the distribution of clean and new underclothing to Units & Division service out. Three carpenters temporarily attached to section engaged in structural alteration at Divisional Laundry LA GORGUE. Fatigue party from Divisional Ambulance engaged in cleaning up Town of LA GORGUE and

1875 Wt. W593/826 1,000,000 4/15 J.B.C. & A. A.D.S.S./Forms/C. 2118.

WAR DIARY or INTELLIGENCE SUMMARY

Army Form C. 2118

Place	Date	Hour	Summary of Events and Information	Remarks and references to Appendices
LA GORGUE	24th March		Sanitary arrangements superintended. Fatigue squad also engaged in clearing up LA BASSÉE Road.	
LA GORGUE	24th March		One squad in North Butts Coy and Field inspected. One squad at PONT DU HEM Baths and one squad at CROIX BARBÉE Baths. The men and boys otherwise clean undertaking & forward baths and collected soiled clothes. Divisional Baths and Laundry at LA GORGUE superintended and the distribution of clean and new underclothing. 8 Units of Divisional Carpenters under O/C 1st Carpenter Stanyan attacked engaged in structural alteration at LA GORGUE Laundry. Two French civilians and one attached man engaged on sanitary work at LA GORGUE and each work superintended. Lieut. Batty and Carpenter visited Trenches as to Sandbag and water experiment.	
LA GORGUE	25th March		Company Orders inspected. One squad in North Butts. One squad at PONT DU HEM Baths and one squad at CROIX BARBÉE Baths. Baths at NEUVE CHAPELLE and LESTREM placed in charge of Section Sergeants. The men and boys otherwise clean undertaking to forward baths over overcoats soiled clothes. Divisional Baths and Laundry at LA GORGUE superintended and the distribution of clean and new underclothing. 8 Units of Divisional Carpenters arrived work. Two carpenter companies attached and one man of section engaged in structural alteration at LA GORGUE Laundry. Two French civilians and one attached man engaged on sanitary work in LA GORGUE and each work superintended. Lieut. Batty accompanied by Corporal visited trenches re Sandbags and water supplies. Report on erection of Field Laundry by 5th Brigade Divisional ADMS investigated. Civilian case of Contra Spinal Meningitis at MERVILLE investigated.	

Army Form C. 2118

WAR DIARY
or
INTELLIGENCE SUMMARY
(Erase heading not required.)

Instructions regarding War Diaries and Intelligence Summaries are contained in F. S. Regs., Part II. and the Staff Manual respectively. Title Pages will be prepared in manuscript.

Place	Date	Hour	Summary of Events and Information	Remarks and references to Appendices
LA GORGUE	26 March		Camps and Billets inspected. One squad on Kella Duties. One squad at PONT DU HEM Baths and one squad at CROIX BARBEE Baths. The men and Lorry delivering clean clothes to, and collected soiled underclothing. Divisional Baths and the distribution of clean and new underclothing to thirds of Divisions carried out. Three carpenters engaged in structural alteration at Divisional Laundry LA GORGUE. Four French civilians and squad of attached men engaged on Laundry work in LA GORGUE and with supervision. Coal & Miocoks at 19 Divisional Train received and their disposal. Four men from 7 East Lancashire Regt attached for instruction in sanitary work and those for instruction in rat-catching.	AWB
LA GORGUE	27 March		Camps and Billets inspected. One squad on Kella Duties. One squad at PONT DU HEM Baths and one squad at CROIX BARBEE Baths. The men and Lorry delivering clean and collected soiled clothes. Divisional Baths and distribution to Divisional Baths and the distribution of clean and new underclothing to thirds of Divisions carried out. Three carpenters temporarily attached engaged on making structural alteration and improvement at Divisional Laundry, LA GORGUE. Four French civilians and squad of attached men engaged on sanitary work at LA GORGUE and work experiment.	RWB
LA GORGUE	28 March		Camps and Billets inspected. One squad on Kella Duties. One squad at Baths CROIX BARBEE. The men and Lorry delivering clean underclothing to Baths at PONT DU HEM and CROIX BARBEE and collected soiled clothes. One L Surgeon	

WAR DIARY or INTELLIGENCE SUMMARY

Army Form C. 2118

(Erase heading not required.)

Instructions regarding War Diaries and Intelligence Summaries are contained in F.S. Regs., Part II. and the Staff Manual respectively. Title Pages will be prepared in manuscript.

Place	Date	Hour	Summary of Events and Information	Remarks and references to Appendices
			and no reinforcement attached to below details for the return of clean underclothing to Baths at ORES STREET and RICHEBOURG. Divisional Baths and Laundry at LAGORGUE superintended and the distribution of clean and new underclothing to them of linen carried out. Wire entanglers temporarily attached engaged in carrying out structural alterations at Divisional Laundry, LAGORGUE. Sun. Dried curtain and square of attached men engaged in sanitary work at LA GORGUE and work superintended. Case of Measles at P.W.Lincolnshire Regt investigated and billet sprayed. Case of Cerebro Spinal Meningitis at MERVILLE further investigated.	
LAGORGUE	29 March		Baths and Billets inspected. One squad on Native Baths. One squad at PONT DU HEM Baths and one squad at PONT DU HEM South. One man and lorry delivering clean underclothing to Baths at CROIX BARBEE and PONT DU HEM and collected soiled clothes. W.S. Wagon delivered clean clothes to Divisional Baths at GRUB STREET and RICHEBOURG. One Carpenter engaged in alteration at Divisional Laundry LAGORGUE. Laundry arrangements at LAGORGUE superintended and fatigue parties of foot trench civilians and Khaymans attached men engaged in cleaning town. One man from 6th Wiltshire Regt attached section for duty.	
LAGORGUE	30 March		Baths and Billets inspected. One squad on Native Baths. One squad at PONT DU HEM Baths and one squad at CROIX BARBEE Baths. One man and lorry delivering clean underclothing to Baths at CROIX BARBEE and PONT DU HEM and collected soiled clothes. One man	

WAR DIARY
or
INTELLIGENCE SUMMARY

(Erase heading not required.)

Army Form C. 2118

Place	Date	Hour	Summary of Events and Information	Remarks and references to Appendices
			and U.S. Wagon delivered clean clothing to Baths on GRUB STREET and RICHEBOURG l'avoué. Carpentin engaged in alteration at Nouveau Monde Camp. Divisional Baths and Laundry at LA GORGUE superintended and the distribution of clean and new clothing to Hand Wash carried out. Four Field Ovens and squad of attached men engaged in cleaning time of LA GORGUE and sanitary arrangements superintended. Baths & Mundres of Base Battalion Regt of Divisional Cavalry superintended and billets inspected.	
LA GORGUE	31st March		Camps and Billets inspected. One squad on Male Baths. One squad at PONT DU HEM Battalion one squad at CROIX BARBEE Baths. One man and boy delivered clean men's clothing to baths at PONT DU HEM and CROIX BARBEE and collected soiled clothes. One man and U.S. Wagon detailed for delivery of clean men's clothing to forward baths at GRUB STREET and RICHEBOURG. Divisional Baths and Laundry at LA GORGUE superintended and the distribution of clean and new men's clothing to Units of Division carried out. Sanitary arrangements at LA GORGUE superintended and fatigue party engaged in cleaning up town. Cases of Scabies from 6th Middlesex Regt and 1st Lincoln Regt investigated and billets sprayed with formalin. Strength of DHQ as to annexure of this record today 4.57" signing, Bingadien, 60 attained from leave.	

WAR DIARY
or
INTELLIGENCE SUMMARY

(Erase heading not required.)

Army Form C. 2118

36 San Sec
Vol 10

Confidential

War Diary
of
Sanitary Section 36
From 1st April to 30 April 1916
(Vol 10)

COMMITTEE FOR THE
MEDICAL HISTORY OF THE WAR
Date 9 - JUN. 1916

Place	Date	Hour	Summary of Events and Information	Remarks and references to Appendices
	April 1916			1916

Army Form C. 2118.

WAR DIARY
or
INTELLIGENCE SUMMARY.
(Erase heading not required.)

Instructions regarding War Diaries and Intelligence Summaries are contained in F. S. Regs., Part II. and the Staff Manual respectively. Title pages will be prepared in manuscript.

Place	Date	Hour	Summary of Events and Information	Remarks and references to Appendices
	1916			
LA GORGUE	1st April		Camps and Billets inspected. One squad on Trek Baths. One squad at PONT DU HEM Baths and one squad at CROIX BARBEE Baths. One man and lorry delivered clean underclothing to Baths at PONT DU HEM and CROIX BARBEE Baths and collected soiled clothes. One man and O.S. Wagon delivered clean underclothing to baths at GRUB STREET and RICHEBOURG and collected soiled clothes. Divisional Baths and Laundry at LA GORGUE superintended and the distribution of clean underclothing to units f/ Division carried out. Three carpenters engaged in making appliances for Divisional Laundry. Four Divnl. Cooker and squad of attached men engaged in sanitary work at LA GORGUE and work superintended. Lieut. Tracy R.A.M.C. returned to duty with 59 Field Ambulance. C.O. visited Curlu-axe 1(?) Dribbletern at PONT RIQUEUL.	
LA GORGUE	2nd	Do	Camps and Billets inspected. One squad on Trek Baths. One squad at CROIX BARBEE Baths. One squad on CROIX BARBEE Baths. One man and lorry delivered clean underclothing to Baths at PONT DU HEM and CROIX BARBEE Baths and collected soiled clothes. One man and O.S. Wagon delivered clean underclothing to GRUB STREET and RICHEBOURG and collected soiled clothes. Divisional Baths and Laundry at LA GORGUE superintended and the distribution of clean and new underclothing to units f/ Division carried out. Three carpenters engaged in making appliances	

WAR DIARY
or
INTELLIGENCE SUMMARY.
(Erase heading not required.)

Army Form C. 2118.

Instructions regarding War Diaries and Intelligence Summaries are contained in F.S. Regs., Part II. and the Staff Manual respectively. Title pages will be prepared in manuscript.

Place	Date	Hour	Summary of Events and Information	Remarks and references to Appendices
			/P. Divisional Laundry, LA GORGUE. 200 French civilians and squad of attached men engaged in sorting work at LA GORGUE and work superintended. Ambulance trooper from. OMP	
LA GORGUE	3rd April		Camps and Billets inspected. The squad on Bath Duties. The squad at PONT DU HEM Baths and one squad at Baths CROIX BARBEE. The man and lorry delivered clean underclothing to Baths at CROIX BARBEE and PONT DU HEM. The man and U.S. wagon delivered clean underclothing to Baths at GREE STREET and RICHEBOURG and collected soiled clothes. Divisional Baths and laundry LA GORGUE superintended and the distribution of clean and new underclothing to Units commented. Three carpenters and attached man engaged in erecting drying shed at Divisional Laundry. 200 French civilians and squad of attached men engaged in sorting work at LA GORGUE and simulation of Town superintended. 6.0. visited MERVILLE and A.D.O.S. referring hymn for Valangé Bath - made arrangements for town drains with civilians and Cpl. of Divison. Ambulance in Workshop. OMP	
LA GORGUE	4. April		Camps and Billets inspected. The squad on Bath Duties. The squad at PONT DU HEM Baths and one squad at CROIX BARBEE. The man and lorry delivered clean underclothing to Baths at	

Army Form C. 2118.

Instructions regarding War Diaries and Intelligence Summaries are contained in F. S. Regs., Part II. and the Staff Manual respectively. Title pages will be prepared in manuscript.

WAR DIARY
or
INTELLIGENCE SUMMARY.
(Erase heading not required.)

Place	Date	Hour	Summary of Events and Information	Remarks and references to Appendices
			CROIX BARBEE and PONT DU HEM. The men and O.S. wagon although clean and clothing to Battn at GRUB STREET and RICHEBURG and collected soiled clothes. Personnel Baths and (Laun) at LA GORGUE superintended and the distribution of clean and new underclothing to Units of Division carried out. Three carpenters and riveters men engaged in erecting drying sheet at Personnel Laundry. Two French curtains and apron factories men engaged in sanitary work in LA GORGUE and environs 1 km superintended. CO visited Kings Post (Yorkshire Regt) at Scarlet Loop and German Muroto cases and inspected billets. CO visited 59 Field Ambulance re Scarlet Loop cases and inspected billets of 8 Staffordshire Regt (LA GORGUE). CO crossed LA GORGUE Bridge of Warwickshire Regt.	
LA GORGUES	April		Trenches and Billets inspected. All quiet in trenches. As gunner at Pont du Hem Battn arms operated at CROIX BARBEE Bath. Personnel Laundry collected clean underclothing to Batts at PONT DU HEM and CROIX BARBEE and accepted soiled clothes. The men and U.S. wagon delivered clean clothes to Batts at GRUB STREET and RICHEBURG and collected soiled clothes. Personnel Baths and Laundry at LA GORGUE superintended and the distribution of clean and new underclothing to Units of Division carried out. Three carpenters and men attached men engaged constructing drying shed at Personnel Laundry. Two French curtain	

WAR DIARY
or
INTELLIGENCE SUMMARY.
(Erase heading not required.)

Army Form C. 2118.

Place	Date	Hour	Summary of Events and Information	Remarks and references to Appendices
			Five squads of attached men engaged in sanitary work at LA GORGUE and escalation. 1 him superintended.	
			(1) escorted afternoon convoy of ammunition before but weather began. One of 88ᵗʰ Bde R.F.A. Ammunition Column D	
			Battery, 88ᵗʰ Sec. B Battery, 88ᵗʰ Bde A Battery, and B Battery 87ᵗʰ Sec. R.F.A. O.N.P.	
LA GORGUE	6ᵗʰ April		Nampo and Billet inspected. One squad on bath duties. One squad at PONT DU HEM Baths and one squad at	
			CROIX BARBEE Bath. One man and boy delivered clean under-clothing to prisoners baths at PONT DU HEM and	
			CROIX BARBEE and collected soiled clothes. One man and US flag-waller in clean men's clothing to	
			Baths at ORIS STREET and RICHEBOURG and collected soiled clothes. Two carpenters and attached	
			men engaged on construction drying shed at Divisional Laundry. One carpenter engaged in making	
			appliances for Divisional Laundry. Divisional Laundry and Baths LA GORGUE superintended	
			and the distribution of clean and new underclothing to Units of Division carried out. Four French	
			civilian and one girl attached men engaged in sanitary work at LA GORGUE and sanitation of	
			town superintended. Cas. 1 military at 1ˢᵗ handicap-station Regt. invalided and billet of major.	
			Enquiries made as to civilian cases of 2 μmiracles at PONT RIQUEUL. O.N.P.	

WAR DIARY
or
INTELLIGENCE SUMMARY.

(Erase heading not required.)

Army Form C. 2118.

Instructions regarding War Diaries and Intelligence Summaries are contained in F. S. Regs., Part II. and the Staff Manual respectively. Title pages will be prepared in manuscript.

Place	Date	Hour	Summary of Events and Information	Remarks and references to Appendices
LA GORGUE	7 April		Lamps and Billets inspected. Bu squad on bathi Baths. One squad at PONT DU HEM Baths and one squad at CROIX BARBEE Baths. One man and lorry delivered clean underclothing to Baths at CROIX BARBEE and PONT DU HEM. One man + C.S. Major delivered clean underclothing to baths at RUE STREET and RICHEBOURG and collected soiled clothes. Divisional Baths and Laundry at LA GORGUE superintended over the distribution of clean and new underclothing to units of Division carried out. Two carpenters attached men engaged in constructing frames and drying shed at Divisional Laundry. Two carpenters engaged in making appliances for Divisional Laundry. Two French civilian women engaged in washing. Two men engaged in laundry work at LA GORGUE and the construction of a new superintendent. Arrangements having been made for Latrine accommodation at LA GORGUE, FOSSE and VIEILLE CHAPELLE & further receptacles for toilet waste for dugouts and trench areas, all specific inspection of latrines made in these districts where it was found scarcity of latrines and that most all latrines had provided a suitable receptacle and was labelled same.	
LA GORGUE	8 April		Lamps and Billets inspected. One squad on baths Baths. One squad at PONT DU HEM Baths and one squad at CROIX BARBEE Baths. One man and lorry delivered clean underclothing to baths at CROIX BARBEE and PONT DU HEM and collected soiled clothes. One man + C.S. Major delivered clean underclothing to	

WAR DIARY or INTELLIGENCE SUMMARY

Army Form C. 2118.

Place	Date	Hour	Summary of Events and Information	Remarks and references to Appendices
			Baths at GRUB STREET and RICHEBOURG and collected soiled clothes. Divisional Baths and Laundry LA GORGUE superintended and the distribution of clean and new underclothing & work carried out. The output of the Divisional Laundry for the week ending the 17 April was 31,960 articles - an increase of 10,100 articles per week since the extension of the Laundry. 10,785 Officers, N.C.Os men bathed at Divisional Baths during the week. Two carpenters and one attached man engaged in drying sheds at Divisional Laundry and no carpenter making apparatus for moving from 1st Worcestershire Regt. Classified as TD attached & technical duty. Four French civilians and squad of attached men engaged in sanitary work at LA GORGUE and demolition of former experimental.	
LA GORGUE.	17 April		Temp. and Butler inspected Dr squad on Water Butts, the squad at PONT DU HEM Baths and one squad at CROIX BARBEE Baths. One man and lorry delivered clean underclothing to baths at CROIX BARBEE and PONT DU HEM. One man and M.S Wagon delivered clean underclothing to Baths at GRUB STREET and RICHE BOURG and collected soiled clothes. Divisional Baths and Laundry superintended and the distribution of cleanwear and underclothing to Units carried out. Divisional Laundry closed for today. Two carpenters engaged in making appliances for laundry. Four French civilians and squad of attached men engaged in sanitary work and demolition of former experiments. Chronicles 6 Yorkshire Regt. ex attached of Batista amongst Officers	

T2131. Wt. W708-776. 50000. 4/15. Sir J. C. & S.

WAR DIARY
or
INTELLIGENCE SUMMARY.
(Erase heading not required.)

Army Form C. 2118.

Place	Date	Hour	Summary of Events and Information	Remarks and references to Appendices
			also case of 2nd Croydon Grenadier Attempth at 7pm Funeral in Rep also sanitary invasion Atuck at CROIX BARBEE and CROIX BARBEE Baths and PONT DU HEM Baths. Report and Returns of Guardroom 15 inches and work of Machine Gun(outpost) of Retriere attacked)	OMP
LA GORGUE	10th April		Company and Billets inspected. The opened on Male Baths. The opened at PONT DU HEM Baths and the opened at CROIX BARBEE Baths. The men and boys attended clean manufacturing at Baths at CROIX BARBEE and PONT DU HEM and collected soiled clothes. The men and US hogm attended clothes to Baths at PIERRESBURG and the STREET and collected soiled clothes. Divisional Baths and Laundry at LA GORGUE superintended and the distribution of clean and new manufacturing to Units carried out. Divisional civilian arose agreed attached now engaged in sanitary work in LA GORGUE and sanitation of town superintended. Laundry engaged in making appliances for laundry.	OMP
LA GORGUE	11th April		Company and Billets inspected. The opened at Male Baths. The opened at PONT DU HEM Baths and the opened at CROIX BARBEE and PONT DU HEM Baths. The men and boys attended clean manufacturing to Baths at CROIX BARBEE and PONT DU HEM and collected soiled clothes. The men and US hogm attended clean clothes to Baths at RICHEBOURG and GRUB STREET and collected soiled clothes. Divisional Baths and Laundry LA GORGUE superintended	

WAR DIARY
or
INTELLIGENCE SUMMARY
(Erase heading not required.)

Army Form C. 2118.

Place	Date	Hour	Summary of Events and Information	Remarks and references to Appendices
			and the distribution of clean and new underclothing to Mens of Divion cantoned. Jun carpenters engaged in making apphones for laundry. Sun French civilians and squad of attached men engaged in sanitary work at LA GORGUE and sanitation of town superintended. EO visited ST VENANT re British laundries and Baths. Billet of 19' Environnat Irac where case of German Measles had occurred disinfected. ONP	
LA GORGUE	12' April		Campaign British inspector. One squad at Baths CROIX BARBEE and PONT DU HEM. One man and lorry delivered clean underclothing to baths at CROIX BARBEE and PONT DU HEM and collected soiled clothes. One man and U.S. Wagon delivered clean underclothing to French baths at GRUB STREET and RICHEBOURG and collected soiled clothes. Divisional Baths and Laundry LA GORGUE superintended and the distribution of clean and new clothing to Units of Division carried out. Sun carpenters engaged in making apphones for laundry. Sun French civilians and squad of attached men engaged in sanitary work in LA GORGUE and sanitation of town superintended. CO inspected Ironbothers Regiment reference German Measles; all Officers and other billets placed Out of Bounds and new billeting arrangements arranged for also few huts and if necessary tents to arrive today. Civilian cases of Typhus and Diphtheria at LESTREM and Appelterre at LA GORGUE investigation. ONP	

T☐34. Wt. W708 -776. 500000. 4/15. Sir J. C. & S.

WAR DIARY
or
INTELLIGENCE SUMMARY.
(Erase heading not required.)

Army Form C. 2118.

Instructions regarding War Diaries and Intelligence Summaries are contained in F.S. Regs., Part II. and the Staff Manual respectively. Title pages will be prepared in manuscript.

Place	Date	Hour	Summary of Events and Information	Remarks and references to Appendices
LA GORGUE	April 13th		Company and Billets inspected. One squad on Fatigue Duties. One squad on Hot Baths at PONT DU HEM and one squad at CROIX BARBEE. One man and lorry delivered clean underclothing to Baths at CROIX BARBEE and PONT DU HEM and collected soiled cloths. One man and US Wagon delivered clean underclothing to baths at RICHEBOURG and GRUB STREET and collected soiled underclothing. Divisional Baths and Laundry LA GORGUE experimented. One carpenter and the distribution of cleaned new underclothing to Wives of Divison experimented. One french civilian and squad of attached men engaged in making appliances for Divisional Laundry. One french civilian and squad of LA GORGUE experimented. One french civilian and conductor of LA GORGUE experimented. Mountjoy's letter at 8PM re: one of Meade's Curates Case of Lychens at BOOTDEVILLE investigated. ODP	
LA GORGUE	April 14th		Company and Billets inspected. One squad on town duties. One squad on Hot Baths at PONT DU HEM and one squad on CROIX BARBEE. One man and lorry delivered clean clothing to Baths at CROIX BARBEE and PONT DU HEM and collected soiled cloths. One man and US Wagon delivered clean underclothing to baths at RICHEBOURG and GRUB STREET and collected soiled clothing. Divisional Baths and Laundry LA GORGUE experimented and the distribution of clean new underclothing to Wives of Divison came in. One carpenter engaged in making appliances for Divisional Laundry. One french civilian and squad of attached men engaged in carrying out at LA GORGUE and conductor of town experimented. Inspection of ADMS of new male appliance for Divisional use and test cases.	

WAR DIARY
or
INTELLIGENCE SUMMARY.
(Erase heading not required.)

Army Form C. 2118.

Place	Date	Hour	Summary of Events and Information	Remarks and references to Appendices
			for testing again in the field. CO inspected inspectors billets at RICHEBOURG & field kitchen re Meade also re-inspected hung Road billets of G. field Regt'n kitchen.	
LA GORGUE	April 15th		Camps and Billets inspected. The squad on Kate duties. The squad at CROIX BARBEE Baths and one against PONT DU HEM Baths. One man and boy allowed clean underclothing to Baths at PONT DU HEM and CROIX BARBEE and collected soiled clothes. One man and W.S. Major allowed clean underclothing to Baths at RICHEBOURG and ORILSSTREET. Divisional Baths and Laundry LA GORGUE superintended and subdivision of clean and rest underclothing to Baths carried out. The carts also engaged in making up stores for Divisional Laundry. Sen Superintendent AM Squad & attached men engaged in sanitary work at LA GORGUE and contain of town superintended. CO inspected billets vacated by wagon lines 88 Brigade RFA D Battery B Battery and C Battery - Wagon lines of 84 Brigade RFA and D Battery - A Bar & C Battery 87 Brigade RFA - Wagon line of 89 Brigade RFA and A Cav. D Battery - Two billets of 5 South Wales Border Regt - 57 Infty. Brigade Reunion Farm. Also inspected intervened sanitary officers of 35 and 38 Divisions referance changing over.	
LA GORGUE	April 16th		Camps and Billets inspected. One squad on Kate duties. One squad at CROIX BARBEE Baths and one against PONT DU HEM Baths. One man and boy allowed clean Clothes to Baths at ORILS STREET and RICHEBOURG and collected soiled clothes.	

WAR DIARY or INTELLIGENCE SUMMARY.

Army Form C. 2118.

(Erase heading not required.)

Instructions regarding War Diaries and Intelligence Summaries are contained in F. S. Regs., Part II. and the Staff Manual respectively. Title pages will be prepared in manuscript.

Place	Date	Hour	Summary of Events and Information	Remarks and references to Appendices
ST VENANT			Divisional Bathouse, Laundry, LA GORGUE superintended and the distribution of linen and new insoles etc. Units of Division carried out Baths at PONT DU HEM handed over to Sanitary Section of 38th Division. Party of Section shirts and equipment and opened men transferred to new billet at ST VENANT. One group of attached men engaged in sanitary work at LA GORGUE upon sanitation of town superintended. Inferior billet at Yorkshire Dragoons (Monetay) discovered and placed out of bounds. CO accompanied touring Engineer upon Inspection of new nature. CO visited ST VENANT and took over Laundry and Bath.	O.P.
	April 17th		Lamps and Billets inspected. As usual on routine duties. LA GORGUE Divisional Baths and Laundry handed over to O/C field Divisional Sanitary Section. Baths at CROIX BARBÉE handed over to 33rd Division. PONT DU HEM Baths and PONT RIQUEUL Baths handed over to 38th Division Sanitary Section. Section equipment and stores transferred to new billet at ST VENANT. Sanitary arrangements at new billet carried out.	O.P.
ST VENANT	April 18th		Lamps and Billets inspected. As usual on routine duties. As guard at ST VENANT Spray Baths Sanitation of town superintended and fatigue party engaged in clearing up dumping of latrine equipment and other transfers from LA GORGUE. CO visited BOURECQ, AUCHY AU BOIS, ELSTREE BLANCHE, RELY, BLESSY, MARTHES, WITTERNESSE and LAMBRES & prince Baths and IVORRENT FONTES	

T2134. Wt. W708-776. 500000. 4/15. Sir J. C. & S.

WAR DIARY
or
INTELLIGENCE SUMMARY.
(Erase heading not required.)

Army Form C. 2118.

Instructions regarding War Diaries and Intelligence Summaries are contained in F. S. Regs., Part II. and the Staff Manual respectively. Title pages will be prepared in manuscript.

Place	Date	Hour	Summary of Events and Information	Remarks and references to Appendices
			Reference Sketch. C.O. inspected huts at LACERODE.	O.H.
NORRENT FONTES	10th April		Camps and Billets inspected. Began in Male Wales. Detain huts and equipment transport from ST VENANT. A new hut at NORRENT FONTES. Sanitary arrangements new on at Detain new huts. Divisional Rosenheim as ST VENANT. Sanitary arrangements carried on at Detain new huts. Divisional Rosenheim attaching me inspection from Sanitary Section to meet Infantry Brigade. Officers and the Royal Artillery.	N.P.
NORRENT FONTES	20th April		Camps and Billets inspected. One spent in trade duties. List of Medical supplies in auraa complete and forwarded to all Medical Officers of Division (Copy attached). Report on sanitary comments of new activity proceeded by Division. Papers and Formation to A.A. & Q.M.G. and A.D.M.S. Further pass of Detain equipment arrived. Transport from ST VENANT. Spent 1 attached companies engaged in attachment at BOURECQ Baths. One spent at BOURECQ Baths and one squadron at ELSTREE BLANCHE. Sanitary arrangements made at Detain huts. C.O. visited AUCHY AU BOIS to both and 58th Infantry Brigade H.Q. at RELY. Leaving company inspection attached. C.O. visited ELSTREE BLANCHE Baths leaving Cpl—— in charge, and then at Aytchken Croix in the turn and 57th Infantry.	

T₹34. Wt. W708-776. 560000. 4/15. Sir J. C. & S.

WAR DIARY
or
INTELLIGENCE SUMMARY.
(Erase heading not required.)

Army Form C. 2118.

Place	Date	Hour	Summary of Events and Information	Remarks and references to Appendices
			Brigade HQ Carrying sanitary inspection attacked around FONTES. Things not look happy. OLP	
NORRENT FONTES	21st April		An agram on Hostil Duties. Sanitation of NORRENT FONTES superintended and agmt of Tenyman attached area engaged in clearing up town. One agmt at Baths BOURECQ and one agmt at Baths ESTRÉE BLANCHE. Agmt of attached contents engaged in structural alteration at BOURECQ Baths. CO around CRECQUE in Baths - men were attained by the Lip-Revis. Billets of the P. Winchester Regt inspected and needs supplies attention reference to their request for same. OLP	
NORRENT FONTES	22nd April		One agmt in Hostil Duties. Sanitation of NORRENT FONTES superintended and agmt of Tenyman attached area engaged in cleaning up town. One agmt at BOURECQ Baths and one agmt at Baths ESTRÉE BLANCHE. Report received from Inspector attached Infantry Brigade as to sanitation. OLP	
NORRENT FONTES	23rd April		One agmt in Hostil Duties. Sanitation of NORRENT FONTES superintended and agmt of Tenyman attached area engaged in cleaning up town. One agmt at BOURECQ Baths and one agmt at ESTRÉE BLANCHE Baths. Billet at NORRENT FONTES where case of Measles occurred disinfected. Another	

WAR DIARY or INTELLIGENCE SUMMARY

Army Form C. 2118.

Place	Date	Hour	Summary of Events and Information	Remarks and references to Appendices
			Civilian cases of Diphtheria at LINGHEM investigated and Huts placed "Out of Bounds". Also one case at	
			COYECQUES. CO visited MO of 172nd Lancashire Regt. 86 & 87 and 88 Brigades R.F.A., M.R.A. refuse sanitary	
			arrangements. Inspected 10th Manchester Regt, 10th Manchester Regt, and R.E. Staffordshire Regt's Billets	
			and enquired into three Measles cases at Manchester Regt. OAP	
NORRENT FONTES	24 April		CO spent in Intel: Andrei Isolation of NORRENT FONTES and surrounding district. Supervision and	
			fatigue party of attached men engaged in clearing up. He opened Baths ESTRÉE BLANCHE. He agreed	
			of dustmen and fire attacked carpenters trapped in renovating Drury system at BOURECQ Baths and	
			siding. Open air Bath at CRECQUE. CO supervised section. Civilian cases of Diphtheria at BONY	
			ERNY, ST JULIAN and BOURECQ investigated. OAP	
NORRENT FONTES	25 April		CO spent in Intel: Andrei Isolation of NORRENT FONTES and district. Supervision and fatigue	
			party of attached men engaged in clearing up. CO agreed at Baths ESTRÉE BLANCHE. As	
			squad of dustmen and fire attached men on open air spray bath at CRECQUE. Billets at Divisional Ammunition	
			Column examined (Cheves Spindle Hemnghis). Billets at 6th Wiltshire Regiment 10th Warwickshire	
			Regt Montford - Measles. CO ordered Divisional Ammunition Column Influenza cases of Austro-Spanish	

WAR DIARY
or
INTELLIGENCE SUMMARY.

(Erase heading not required.)

Army Form C. 2118.

Place	Date	Hour	Summary of Events and Information	Remarks and references to Appendices
			Motorcyclist. CO inspected Gr Transport M.T. Section 6 N. Staffs Regt and 7th Loyal North Lancashire Regt.	
			CO visited baths at CREGONS and ESTREE BLANCHE.	O.N.P
NORRENT FONTES	26th April		Found guard on Rue Dixer. One guard at CREQUE Rack. One guard at Berlles ESTREE BLANCHE. Sanitation of NORRENT FONTES superintended and fatigue party of attached men engaged in cleaning up town and surrounding district. Six men and two engineers in cleaning clean and clothing to Baths. Infantry Brigade and Divisional Artillery inspected. Six men on Injection. Advance Slow.	O.N.P
NORRENT FONTES	27th April		One guard on Rue Dixer. Sanitation of NORRENT FONTES superintended and fatigue party engaged in cleaning up town and surrounding district. One guard at CREQUE Baths and one guard at ESTREE BLANCHE Baths. Six men and two orderlies from Rest Park for attending and collection of instructing. Infantry Brigade and Divisional Artillery inspected. Billets at 119th Divisional Ammunition Column and 5th Machine Gun Co. & line- examined. Billets at 7th Loyal North Lancashire Regt disinfected.- ? Rubella. All made arrangement with French Mission as to removal of manure to civilian.	O.N.P

Army Form C. 2118.

WAR DIARY
or
INTELLIGENCE SUMMARY.
(Erase heading not required.)

Instructions regarding War Diaries and Intelligence Summaries are contained in F. S. Regs., Part II. and the Staff Manual respectively. Title pages will be prepared in manuscript.

Place	Date	Hour	Summary of Events and Information	Remarks and references to Appendices
NORRENT FONTES	28 April		One squad on Batta. Duties. Remainder of NORRENT FONTES experienced and fatigue party of Temporarily attached men engaged in clearing up town and surrounding district. One squad at CRECQUES Baths and one squad at ESTREE BLANCHE Baths. Remainder lorry engaged in delivering clean underclothing to Baths. One lorry from Divisional Dirt Park detailed for collection of soiled underclothing from Baths. Infantry Brigades and Divisional Artillery inspected front tank which had been erected at CRECQUES (photos reproduced/copy attached) Divisional BAILLIEU. ONP	
NORRENT FONTES	29 April		One squad on Water Duties. Remainder of NORRENT FONTES experienced and fatigue squad of attached men engaged in clearing up town and surrounding district. One squad at ESTREE BLANCHE Baths and one squad at Baths CRECQUES. One man and detainee lorry engaged in delivering clean under-clothing to Baths and one lorry detailed from Divisional Dirt Park collected soiled underclothing. Infantry Brigade and Divisional Artillery inspected. Supplementary List of Kabi supplies furnished A.P.M. Di (copy attached) to Composite Learning Area during manoeuvres ONP	
NORRENT FONTES	30 April		One squad on Water Duties. One squad at CRECQUE Baths and one squad at ESTREE BLANCHE Baths. Remainder of NORRENT FONTES experienced and fatigue party of temporary attached men engaged in	

WAR DIARY
or
INTELLIGENCE SUMMARY.
(Erase heading not required.)

Army Form C. 2118.

Place	Date	Hour	Summary of Events and Information	Remarks and references to Appendices
			Cleaning up Town. No rum and returns being allowed. Clean underclothing to Baths and no dirty clothes from Divisional Suit Park for collection. 4 ordered underclothing. One man in H.E. column. Disease Chart. 6.O. received refunds from Inspection of Infantry and Artillery Brigades and gave direction for future inspection. OWP	

Confidential

First Army Training Area

Amended List of Water Supplies in each Village

No.	Source of Supply and Locality	Treatment	Remarks
1	Crecques. Outside Estaminet Joly Robilliard in main	½ Scoop	Pump
2	" " " " Mr Minchin	Scoop	Pump
3	" " " Lemaitre Familles	1½ Scoops	Pump
4	Rely. Brassèrie	Scoop	Tap
5	Erny. Outside Estaminet "Pinchebourg"	1½ Scoops	Pump
6	" " " Grade Joyeux	Scoop	Pump
7	Crestaux. Opposite Estaminet Crepies Buch	1½ Scoops	Tap
8	Fleckinelle. Communal Well. In main St.	1 Scoop	Civil
9	Eny-les-Mines, at. use of Madame Payet	1 Scoop	Well
10	Estree Blanche, at Farm of Madame Wattier. White House with large entrance 100 yds S.E. of Church	1 Scoop	Pump
11	La Dommart. At T Rd. Outside Home of Madame Leon	1 Scoop	Well
12	Ligny-leguire. In road at Home of Madame Mueller 200 yards north of Church. Communal supply	2 Scoops	Well
13	Ligny-leguire Communal Well in Main Road	1½ Scoops	Well
14	Auchy-aux-Bois " " 300 yds SW of Church	1 Scoop	Well
15	" Brasserie (Good Supply)	1 Scoop	Tap
16	Norrent-Fontes. At Estaminet A la Marne (Good Supply)	1 Scoop	Pump

Note:— Owing to the difference in the strength of the Chloride of Lime supplied to units, and the variation in quality of small water supplies from time to time, the above figures for chlorination are only suggestive. Standards should be readjusted with the sample of lime to be used.

C.H. Peters Capt
O.C. Sanitary Section

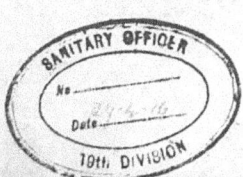

Confidential   First Army Training Area.
   List of Water Supplies in and adjacent

No	Map Ref	Source of supply & Locality	Treatment	Remarks
1	O16a8.2	Berguette Pump south of Rd opposite Drying Room	1 scoop	
2	O27 d.	Ham en Artois Brasserie	1 scoop	Deep well
3	U3b77	Mangueville Constant running Artesian well on Roadside next to Estaminet "Leclerq-Dubuille"	1 scoop	Artesian
4	U1a8.2	Bourecq, Brasserie (Draw from Tap)	1 scoop	Artesian
5	T5d67	St Hilaire Pump in Archway of Wineshop (West of Rd)	1½ scoops	Pump
6	"	" " next door. North of above.	1 scoop	Pump
7	N35d3.9	Norrent Fontes Farm of Bengin-Bellanger (East of road)	1 scoop	Pump
8	"	At Estaminet De la Mairie East of DE O.S. good supply	1 scoop	Pump
9	N29a5.2	Fontes (At Estaminet "Legrain-Decobert" (necessary to) carry water in buckets through passage	1 scoop	Pump
10	N10b6.1	Lambres Brasserie Good supply	1 scoop	Pump
11	O14913	Quernes. Pump at Estaminet "Gaqueire-Ducocq"	1 scoop	Pump
12	M13d	Quernes " " "Martel-Delmair"	1 scoop	Pump
13	M913	Quernes Pump at Estaminet (between Church & Railway) "Duming-Bocquillo"	1 scoop	Pump
14	M8c1.1	Witternesse. Pump at Farmhouse (East side of church)	1 scoop	Pump
15	M24c9.7	Lieltres Pump at Farm of Madam Deron	1 scoop	Pump
16	"	" Pump at Farmhouse opposite above	2 scoops	Pump
17	M22d5.2	Ethée-Blanche Brasserie (Draw from Tap)	1 scoop	Deep well
18	M33a8.3	Flechinelle. Pump in Woodyard	1 scoop	Pump
19	M11b3.5	Blessy Pump at house opposite East gate of church at T road	1 scoop	Pump
20	H32d1.10	St Quentin Pump outside Estaminet "Pont de Folie" (800 yds East of church)	1½ scoops	Pump
21	H32b3.3	St Quentin Pump at Estaminet "Hahann-Brassert"	2 scoops	Pump
22	"	" " " " " "A la arrivée Voyageurs"	1 scoop	Pump
23	H? ?.8.8	" Communal Pump Rue de Bas opposite Estaminet "Lefoure. Baily"	1½ scoops	Pump
24	M .1	La Lacque. Pump at Estaminet "Louis Dulonginstij"	1 scoop	Pump
25	I33d.1.1.	Isbergues Brasserie	1 scoop	Artesian
26	O12a3.1.	Le Pont à Balgne. Communal pump at T road	1 scoop	Pump
27	O17 c.	Guarbecque at Estaminet "Marien-Ray"	2 scoops	Pump
28	"	" at Estaminet "A la Reunion du Fermier"	2 scoops	Pump

Note:— Owing to the difference in the strength of the Chloride of lime supplied to Units, and the variation in quality of small water supplies from time to time, the above figures for Chlorination are only suggestive Standards should be re-adjusted with the sample of lime to be used.

A. Peters Capt.

(1)

36th SANITARY SECTION.
(19th Division)

PERSONNEL and DUTIES.

(a) Sanitary Section (R.A.M.C.)- 1 Officer and 24 men (wanted to complete 1)
(b) Attachments -military- 1 Officer (R.A.M.C.) and 68 men.
(c) Civilian Labour- 5 men and 163 women.

DUTIES	NUMBER OF PERSONNEL	DESCRIPTION.
"A" Sanitary Section (R.A.M.C.)		
Senior N.C.O.	1	1 Staff Sergeant (administration and discipline)
Office	1	1 L/cpl (Clerical work)
Q.M. Duties	1	1 Cpl.
Inspectors	9	1 Sgt, 3 Cpls, 5 L/cpls.
Baths and Laundry	7	1 Sgt, 1 L/cpl, 5 men.
Batman (Storekeeper)	1	1 man.
Billet Orderly, messenger, fatigues, etc.	2	2 men.
Cook	1	1 man.
Total	24	
"B" Attachments- Military.		
La Gorgue Laundry-Bath	18	P.B. 1 Sgt, 1 Cpl, 13 men, and 3 barbers (plus 2 San.Sec.)
Croix Barbee Bath	2	P.B. men. (plus 4 San: Sec:)
Pont du Hem Bath	3	P.B. 1 Cpl and 2 men. (plus 1 San. Sec.)
Pont Riqueul Bath	4	P.B. 1 Sgt, 1 Cpl and 2 men.
Lestrem Bath	2	P.B. 1 Cpl and 1 man.
Vielle Chapelle Bath	6	P.B. 1 Sgt, 1 Cpl and 4 men.
Daimler Lorry	2	A.S.C. men.
Foden Disinfector	2	A.S.C. men.
Ford Car	2	1 A.S.C. and 1 R.A.M.C. man.
V'l Chapelle Water Tks	5	35th Dvnl Fatigue,-1 Cpl and 4 men.
Carpenters.	4	1 Sgt and 3 men.
Boot Repairer	1	1 T.U. man.
3 Horsfall Destructors	3	P.B. men.
Special Sanitary Fatigue	14	T.U. 1 Sgt, 1 Cpl, and 12 men
Total	68	
"C" Civilian Labour.		
Street Scavenging	3	3 men, 1 horse, 1 cart.
La Gorgue Laundry	165	2 men and 163 women.
Total	168	

(2)

DEPARTMENTS:- The work of the Sanitary Section is divided up into 8 Departments with an N.C.O. and men definitely detailed and held responsible in each.

I. Sanitary Department (under the "Sanitary Sergeant")
II. Water " (under the "Water Corporal")
III. Infectious Disease " . (under the "Infectious Diseases Corporal")
IV. Baths and Laundry " . (under the " Baths Sergeant")
V. Waterways and Drainage Dept.
VI. Food Inspection " .
VII. Constructional " .
VIII. Clerical and Draughtsman's" . printing , mapping, etc.

===

SYSTEM OF INSPECTIONS.

Inspectors are divided up into "Working Groups" for Inspection in Brigades ,or "Districts".

	Sanitary Duties	Special Duties	Other Special Duties
I 1 Sergt and 1 L/cpl.	Headquarters & Divnl Units	Sgt acts as Senior Sanitary Inspector(receives reports, etc.)	From any who happen to be available are
II 1 Cpl. 1 L/cpl	56th Bde	Cpl acts as Special Inspector of H.Q.Town.	detailed 3 Special helpers of the
III 1 Cpl,1 L/cpl	57th Bde	Cpl acts as Reserve for special Sanitary jobs.	"Water Corporal" when supplies of a new district
IV 1 Cpl,1 L/cpl.	58th Bde	Cpl and L/cpl are 2 specialists in Infectious Disease work.	have to be opened up.
V 1 Cpl.		Always on Water Duties.	

(1 or 2 more inspectors should be available as a reserve.)

(3)

WORK OF THE 8 DEPARTMENTS.

I SANITARY   (a) Sanitation of D.H.Q.Town.
                (b) . "   " Divisional Area.

(a) D.H.Q. Town . (La Gorgue)
                             (I) H.Q.Billets and Offices.
                             (II) Scavenging of Town.

The Sanitation of the H.Q.Town is arranged for by:-

1 Cpl (San Sec. s.p.1) in charge-
Special Fatigue Squad of about 12 T.U.men.
3 P.B. men working the 3 Horsfall Destructors.
3 Civilians with horse and cart(paid by Division) for emptying privy pits and carting away military horse litter.
Military Vidange cart for emptying water-logged middens and ditches.
1 Military Rotary Broom for streets.
Civilian Authorities collect civilian refuse twice a week.
Departmental (French) Authorities have Rotary Broom for main road.
Civilian Authorities have undertaken clearing out of the main culverts and ditches of the town.

(b) The DIVISIONAL Area has been divided up into 5 Inspection Districts- 4 outlying districts with one Sanitary Inspector (4 Cpls from Sfns. I,II,III and IV) to each.
1 District including units immediately around H.Q. Town- the Sanitary Sergeant (s.p.I) acting as Inspector.

Fortnightly reports are made by the 5 Inspectors for forwarding to D.H.Q.

Special Reports are called for by D.H.Q. as to state in which billets arex left by units at each Divisional "move".

A daily record of Disinfectants drawn by each unit of Division is obtained from refilling points by O.R. Corporal.

(4)

II. WATER.

Staff- 1 "Water Corporal", who may have three other assistants detailed from amongst Inspectors.

R.M.O's are circularized when the Division moves as to position and quality of water supplies of the new area.

Office records are kept of all water supplies, water carts and water personnel and Inspectors and printed notices are attached to all important supplies.

"Water Corporal" exercises supervision over work of water orderlies of units and takes test samples of water from carts as to chlorination.

Records are kept of trench water supplies.

III. INFECTIOUS DISEASE.

Staff- 1 "Infectious Disease Corporal" with 1 L/cpl (s.p.IV) specially trained to assist in emergency.

All notifications of Infectious Disease in the Division are received through A.D.M.S.

These cases are visited by Corporal and disinfected, and records kept, and data on completion forwarded to A.D.M.S.

All civilian cases are investigated and civilian and military cases notified to Mayor & Sub Prefect of District.)

Sick Reports from M.O's received through A.D.M.S., and sick data compiled, and daily records charted in Sanitary and A.D.M.S.office.

Meteorological data (max. and min. Temp, and rainfall) are taken daily and also, in Summer, Fly Counts are taken.
These data are also charted.

IV. BATHS AND LAUNDRY.

Staff- (a) Laundry. (See list of Personnel)-20 military and 165 civilians.
(b) 6 Baths.(see list of Personnel P.I)- 22 military.

V. WATERWAYS AND DRAINAGE.

Staff- One Inspector (L/cpl) formerly for six years a surveyor in charge of roads and drainage of urban district in England.
At the beginning of Winter, he directed large squads of pioneers provided by D.H.Q. for cutting drainage channels where billeting district was flooded.

VI. FOOD INSPECTION.

No Inspectors provided. Cook houses and stores inspected in the course of usual Sanitary inspection. Divnl San. Off. inspects Refilling points from time to time, and represents Medical Department on Boards of Enquiry into condition of Food stuffs.

VII. CONSTRUCTIONAL.

This is an important department. A squad of 4 carpenters were attached 4 months back, and with 2 plumbers and handy men from the Sanitary Section, have been continuously engaged in alterations to Baths and Laundries, constructing refuse bins, drains, etc,-
Since August 1915, eleven baths have been put up or extended, and two laundries.

VIII. DRAUGHTSMAN'S and CLERICAL.

Maps for Inspectors in each new district.
Plans of model sanitary structures and baths.
Printed notices for "Water boards".
Two first class clerks are necessary when baths and laundry are in full swing.

H. Peters
Captain.
O.C. No 36 Sanitary Section.
19th Division.

In the Field.
April . 1916.

To: The D.D.M.S.
    2nd Echelon

I beg to forward herewith
War Diary for the month of
May.

O.H. Peters Capt
O/C 86th Sanitary Section

Army Form C. 2118

WAR DIARY
or
INTELLIGENCE SUMMARY
(Erase heading not required.)

19th Do   36 Som San Lee   Vol 11

Confidential

War Diary

of

Sanitary Section 36.

from 1st May to 31st May 1916.

(Vol 11)

COMMITTEE FOR THE
MEDICAL HISTORY OF THE WAR
Date 26 JUN 1915

May 1916

Army Form C. 2118.

WAR DIARY
or
INTELLIGENCE SUMMARY.
(Erase heading not required.)

Instructions regarding War Diaries and Intelligence Summaries are contained in F. S. Regs., Part II. and the Staff Manual respectively. Title pages will be prepared in manuscript.

Place	Date	Hour	Summary of Events and Information	Remarks and references to Appendices
	1916			
NORRENT FONTES	1st May		One squad on Batt. Duties. Remainder of NORRENT FONTES superintended and fatigue party of Emigrants attached were engaged in cleaning up town. One squad at ESTREE BLANCHE Baths and one squad at CRECQUES Baths. One man and lorry allowed steam underclothing at Baths. One lorry detailed from Sub-Park for collection of soiled underclothing. CO inspected 8th Bde R.F.A., 87 Brigade R.F.A., 6th Wiltshire Regt. and CRECQUES Baths in company with A.D.M.S. 4 Division. Fourteen cases of Diphtheria at DELIETTE investigated and Adults where German Measles had occurred disinfected.	OMP
NORRENT FONTES	2nd May		One squad on Batt. Duties. Remainder of NORRENT FONTES superintended and fatigue party of Emigrants attached were engaged in cleaning up town and surrounding district. One squad at ESTREE BLANCHE Baths and one squad at CRECQUES Baths. One man and lorry allowed steam underclothing at Baths. One lorry detailed from Divisional Sub-Park for collection of soiled underclothing. One man at Infectious Disease Chart.	OMP
NORRENT FONTES	3rd May		One squad on Batt. Duties. Remainder of NORRENT FONTES superintended and fatigue party of men Emigrants attached engaged in cleaning up town and surrounding district. One squad at CRECQUES Baths and one squad at ESTREE BLANCHE Baths. One man and lorry allowed for delivering clean underclothing to Baths. One lorry detailed from Divisional Sub-Park for collecting of soiled underclothing	

T2134. Wt. W708—776. 500000. 4/15. Sir J. C. & S.

Army Form C. 2118.

WAR DIARY
or
INTELLIGENCE SUMMARY.
(Erase heading not required.)

Instructions regarding War Diaries and Intelligence Summaries are contained in F. S. Regs., Part II. and the Staff Manual respectively. Title pages will be prepared in manuscript.

Place	Date	Hour	Summary of Events and Information	Remarks and references to Appendices
NORRENT FONTES	4th April		Brussels of G. field Ambulance disinfected area of Battn.	OAP
			Bn opened in Battn Baths. Simulation of NORRENTFONTES superintended and fatigue squad of men furnished, attached engaged in clearing up town and district. Bn opened at CRECQUES Baths and one opened at ESTREE BLANCHE Baths. The men and boys returned clean clothing to Baths. Bn. liny obtained from Divisional Ord. Park for collection of soiled underclothing. Reports received from Inspector with Infantry Brigades and Divisional Artillery re OC anspected ground of Divisional manoeuvres. CO visited MERVILLE and settled account for purchase of engine for STVENANT foundry.	
				OAP
NORRENT FONTES	5th May		Sanitation of NORRENT FONTES superintended and one fatigue squad of men temporarily attached engaged in clearing up town and district. Baths Enfinal [?] proceeded to make liny & new over wheels supplies. Bath at CRECQUES dismantled and squad of attached carpenters engaged in such work. Bn opened at ESTREE BLANCHE Baths. Inspection of manoeuvres of Divisional Artillery and Infantry Brigades.	
				OAP
NORRENT FONTES	6th May		Sanitation of NORRENT FONTES superintended and squad of attached men engaged in cleaning up town and district. Water supplies in new over wheels and supplies fitted and removed.	

T2124. Wt. W708—776. 500/300. 4/15. Sir J. C. & S.

WAR DIARY
or
INTELLIGENCE SUMMARY.
(Erase heading not required.)

Army Form C. 2118.

Instructions regarding War Diaries and Intelligence Summaries are contained in F. S. Regs., Part II. and the Staff Manual respectively. Title pages will be prepared in manuscript.

Place	Date	Hour	Summary of Events and Information	Remarks and references to Appendices
			Part of Section stores and equipment transferred with hire men in lorry to FLESSELLES. Up not 1 man engaged at ESTREE BLANCHE Bath. Reports received from Inspector with Armoured artillery and Infantry Brigade.	O.N.P.
NORRENT FONTES	7ᵗʰ May		Batt'n supplies in men's area received and supplies todat area removed. Billets at NORRENT FONTES cleaned and on-whing in view of move on the morning of the 8ᵗʰ May. Inspection with Infantry Brigade and Armoured Artillery formation reports. C.O. proceeded by road to FLESSELLES.	O.N.P.
NORRENT FONTES & FLESSELLES	8ᵗʰ May		Together with Part of Section of two and equipment with four men transferred in motor lorry to FLESSELLES. Rest of section and attached men marched to LILLERS and entrained for LONGUEAU arriving on the latter time at 2/30 am and then marched to FLESSELLES. C.O. inspected Bath supplies and those en te for Bath.	O.N.P.
FLESSELLES	9ᵗʰ May		Bath lamps and Builth inspected. Inspection in Water Drains. Remainder of FLESSELLES accommenced and fatigue squad of Stonemount attached men engaged in cleaning up tom and district. Section Billets non-commissioned cleaned and put in sanitary condition. Present Officer of Regiment

Army Form C. 2118.

WAR DIARY
or
INTELLIGENCE—SUMMARY.
(Erase heading not required.)

Instructions regarding War Diaries and Intelligence Summaries are contained in F. S. Regs., Part II. and the Staff Manual respectively. Title pages will be prepared in manuscript.

Place	Date	Hour	Summary of Events and Information	Remarks and references to Appendices
			Continued work line of water supplies in area occupied by the Division (Copy of Lieut Locker) to G O inspected Billets of 6 N Stafford Regt.	OAP
FLESSELLES	10th May		Camps and Billets inspected. One squadron Native Cavalry Division of FLESSELLES superintended one fatigue squad of Engineers attached men engaged in clearing up town and surrounding district. Billets of 10th Royal Warwickshire Regiment where three cases of measles had occurred disinfected. Refuse from sanitary trenches emptied as to division of area recently vacated by the Division.	OAP
FLESSELLES	11th May		Camps and Billets inspected. One squadron Native British Cavalry Division of FLESSELLES superintended and fatigue squad of men temporarily attached engaged in clearing up town and surrounding district. Billets at 5th Machine Gun Corps (Ricardo) disinfected. Lieut Spurr-Menengha (Dane at General Jesus) med transferred. By Motor to Flesselles attached to General Artillery and on horseback also attached to 57th Infantry Brigade. CO explored the water outfit of the Divisional area. Me visiting of ST VAST EN CHAUSSEE also trucks of Piver Somme. Co visited 56th Infantry Brigade Buckets and Artillery Headquarters at BELLOY.	OAP

WAR DIARY
or
INTELLIGENCE SUMMARY.
(Erase heading not required.)

Army Form C. 2118.

Place	Date	Hour	Summary of Events and Information	Remarks and references to Appendices
FLESSELLES	12th May		Camps and billets inspected. One squad in Walle Butler. Remainder of FLESSELLES superintendent and fatigue squad temporarily attached men engaged in clearing up town and surrounding district. Reports received from inspector with 5th Infantry Brigade as to condition of market village RAINNEVILLE and VILLERS BOCAGE.	O.M.P.
FLESSELLES	13th May		Camps and Billets inspected. One squad in Walle Butler. Remainder of FLESSELLES superintendent and fatigue squad of temporarily attached men engaged in clearing up town and district. Visit to FLESSELLES scated. C.O. visited BOVES to arrange ration for washing arrangements. I.O. visited RAVERNESS, NAVIERS and CANAPLES re Walle and VIGNACOURT re safeguarding certain supply in forest.	O.M.P.
FLESSELLES	14th May		Camps and Billets inspected. One squad in Walle Butler. Remainder of FLESSELLES superintendent and fatigue squad engaged in clearing up town and district. Butler at 5th Anti Walle Brothers (Muastie) also here. Interview at 10 Royal Warwickshire Regt (Meadle). One man on Infectum diseases chart	O.M.P.

Army Form C. 2118.

WAR DIARY
INTELLIGENCE SUMMARY.
(Erase heading not required.)

Instructions regarding War Diaries and Intelligence Summaries are contained in F. S. Regs., Part II. and the Staff Manual respectively. Title pages will be prepared in manuscript.

Place	Date	Hour	Summary of Events and Information	Remarks and references to Appendices
FLESSELLES	15th May		Camps and Billets inspected. One squad in Rocks Duties. Sanitation of FLESSELLES supervised and fatigue squad of Kinsmen's attached men engaged in cleaning up town and surrounding district. One man in Infectious Diseases Hospital. Billets at & Willshire Regiment sprayed and cleaned (Measles) also trace ok 5th Infantry Brigade Headquarters (Measles). Return received from hospital with Armoured Artillery and 5th Infantry Brigade. M.O. visited BOVES and made contract with civilian for washing 6,000 articles of underclothing.	OMP
FLESSELLES	16th May		Camps and Billets inspected. One squad in Rocks Duties. One man in Infectious Diseases Camp. Sanitation of FLESSELLES supervised and fatigue party of Temporary attached men engaged in cleaning up town and district. Arrangements made for washing of underclothing and amount of underclothing from Field Ambulances at Lechuin Obus. M.O. inspected Barracks and attache of 5th Infantry Brigade. Also No.2 Company of Divisional Train. Billets of 19th Divisional Ammunition Column inspected. Road of Rubio-Spinal-Harringha. The civilian cases of Measles at FLESSELLES investigated.	OMP
FLESSELLES	17th May		Camps and Billets inspected. One squad in Rocks Duties. Sanitation of FLESSELLES supervised and	

Army Form C. 2118.

WAR DIARY
or
INTELLIGENCE SUMMARY.
(Erase heading not required.)

Instructions regarding War Diaries and Intelligence
Summaries are contained in F. S. Regs., Part II.
and the Staff Manual respectively. Title pages
will be prepared in manuscript.

Place	Date	Hour	Summary of Events and Information	Remarks and references to Appendices
			Fatigue squad & one Corporal attached engaged in cleaning up town and district. One carpenter engaged in preparing hurdles for proposed Bath. Two men of Section at BOVES attending that of further section who was prepared & made manufacturing. All attached men for baths at HAVERNAS. Further report forward on to Divisional Sanitation.	OPP
FLESSELLES	18th May		Temps and Butter inspected. One officer on Water duties. Remainder of FLESSELLES attended Fatigue squad of temporarily attached men engaged in cleaning up town and district. The squad engaged in erecting temporary bath at HAVERNAS. As lorry from Last Park available for carrying section ammunition. L. BOVES and three men of Section engaged in disinfecting clothes & section for washing. C.O. inspected 10th Worcestershire Regiment and received main column at STEVEN.	OPP
FLESSELLES	19th May		Temps and Butter inspected. The squad on Water duties. Remainder of FLESSELLES attended and fatigue squad of temporarily attached men engaged in cleaning up town and district. The squad engaged in erecting temporary bath at HAVERNAS. We have from the Park services for carrying section ammunition. L. BOVES and two men of Section engaged in disinfecting clothes & section for washing. C.O. inspected encounter in divisional Sanitation and quarter	

T2134. Wt. W708—776. 500090. 4/15. Sir J. C. & S.

Army Form C. 2118.

WAR DIARY
or
INTELLIGENCE SUMMARY.
(Erase heading not required.)

Instructions regarding War Diaries and Intelligence Summaries are contained in F. S. Regs., Part II. and the Staff Manual respectively. Title pages will be prepared in manuscript.

Place	Date	Hour	Summary of Events and Information	Remarks and references to Appendices
AMIENS			Laundry Recruit & Wilshire Regiment Medical inspected.	CNP
FLESSELLES	20th May		The squad on Main Road. Camps and Billets inspected. Remainder of FLESSELLES surroundings and squad of temporary attached men engaged in clearing of lines and ditches. Baths at HAVERNAS inspected and one squad of men engaged in supervising. The squad engaged in erecting carpenter bath at LA CHAUSSEE. Billets at Wilshire Regiment inspected. Parties.	CNP
FLESSELLES	21st May		One squad on Main Road. Camps and Billets inspected. One squad at Baths HAVERNAS. Squad of carpenters and temporary attached men engaged in erecting Bath at LA CHAUSSEE. Remainder of FLESSELLES surroundings and squad of temporary attached men engaged in clearing of lines and surrounding ditches. Refuse received from Inspector and St Infants Brigade and Divisional Artillery. O.C. proceeded to PARIS to purchase Spray Bath.	CNP
FLESSELLES	22nd May		Camps and Billets inspected. One squad on Main Road. One squad at Baths Haverna. Squad of carpenters and temporary attached men engaged in erecting Carpenter Bath at LA CHAUSSEE. Remainder of FLESSELLES surroundings and squad of temporary attached men engaged in clearing of lines and	

WAR DIARY
INTELLIGENCE SUMMARY.
(Erase heading not required.)

Army Form C. 2118.

Instructions regarding War Diaries and Intelligence Summaries are contained in F. S. Regs., Part II. and the Staff Manual respectively. Title pages will be prepared in manuscript.

Place	Date	Hour	Summary of Events and Information	Remarks and references to Appendices
			surrounding district. O.C. in PARIS purchasing spong baths.	O.C.P
FLESSELLES	23rd May		No. 1 group at Water Billets. Camp and Billets inspected. No. 2 group at Baths TAVERNAS. Carrying on of FLESSELLES superintended and spare of temporary attached men engaged in clearing up farm and surrounding district. No. 3 group at Bath LACHAUSSEE. A party of carpenters and men employed in temporary attached copper on erecting baths at OLINCOURT. Man undertaking collected from BOVES and thus men and lorry engaged in usual work. O.C. returned from PARIS.	O.C.P
FLESSELLES	24th May		No. 1 group in Water Works. Carpenters Billets inspected. No. 2 group at Baths TAVERNAS. A group of fatigue men Baths LACHAUSSEE. Carrying on of FLESSELLES superintended and spare of fatigue men temporarily attached engaged in clearing up farm. A party of carpenters and men engaged in erecting baths at OLINCOURT. Drill undertaken received from 8th Lieut. G. Royal Engineers and 40 Royal Warwickshire Regiment. Lorry dispatched to OLINCOURT spong baths. Lorry proceeded to LONGPRÉ and collected spong bath.	O.C.P

T2134. Wt. W708—776. 500000. 4/15. Sir J. C. & S.

Army Form C. 2118.

WAR DIARY
INTELLIGENCE SUMMARY.
(Erase heading not required.)

Place	Date	Hour	Summary of Events and Information	Remarks and references to Appendices
FLESSELLES	25th May		Troops and Billets inspected. The squad on Baths LA CHAUSSEE. The squad at CLINCOURT Upper Baths. Remainder of FLESSELLES superintended and squad of Improvements attached men engaged in cleaning up Horse and Cow stables. Squad of Carpenters engaged on construction of CLINCOURT Baths. Baths at HAVERNAS dismantled. Lorry and two men proceeded to BOYES and collected washed underclothing. Reinforcement - 2 men from 1st London (City of London) Sanitary Company reports for duty with detm. 66 washers from 1st Lincolns Regiment, 10 Staffordshire Regiment and 10 Royal Hussars and carried Medical Officers 1st Lincolns Regiments. Inspections made of three tins of Units. Also visited LA CHAUSSEE and CLINCOURT and inspection Baths.	OpP
FLESSELLES	26th May		The squad on Baths LA CHAUSSEE. The squad on Baths at CLINCOURT. Remainder of FLESSELLES superintended and squad of temporary attached men engaged in cleaning up Horse and Cow stables. Lorry and three men proceeded to BOYES and collected washed underclothing. Dirties underclothing received from Units of Division and issue of clean underclothing. Inspection made of creation of tents & c O facilitating the washing of underclothing. Inspected 5 Welch Regiment and 2 North Staffordshire Regiment and visited C.R.E. Supreme Command.	OpP

T2134. Wt. W708 – 776. 500000. 4/15. Sir J. C. & S.

WAR DIARY
INTELLIGENCE SUMMARY.
(Erase heading not required.)

Army Form C. 2118.

Place	Date	Hour	Summary of Events and Information	Remarks and references to Appendices
FLESSELLES	27th May		Range and Bullets inspected. One squad on Water Duties. One squad at Baths OLINCOURT. The squad at LA CHAUSSEE Baths. Reports received from Inspector with St H Sands Engineers on Divisional Artillery. Units medicals/clothing received from Units of Division. Lorry and two men proceeded to BOVES and distributed soiled clothing and collected clean. Town Camp Disinfectors attached to Division 6 Coy continued taking supplies to Units. Remainder of FLESSELLES experimented on fatigue squad of Captured/attached men engaged in cleaning up town and practice. Further inspection made of the Mess Room of Units, Billets of 10th Royal Warwickshire Regiment, 16th Divisional Train and own S.T. Machine Gun baths where throats had examined disinfected 166 quarters CAGNY and made arrangement for 3000 articles per day to be washed.	OMP
FLESSELLES	28th May		Range and Bullets inspected. One squad on Water Duties. One squad at Baths OLINCOURT. One squad at LA CHAUSSEE Baths. Reports received from Inspector with 86th Infantry Brigade. Soiled under-clothing received from Units of Division and lorry transport attached to Division for conveyance or orders conveyed to BOVES and three men of Section engaged in disinfecting same to civilian. Remainder of FLESSELLES experimented on new fatigue squad of Non-Commis attached men engaged in cleaning up town. Sec men of Section engaged in Field Army Disinfector.	OMP

WAR DIARY
INTELLIGENCE SUMMARY

Army Form C. 2118.

Place	Date	Hour	Summary of Events and Information	Remarks and references to Appendices
FLESSELLES	29th May		Horses and Billets inspected. One squadron taken to Squadron Baths. LA CHAUSSEE. One squad at OLINCOURT Baths. Remainder of FLESSELLES Squadrons and Fatigue squad if temporarily attached men engaged in cleaning up horse and district lines, also underclothing received from Divn. Baths, underclothing and S.D. Clothing disinfected and 2 men engaged in Tailoring if Brown Army Workshops. "A" Coy. Inspected, attached section provided to CAGNY and orderlies, one also provided to BOVES with horse and Limber Wagon. Lieut. of Inspired Regiment and Railways Company when came to billets - Billets at the Medical Regiment and Railways Company when came of Master had occurred of injured and disinfected. All Officers out of Bath at CHOURS and more or arrangements were truck for everything made available of NULoD Regt on arrival half distance to Learning Also inspected of NULoD Regt on arrival half distance to Learning Area.	OAP
FLESSELLES	30th May		Horses and Billets inspected. One squad engaged in treating water supplies in Learning Area. One squad. Supplies provided to R.M.O's (carry first attached.) One squad at Baths LA CHAUSSEE. Baths at CHACOURT dismantled and erected at CHOURS. Squad of carpenters and attached grow engaged in road work. Section Lorry sent two men forward to CHOURS with underclothing, soiled underclothing received from Units and underclothes S.D. Clothing disinfected - Two men engaged in assisting with Water Lorry Disinfector. Sanitary Inspector attached to 58th Infantry Brigade on leaving Area	

WAR DIARY
or
INTELLIGENCE—SUMMARY.
(Erase heading not required.)

Army Form C. 2118.

Place	Date	Hour	Summary of Events and Information	Remarks and references to Appendices
			Vandohm. 1/ FLESSELLES experimented and fatigue og not engaged in cleaning up town and erection of 6 inch Training Area and experimented construction of Boths at CAOURS. Also inspected 58' Infantry Brigade on the march so as to regain of the march and sanitary arrangements during halt. OMP	
FLESSELLES	30th May		Camps and Billets inspected. Two a quad in rehabilita. One squad at LA CHAUSSEE Baths. One quad at Baths CAOURS. Remainder of FLESSELLES experimented and fatigue squad engaged in cleaning up town. Sanitary report and two fatigue men detailed to Divisional Headquarters in Training Area Villes. Ambulances received from Kants and evacuated. Two men engaged in washing from Kerry. Dispensation, horse and two men proceeded to CAOURS with load of ammunition and medical stores to proceed. Report as to condition of men sick and sent home enquired and forwarded to ADMS of Division. A.A visited Headquarters of Division in Training Area. Baths on CAOURS and 58' Field Ambulance. OMP	

Confidential

List of Main Water Supplies in New Area ..... District.

No.	Source of Supply & Locality			...ent	Remarks
(1)	Hesselles	Communal Well	in Church Square.	1 Scoop	Well
(2)	Hesselles	"	" Outside Cafe de la Reunion	2 Scoops	Well
(3)	Hesselles	"	" Opposite D.H.Q	1 Scoop	Well
(4)	St. Vaet en Chaussee	"	" in Main Rd.	1 Scoop	Well
(5)	La Chaussee	Communal Well	in Main Rd. near Church	1 Scoop	Well
(6)	La Chaussee	"	" in Rue d'Amiens	1 Scoop	Well
(7)	La Chaussee	"	" in Rue de Lille	1 Scoop	Well
(8)	Picquigny	"	Pump in La Place, near Zinnerie	2 Scoops	Pump
(9)	Picquigny	"	" " " " Cafe Ed Beguin	2 Scoops	Pump
(10)	Picquigny	"	" " " " Bakery	2 Scoops	Pump
(11)	Belloy	Communal Well at X Rds. near Church		1 Scoop	Well
(12)	Belloy	"	" 30 yards from above	1 Scoop	Well
(13)	Belloy	"	" 40 yards North of Church	1 Scoop	Well
(14)	Yzeux	"	" in Road, near Church	1 Scoop	Well
(15)	Vignacourt	"	" in main Rd. S.E. of Village	2 Scoops	Well
(16)	Vignacourt	"	" in Fork Rd. " "	2 Scoops	Well
(17)	Vignacourt	"	" in Rd. West of Village	1 Scoop	Well
(18)	Vignacourt	"	" in Rd. Next to Railway	1 Scoop	Well
(19)	Bertangles	"	" " " West of Village	1 Scoop	Well
(20)	Bertangles	"	" " " East of Village	1 Scoop	Well
(21)	Coisy	"	" In Montrose Rd.	1 Scoop	Well
(22)	Rainneville	2 Storage Tanks in Main Rd. fed by pump from well.		1 Scoop	Well
(23)	Villers-Bocage	Communal Well in Argyll St.		2 Scoops	Well

Note:-

(1) Water at Frement & Amiensis not recommended.

(2) A 2¾" disc, as shewn in diagram, indicating the number of Scoops required, has been fixed to supplies marked with X.

3. Owing to the difference in the strength of the Chloride of Lime supplied to units, and the variation in quality of small Water Supplies from time to time, the above figures for chlorination are only suggestive. Standards should be re-adjusted with the sample of Lime to be used.

O.H. Peters Capt
O.C. 19th Divisnl. San. Sec.

New 57th & 58th Brigades &c.

Listing of available supplies of water adjacent

(1)	Mt Bernard. Running stream	1 Scoop
(2)	Neuf Berquin. Running stream	1 Scoop
(3)	Caruse. Running stream	1 Scoop
(4)	Caruse. Communal Well in yard of School	2 Scoops
(5)	Doulieu. Running stream	1 Scoop
(6)	Doulieu. Communal Well in Doulieu Square	1 Scoop
(7)	Doulieu. Well opposite Church N.E.	1 Scoop
(8)	Neuilly l'Hôpital. Well at house of Madame Baillon	1 Scoop
(9)	Neuilly l'Hôpital. Well at house of Madame Caux Jacques	1 Scoop
(10)	Neuilly l'Hôpital. Well at g? West 4th house W of R?	1 Scoop
(11)	Neuilly l'Hôpital. Well at 2nd farmhouse East of Church on right	1 Scoop
(12)	Neuilly l'Hôpital. Well East of Church Opposite Church gate	1 Scoop
(13)	Millbrouck. Communal Well in road between Church and X Road	2 Scoops

Note:—

(1) Chlorification of the above Stream Water is Recommended.

(2) Owing to the poor or low strength of the chloride of lime supplied to units in the Divisional in quantities of small packets supplied from time to time. Admix? for Chlorination are not sufficient. Chlorides could be used for and? with this purpose I would suggest.

O.H. ???, Capt
R.E. 19th Divisional ?????

No. 36 Sanitary Section

June 1916

The DAG
3rd Echelon

I beg to forward herewith War Diary for this Unit for the month of June.

A H Peters Capt
O/C Sanitary Section 86
and 19 Division

No. 36 Sanitary
Vol 12
June

WAR DIARY
or
INTELLIGENCE SUMMARY.

Confidential

War Diary

Sanitary Section 36.

From 1st June to 30th June 1916.

Vol 12

WAR DIARY
or
INTELLIGENCE SUMMARY.
(Erase heading not required.)

Army Form C. 2118.

Place	Date	Hour	Summary of Events and Information	Remarks and references to Appendices
FLESSELLES	1st June		One squad in Nath. Baths. One squad at Baths, LA CHAUSSEE, agreed. Baths, CAOURS. Monsieur of FLESSELLES superintended and squad of temporaries attached men engaged in cleaning of town. Sanitary temporaries with Infantry Brigades and Royal Artillery. One bugler and his temporary attached men at Divisional Headquarters in Training Area. Dental manufacturing received from Units and disinfected. Two men engaged in Divr. Army Workshops. Socks manufacturing taken from CAOURS Bath to ABBEVILLE for washing. Supply of new manufacturing received from SCABIES IC Division and taken by Motor Lorry to CAOURS. 160 repaired monthly after a hair cut for fumigating to DMS 1st C.A.R.	O.K.P.
FLESSELLES	2nd June		One squad in Nath. Baths. One squad at Baths, LA CHAUSSEE. One squad of Section and temporaries attached men at CAOURS Bath. Monsieur of FLESSELLES superintended and squad of temporaries attached men engaged in cleaning up town and streets. Sanitary temporaries with Infantry Brigades and Divisional Artillery. One bugler and his attached men at Divisional Headquarters in Training Area. Worn manufacturing received from Units and disinfected. One or two attached D.A.D.M.S. Clambetter on Baths Army Workshops. Unserviceable S.D. clothing disinfected. 160 arrived D.A.D.M.S. Clambetter of 1st M. Army.	O.K.P.

Army Form C. 2118.

WAR DIARY
or
INTELLIGENCE SUMMARY.
(Erase heading not required.)

Instructions regarding War Diaries and Intelligence Summaries are contained in F. S. Regs., Part II. and the Staff Manual respectively. Title pages will be prepared in manuscript.

Place	Date	Hour	Summary of Events and Information	Remarks and references to Appendices
FLESSELLES	3rd June		One squad on Water Duties. One squad at CHOURS Baths. One squad at LA CHAUSSEE Baths. Sanitation of FLESSELLES superintended and squad of attached men engaged in cleaning up town and district. One Corporal and two fatigue men engaged at Divisional Headquarters on Training Area. Sanitary Inspection with Brigade and divisional Artillery. Willed underclothing received from Units of known and disinfected. Two men engaged in Green Lamp Disinfector. Lorry and three men procured 1730 YDS with orders underclothing and brought back load of clean underclothing. Squad of attached carpenters engaged in making alterations at LA CHAUSSEE Baths. S.O. inspected all Units of 38th Infantry Brigade and of Royal Field Artillery Brigades of Brigade Headquarters. Royal Artillery Headquarters, 19th Divisional Ammunition Column from LA CHAUSSEE. O.P.	
FLESSELLES	4th June		One squad on Water Duties. One squad at LA CHAUSSEE Bath. One squad at CHOURS Baths. Sanitation of FLESSELLES superintended and fatigue party from Divisional Salvage Co. engaged in cleaning up town. Sanitary Inspection with Infantry Brigade and Divisional Artillery. One Corporal and two fatigue men at Divisional Headquarters in Training Area. Soiled underclothing received from Units of known and disinfected. Soilure blankets from Ambulance disinfected. Two men engaged in Green Lamp Disinfector. Squad of carpenters engaged in alterations at LA CHAUSSEE Baths.	

T2134. Wt. W708—776. 560090. 4/15. Sir J. C. & S.

WAR DIARY
OR
INTELLIGENCE SUMMARY.
(Erase heading not required.)

Army Form C. 2118.

Place	Date	Hour	Summary of Events and Information	Remarks and references to Appendices
FLESS			C.O. superintended cleaning up of FLESSELLES.	OMP
FLESSELLES	5th June		One squad in Water Drills. Remainder of FLESSELLES superintended and agreed of Linfantry attached men engaged in cleaning up town. Occupied at LACHAN & E.E Baths. One squad at CROUY. Baths. One Corporal and two fatigue men engaged at Divisional Headquarters in Laundry Area. Sanitary Inspection with Infantry Brigades and Divisional Artillery Units manufactured. Water from CROUY. Bath at ABBEVILLE for washing. Lorry proceeded to BOVES with load of soiled underclothing and returned clean one exchange. One lorry returned from Supply Column and proceeded to CAGNY and collected clean underclothing. Indian Army Transports procured KIREMONT is exempted the S.D. clothing of 7th Loyal North Lancashire Regt. K.O. on company with ADMS of Division and DADMS (Sanitary) of 4th Army inspected billets at FLESSELLES, VAST FREMONT and LA CHAUSSÉE.	OMP

WAR DIARY
or
INTELLIGENCE SUMMARY.

(Erase heading not required.)

Army Form C. 2118.

Instructions regarding War Diaries and Intelligence Summaries are contained in F. S. Regs., Part II. and the Staff Manual respectively. Title pages will be prepared in manuscript.

Place	Date	Hour	Summary of Events and Information	Remarks and references to Appendices
FLESSELLES	6th June.		As agreed on Watie Roster. One agreed on LA CHAUSSEE Baths. One agreed on CROUY Bath. Iodid and washclothing taken from CROUY Bath. IVABBEVILLE for washing, and clean clothing collected. One Corporal and two fatigue men at Divisional Headquarters on Training Area. Sanitary duties with Infantry Brigades and Divisional Artillery. Two men engaged on Divisional Horse Transport. Sanitary Inspections, Inspection Manures and Manures of Latrine Latrines inaugurated. Inhabitants of FLESSELLES unimpressed and fatigue parties of temporary attached men engaged in cleaning up town and district. 6 Carpenters worked at CROUY – also inspected billets of 10 Worcestershire Regiment 2/0 advanced latrines in field. Sanitation at Divisional School of Instruction.	O.P.
FLESSELLES	7th June.		As agreed on Watie Roster. One agreed on LA CHAUSSEE Baths. Squad of carpenters engaged in erecting canvas shelter at LACHAUSSEE Bath. One agreed on CROUY Bath. Soiled underclothing taken from CROUY Bath. IVABBEVILLE for washing. The A.C.O. of Section reported to Headquarters of McDonnell as special intelligence on instruction received from Divisional Headquarters, scales undertaking and Manures of Latrine Formula accompanied. Two men engaged on Divisional Horse Transport. Inspection Sanitation of FLESSELLES superintended. One Corporal and two fatigue men at	

WAR DIARY
or
INTELLIGENCE SUMMARY.
(Erase heading not required.)

Army Form C. 2118.

Instructions regarding War Diaries and Intelligence Summaries are contained in F. S. Regs., Part II. and the Staff Manual respectively. Title pages will be prepared in manuscript.

Place	Date	Hour	Summary of Events and Information	Remarks and references to Appendices
			Divisional Headquarters in Training Area. Sanitary Inspection with Infantry Brigades and Divisional Artillery. Army forwarded to BOVES with order amendments for distribution & services for washing. A.C. inspected all March & 57 Infantry Brigades and of Corps West Section in Training Area. CWP	
FLESSELLES	8 June		Div agroot in Nabn Ruetin. The agroot at LA CHAUSSÉE Baths. Div agroot at CHOURS Baths. Order amendments taken from CHOURS Baths to ABBEVILLE for washing. Inspection of FLESSELLES superintended and no temporary attached men engaged in training grooms and antick. The Corpses and two fatigue men at Divisional Headquarters in Training Area. Blanket and boots returns and order amendments distributed by Indian Army transport. Men now engaged on such work. Sanitary Inspection with Infantry Brigades and Divisional Artillery. A.C. inspected Divisional Headquarters in Training Area, 1st Wiltshire Regiment, 9th Cheshire Regiment, 9th Milot Regiment, 10th Warwickshire Regiment, 10th Worcestershire Regiment in Training Area. Baths at CHOURS inspected. CWP	
FLESSELLES	9 June		Div agroot in Nabn Ruetin. Div agroot at LA CHAUSSÉE Baths. Div agroot at CHOURS Baths. Inspection of FLESSELLES superintended and no temporary attached men engaged in training.	

WAR DIARY
INTELLIGENCE SUMMARY

Army Form C. 2118.

Place	Date	Hour	Summary of Events and Information	Remarks and references to Appendices
			arrived and unload. One Sanitary Squad and two Companys attached men continuance Headquarters in Learning Area. Sanitary Inspector with Divisional Artillery and Infantry Brigade. Scabies Patients Blankets and other underclothing disinfected. No men engaged on Latrine Lorry Disinfector. Lorry proceeded to BOVES with oral underclothing and collects clean washing. Lorry proceeded with squad of carpenter to CROUY for purpose of disinfecting Hospl. C.O. visits unit Sanitary Reports. OMP	
FLESSELLES	10th June		One squad on Water duties. One squad at LACHAUSSEE Baths. Baths at CROUY disinfected and transported together with squad of carpenter to OLINCOURT. One man engaged on training manure and refuse at FLESSELLES and sandown of town superintended. Sanitary Inspector with Infantry Brigades and Divisional Artillery. Underclothing and Blankets disinfected. Two men engaged on Adam Lorry Disinfector. Return Lorry proceeded to BOVES with oral underclothing and collected clean sets from civilians. I.O. inspected Billets of 7th East Lancashire Regiment and Royal Marine Artillery at FLESSELLES. OMP	

Army Form C. 2118.

WAR DIARY
INTELLIGENCE SUMMARY
(Erase heading not required.)

Instructions regarding War Diaries and Intelligence Summaries are contained in F. S. Regs., Part II. and the Staff Manual respectively. Title pages will be prepared in manuscript.

Place	Date	Hour	Summary of Events and Information	Remarks and references to Appendices
FLESSELLES	11th June		One squad on Nalu Duties. One squad at LA CHAUSSEE Baths. One squad at OLINCOURT Baths. Arted underclothing brought from Divisional Baths and disinfected. Two men engaged in Straw Fumy Disinfector. Sanitary Inspection with Infantry Brigades and Divisional Armoured Artillery – reports received from Inspection. Commandm of FLESSELLES superintendent and one attached man engaged in running manure and straw refuse from bivouacs to BOVES noth carted underclothing and collected clean underclothing from overlaine. 1.0. inspected ST GRATIEN (area Town Major). Anted of 33rd Company Army Service Corps. 5th Anst. Water Boiler Regiment, FRECHENCOURT (area Town Major). Anted of 52nd Company Royal Engineers also 281st Company. Inoka Town Major at BEHENCOURT, Part in squad of 10 men to clean up ST GRATIEN under supervision of Captain of Station.	
FLESSELLES	12th June		One squad on Nalu Duties. One squad at LA CHAUSSEE Baths. One squad at OLINCOURT Baths. One squad at OLINCOURT Baths. One squad at OLINCOURT Baths. Arted underclothing from Divisional Baths and disinfected – two men of section engaged on Straw Furny Disinfector. Sanitary Inspection with Infantry Brigades and Divisional Artillery – reports received from Inspection. One man temporary attached engaged on incinerating manure and refuse at FLESSELLES and command of station superintended.	

WAR DIARY
or
INTELLIGENCE SUMMARY.
(Erase heading not required.)

Army Form C. 2118.

Instructions regarding War Diaries and Intelligence Summaries are contained in F. S. Regs., Part II. and the Staff Manual respectively. Title pages will be prepared in manuscript.

Place	Date	Hour	Summary of Events and Information	Remarks and references to Appendices
			Return lorry proceeded to BOVES with soiled underclothing and arrived clean ditto from civilians. Lorry arrived from Divisional Supply Column and two men / Section proceeded to ABBEVILLE and CAOURS for collection of clean underclothing &c. CO inspected 7th South Lancashire Regiment and moved from Mayor MYERS-BOCAGE and inspected 3rd Battalion Royal Engineers and Ancillary Transport &c. CO wrote MONTONVILLERS.	ONP
FLESSELLES	13th June		Bantyn and Bicetti inspected Sanitary Outposts with Infantry Brigades and Divisional Artillery. One Squad on water duties. Remainder of FLESSELLES Superintendent and one attached men engaged in turning manure and lime refuse. One Squad at OLINCOURT Baths. One Squad at LA CHAUSSEE Baths. Blankets of Section Returned and soiled underclothing disinfected. Two men / Section engaged in Section Army transports. Return lorry and two men proceeded to BOVES with bags of soiled underclothing for washing by civilians. On arrival Superintendent fatigue party cleaning up St GRATIEN. CO inspected 86th, 87th, 89th and parts of 88th Brigades Royal Field Artillery, also Baths at OLINCOURT and LA CHAUSSEE.	ONP

Army Form C. 2118.

WAR DIARY
or
INTELLIGENCE SUMMARY.
(Erase heading not required.)

Instructions regarding War Diaries and Intelligence Summaries are contained in F.S. Regs., Part II. and the Staff Manual respectively. Title pages will be prepared in manuscript.

Place	Date	Hour	Summary of Events and Information	Remarks and references to Appendices
FLESSELLES	14th June.		One squadron Native British Field Ambulance at OHINCOURT Baths. One squadron at LACHAUSSEE Baths. Inspection of FLESSELLES encampment and one man Temporary attached to Personnel Baths and turn in report and manner. Tried underclothing extracted from Personnel Baths and disinfected, also blankets from these Ambulances. Two men of section engaged in London Army Disinfector. Sanitary Corporals with Infantry Brigade and Divisional Artillery. Reports received from Inspection. Section Army and his men proceeded to BOVES with order underclothing and extracted clean underclothing. Voluntarism and tested Person Test Coal designed by Warrant Surgeon of Section and sent forward through A.D.M.S. of Division to D.D.M.S. (Offr of Inspection of Coal arrested). A.D.S. involved new district and inspected MAILHIEN LA BOIS and RAINNEVILLE. Others are for baths at BEHENCOURT and arranged for baths at MAILHIEN LA BOIS and RAINNEVILLE.	OMP
FLESSELLES	15th June.		One squadron in Native British. One squadron at OHIN COURT Baths. One squadron at LACHAUSSEE. Inspection of FLESSELLES superintended and one man engaged in turning manner and turn refuse. Under underclothing extracted from Personnel Baths and	

T2134. Wt. W708-776. 500000. 4/15. Sir J.C.&B.

WAR DIARY
or
INTELLIGENCE SUMMARY
(Erase heading not required.)

Army Form C. 2118.

Instructions regarding War Diaries and Intelligence Summaries are contained in F.S. Regs., Part II. and the Staff Manual respectively. Title pages will be prepared in manuscript.

Place	Date	Hour	Summary of Events and Information	Remarks and references to Appendices
			transferred also blankets from Field Ambulance. Two men of Bedns engaged on drawn lorry transport. Sanitary personel with Infantry Brigades and abnormal drilling - reports received from hospitals. Returns lorry one two men proceed to BOYES and that I cried undercloth and clean washing. Nos of Water supplies in new area sent 178 Regimental Medical Officers (attached). C.O. inspected 56 Brigade Medical Arrants and A.D.V.S. arrangement for existing of Venereal Spreads and Preparation of Anti-Gas schemes.	
S.T GRATIEN	16th June		One engaged on Bath Rolls. One engaged on OLINCOURT Baths. Bath at "LA CHAUSSEE" dismantled and open bath equipment manufactured brought in. Return lorry to FRESSELLES, soiled underclothing collected from BLINCOURT Posts. Blankets from Field Ambulance and soiled underclothing disinfected. Two men of Bedns engaged on lorry long transport. Part of clothing equipment and stores removed to ST. GRATIEN. Lorry Bath transport on lorry A BEAUCOURT and coloured washing A CORBIE on Monday. Blankets of Division disinfected	

WAR DIARY or INTELLIGENCE SUMMARY

Army Form C. 2118

Place	Date	Hour	Summary of Events and Information	Remarks and references to Appendices
			after things had moved out spinto [submitted]. One room of boohin left in charge of stone dumper at FLESSELLES. Boohin mess tries cleaned and latrine erected. C.O. inspected 9th Cheshire Regiment, 9th Royal Welsh Fusiliers and 8th Brigade, Royal Field Artillery, superintended erection of spray bath at BEHENCOURT. C.O. interviewed from Major ST GRATIEN reference future latrines of	
ST GRATIEN	17th June		One squad in Water Duties. Evacuation of ST GRATIEN superintended. One squad at OLINCOURT Baths and one squad at BEHENCOURT Baths. Further part of Boohin equipment and other removed from FLESSELLES. John Long Thompson processed from FLESSELLES to ST GRATIEN. OLINCOURT Baths dismantled. Sanitary Corporals inspected truck of division on arrival in our billets. Long / Section proceeded to FLESSELLES and collected orderlies outstanding. I.O. inspected 7th South Lancashire Regiment, 7th Loyal North Lancashire Regiment, 56th Infantry Brigade Headquarters, 59th Infantry Brigade Headquarters and 9th Worcestershire Regiment. A.O. visited FLESSELLES reference materials dumped and BEHENCOURT Baths and inspected camp at PERTHAM FRECHENCOURT.	
ST GRATIEN	18th June		One squad in Water Duties. One squad at BEHENCOURT Baths. Extra long Thompson supply disinfecting Mantles from Ambulances and sorted same clothing. Evacuation of ST GRATIEN superintended and squad of temporarily attached	

WAR DIARY
INTELLIGENCE SUMMARY
(Erase heading not required.)

Army Form C. 2118

Place	Date	Hour	Summary of Events and Information	Remarks and references to Appendices
			men engaged in cleaning up town. Two men of sections engaged in Section Party Transport. Section Lorry proceeded to PLESSETTES and collected for the load of section shoes and underclothing. Section lorry proceeded to BOVES with load of soiled underclothing and collected clean clothing. It proceeded forward. Men are inspected 8th & 10th Staffordshire Regt 10th inniskillin Regt 8th Irish Hallo Borders and 10th Hampshire Regt. 60 men of 85th Brigade RFA and engineer not fit for the of them at BEHENCOURT. CNP	
ST. GRATIEN	10 June		One squad at BEHENCOURT Baths. One squad on Water Duties. One squad of Maynards attached men engaged in cleaning up ST GRATIEN and continued from experiment. One squad of attached men erecting further latrines. Further underclothing and blankets from Ambulance disinfected. Two men of section engaged in Section Lorry transport. Lorry with two men proceeded to BEHENCOURT with load of clean clothing. Lorry with two men proceeded to BOVES with load of soiled underclothing and collected clean clothing. Party again received from Sunday inspect. L.C. inspected 83rd and 69th Brigade Royal Field Artillery. Sum Major of MILLENCOURT and investigated water supply. CNP	

WAR DIARY or INTELLIGENCE SUMMARY

(Erase heading not required.)

Army Form C. 2118

Instructions regarding War Diaries and Intelligence Summaries are contained in F.S. Regs., Part II. and the Staff Manual respectively. Title Pages will be prepared in manuscript.

Place	Date	Hour	Summary of Events and Information	Remarks and references to Appendices
ST GRATIEN	20th June		One squad at BEHENCOURT Baths. One squad on Motor Lorries. One squad of temporary attached men engaged in cleaning up ST GRATIEN and sanitation of town superintended. Blankets from Field Ambulances and extra underclothing disinfected. Two men of Section engaged in Motor Lorry transport. Lorry with two men proceeded to BEHENCOURT with clean underclothing. Lorry with two men proceeded to BOVES with soiled underclothing, and collected clean underclothing from civilians. Anti-Lice Water Supplies in Divisional Area sent to Regimental Medical Officers App.7 (last attached). C.O. visited Units at LAVIEVILLE and FRECHENCOURT including 19th Divisional Ammunition Column 22nd Coy Royal Engineers, 58th Brigade Headquarters, Machine Gun Coys, Trench Mortar Battery, also enquired into case of Scarlet Fever at LAVIEVILLE.	
ST GRATIEN	21st June		One squad at BEHENCOURT Baths. One squad on North Lorries. One squad of temporary attached men engaged in cleaning up from of ST GRATIEN and surrounding country and sanitation of Town superintended. Blankets from Field Ambulances and soiled underclothing disinfected. Two men of Section engaged in Motor Lorry transport. Lorry and two men proceeded to BEHENCOURT with clean underclothing. Lorry with two men proceeded to BOVES	

WAR DIARY
or
INTELLIGENCE SUMMARY
(Erase heading not required.)

Army Form C. 2118

Instructions regarding War Diaries and Intelligence Summaries are contained in F.S. Regs., Part II. and the Staff Manual respectively. Title Pages will be prepared in manuscript.

Place	Date	Hour	Summary of Events and Information	Remarks and references to Appendices
			with soiled underclothing and collected clean washing from civilian. Return received from Inspection. O.C. made arrangements for issue of both the Douche and inspected bath of ST GRATIEN with Town Mayor. Squad of men engaged in mixing anti-gas solution. CNP	
ST GRATIEN	22nd June		One squad in Main Rue. One squad at BEHENCOURT Baths. Remainder of STGRATIEN superintended and squad of temporarily attached men engaged in clearing up town and district. Blankets received from Commander and soiled underclothing disinfected. Two men of Section engaged in Stores from Brouifects. Return from and his men proceeded to BEHENCOURT with clean underclothing. Section lorry proceeded to BOVES with soiled underclothing and collected clean under-clothing from civilians. O.C. inspected STGRATIEN with Sanitary Officer of Fourth Army and instructed Medical Officers on use of new Bath Apparatus and made arrangements for issue of anti-gas solution. CNP	

WAR DIARY
or
INTELLIGENCE SUMMARY
(Erase heading not required.)

Army Form C. 2118

Place	Date	Hour	Summary of Events and Information	Remarks and references to Appendices
ST GRATIEN	23rd June		Section engaged on Water Duties. One squad at BEHENCOURT Baths. Bath and Billet Inspected and defects reported from Inspection. Rations from Ambulances and order ammunition disinfected. Two men of Section engaged on Rum Issue, Disinfestor. Garrison of ST GRATIEN disinfected and squad of men Tomorrow attached engaged on clearing up huts, Section Lorry with two men proceeded to BEHENCOURT with clean ammunitions for Baths. Lorry on return engaged in preparation of Anti Gas solution. One men of Section working in Bean the Water Testing Apparatus. A.C. Inspected 9th West Regiment, 5th South Wales Border Regiment, 6th Wiltshire Regiment and Trenches N.W. of ALBERT. Section from Divisional to BOVES and secured clean underclothing. O.N.P.	
ST GRATIEN	24th June		Section engaged on Water Duties. One squad at BEHENCOURT Baths. Blankets from Inspection. One squad at BEHENCOURT Baths. Blankets from Field Ambulances and soiled underclothing disinfected. Two men of Section engaged on Rum Issue Disinfector. Garrison of ST GRATIEN disinfected and squad of men Tomorrow attached men engaged in clearing up huts. Section Lorry proceeded with two men to BEHENCOURT with clean underclothing for Baths. One man of Section returning lorry for new water testing apparatus. Section Lorry with two men proceeded to BOVES with soiled underclothing and secured clean underclothing. A.C. visited 151/14 Returned Richard Depot at CORBIE on	

WAR DIARY
or
INTELLIGENCE SUMMARY

(Erase heading not required.)

Army Form C. 2118

Place	Date	Hour	Summary of Events and Information	Remarks and references to Appendices
S^T GRATIEN	25 June		Water Apparatus. Inspected 9th Welch Regiment & found Water leaking in the Urns & an entrance Rats Traps and Black Infantant to be emery of an advance.	CNP
			One squad on Water duties. One squad at BEHENCOURT Baths. Garrison of S^T GRATIEN disinfected and squad of Regiments attached men engaged in clearing up town and district. Work of Unknown inspected and report on sanitary condition received. Latrines have overseen at BEHENCOURT will clear manipulations for Baths. Blankets from Field Ambulance and section inspection disinfected. Two men engaged in emptying Soda Lime Disinfector. One man of section engaged in emptying and filling cases for new Water and Power testing base. N.C.O in charge filling up of Water Apparatus for Water and Power testing took in rear of advance. Temporary sniper over attacks to section in rear of advance.	CNP
S^T GRATIEN	26 June		One squad on Water duties. One squad at BEHENCOURT Baths. One squad of Regiments attached men engaged in clearing up S^T GRATIEN and remainder of men superintendent. Work of Unknown inspected as to sanitary of town, Lorry and the	

WAR DIARY
or
INTELLIGENCE SUMMARY
(Erase heading not required.)

Army Form C. 2118

Place	Date	Hour	Summary of Events and Information	Remarks and references to Appendices
			Men proceeded to BEHENCOURT with clean underclothing for Bath. Blankets from Field Ambulance and soiled underclothing disinfected. Two men of Section engaged in Grain Barn disinfector. Section Lorry with two men proceeded to BOVES with soiled underclothing and collected clean washing. The men of Section engaged in making and fitting up cases for new Walls and Boiler for Disinfector. C.O. continued arrangements and organization for further advance. OKP	
ST GRATIEN	27th June		One squad in Walla Dretu. One squad at BEHENCOURT. One squad of Employed attached men engaged in cleaning up ST GRATIEN and sanitation of Town and district superintended. Blankets from Field Ambulances and soiled underclothing disinfected. Two men of Section engaged in Grain Lorry Disinfector. Section Lorry and two men proceeded to BEHENCOURT with clean underclothing for Baths. Work of Division inspected and reports received as to Sanitary arrangements. C.O. visited MILLENCOURT and LAVIEVILLE reference billets and arms for Sanitary material. Continues Instructions for leaving stores and organizing work of Section. OKP	

WAR DIARY
or
INTELLIGENCE SUMMARY
(Erase heading not required.)

Army Form C. 2118

Place	Date	Hour	Summary of Events and Information	Remarks and references to Appendices
ST GRATIEN	28th June		One squad on Motor Duties. One squad of men temporarily attached engaged in clearing up ST GRATIEN and area and work experienced. Horses inspected and report received as to condiment. Blankets from Field Ambulances and cycles monoclothing disinfected. Two men of Section engaged in Salv. from Dourfoin. Section Army and two men proceeded to BEHENCOURT with clean monoclothing for Bath. C.O. continued preparation for possible advance. OhP	
ST GRATIEN	29th June		One squad on Motor Duties. One squad at BEHENCOURT Baths. One squad of temporarily attached men engaged in clearing up ST GRATIEN area, billets and work experienced. Blankets from Field Ambulances disinfected. Two men engaged in salving Salv. from Dourfoin. Section Army and two men proceeded to BOVES and collected clean monoclothing from Civilians. C.O. continued preparation for possible advance. OhP	

1875 Wt. W593/826 1,000,000 4/15   J.B.C. & A.   A.D.S.S./Forms/C. 2118.

WAR DIARY
or
INTELLIGENCE SUMMARY

Army Form C. 2118

Place	Date	Hour	Summary of Events and Information	Remarks and references to Appendices
ST GRATIEN	30 June		C.O. continues preparation for advance. Section equipment the single men moved forward to MILLENCOURT. On march Section in charge of material dumped at FRECHENCOURT. Squad of men at Bath at BEHENCOURT.	OLP

List of Main Water Supplies in the Forward Area.

Nº	Source of Supply and Locality.		Treatment	Remarks
1.	Franvillers	Piped supply at Church	2 scops	Well
2.	Dº	Piped supply between Franvillers & Hielles	1 scop	Tanks
3.	Hielles	Running stream.	2 scops	Stream
4.	Dº	Piped supply in main road near Station Rd.	½ scop	Spring
5.	Ribemont	Running stream.	1 scop	Stream
6.	Dº	Pump in R.E. yard. In Main Road	2½ scops	Pump.
7.	Buire-sur-Lancre	Running stream - draws from tank near Railway.	1½ scops	Stream
8.	Ville-sous-Corbie	Pump in Y.M.C.A. yard, Queen Street	1 scop	Pump
9.	Dº	Pumped supply at Cross Roads - ½ mile East of Village.	2 scops	Tank.
10.	Bonnancourt	Running stream.	1 scop	Stream.
11.	Albert	Large piped supply near Church in Square	1 scop	Tank.
12.	Boozencourt	Piped supply in Main Road ½ mile towards Albert.	1 scop	Tanks.
13.	Dº	Communal Well in Triangle near Church	2 scops	Well
14.	Dº	Piped supply on bridge - opposite Church	2 scops	Tap
15.	Martinsart	Dº off Main Road	1 scop	Tanks.
16.	Millencourt	Well at Church - fitted with horse-pump	1 scop	Tap
17.	Aveluy	Well Nº3 - first house on left passed Railway	1 scop	Well
18.	Lavieville	Piped supply in Main Road	2 scops	Tank.
19.	Dº	Communal Well in Main Road	1 scop	Well.
20.	Bresle	Piped supply.	2 scops	Tank
21.	Piped supply in road between St Gratien & Rainneville		1 scop	Tank
22.	Frechencourt	Piped supply in Main Road near Chateau	1 scop	Tanks.
23.	Henencourt	Piped supply in Road next to Chateau	1 scop	Tanks.
24.	Senlis	Dº in Henencourt Road	1 scop	Tanks.
25.	Warloy-Baillon	Piped supply in Rue de la Croix	1 scop	Tank
26.	Frechencourt	Dº in T Road at Railway	1 scop	Tank

Note:-
See Foot Notes of previous List.

Capt:
O.C. 19th Divisional Sanitary Section.

29/6/16.

List of Main Water Supplies in New Area of position and District.

No.	Source of Supply and Locality			Remarks
(1)	Behencourt	Running Stream		1 Scoop Stream
(2)	Frechencourt	" " Near Railway		1 Scoop "
(3)	"	" " Near Mill		1 Scoop "
(4)	Pont Noyelles	" " Side of Bridge St.		1 Scoop "
(5)	St. Gratien	Piped Supply in Tanks in Main Road. South of Village.		1 Scoop Tanks
(6)	Montigny	Communal Pump in Church Sq.		1 Scoop Pump
(7)	"	Running Stream.		1 Scoop Stream
(8)	Bazieux	Piped Supply at School. York St.		1 Scoop Tanks
(9)	Contay	Running Stream		1 Scoop Stream
(10)	Beaucourt	Draw from Stream at Behencourt		1 Scoop Stream
(11)	Molheim-au-Bois	Piped Supply in Wick Rd.		1 Scoop Tanks
(12)	Mirvaux	Communal Well. Opposite Café de la Place		1 Scoop Well
(13)	Pierregot	Piped Supply in Shuttle Lane.		1½ Scoops Tanks
(14)	Mirvaux	" " Near Church		1½ Scoops "
(15)	Rubempre	Communal Well in Main Rd. S.E. of Village.		1½ Scoops Well
(16)	"	Piped Supply in Villers-Bocage Rd.		Not Tested.
(17)	Villers-Bocage	Piped Supply at Gendarmerie.		1½ Scoops Tanks
(18)	"	Communal Well in Argyll St.		2 Scoops Well
(19)	Raineville	Piped Supply in Main Rd.		1 Scoop Tanks

Piped Supply in Main Rd. between Frechencourt and Pont Noyelles not recommended. Bad Water (11 Scoops)

Note:- (1) Clarification of the above stream water is recommended.
(2) Owing to the difference in the strength of the Chloride of Lime supplied to units, and the variation in quality of small water supplies from time to time the above figures for chlorination are only suggestive. Standard should be verified with the sample of lime to be used.

O.H. Sckers, Capt.
O.C. 19th Divisional Sanitary Section.

A NEW CHLORINATION & METAL POISON TEST CASE.

Experience has shown that a light and portable Water-Testing Apparatus is required, and one capable of rapid examination of Water Supplies in the Field. When opening up an area recently evacuated by the enemy, it is also essential that Water Supplies should be tested for chemical poisons as well as bacteriological contamination, and the boxes of apparatus supplied at present for this purpose are too bulky to be easily carried about between different supplies of water. The combined Test Case here described fulfils all these conditions as regards portability, since its weight is one fifth, and its cubic capacity less than one fifth of the apparatus referred to. All the essential features of the Chlorination and Metal Poison Tests are combined in a case of two compartments easily detachable when occasion requires for separate use. The case allows of great rapidity of manipulation and examination, is found to be in every way as efficient as, and is put forward as a substitute for, the two boxes of apparatus at present in use.

DESCRIPTION of TEST CASE

Dimensions of case:-

Height........7½ inches.
Breadth........8 inches.
Depth..........5¼ inches.

Weight, complete with Reagents:- 4 lbs.

CONTENTS

Chlorination Compartment:-

1 8 ozs Medicine Bottle.
1 Corked Test Tube containing stock of Bleaching Powder.
1 Test Tube for stock solution of Bleaching Powder, fitted

with rings and test for chlorine solution.

1 Test Tube containing test solution of Potassium Iodide and Starch, also fitted with pipette and test.

1 Spare pipette.

1 Stirring rod.

1 Cup, white enamel (cup)

1 Measuring scoop, adapted from scoop taken from tin of Bleaching Powder.

Metal Poison Compartment:-

1 Test Tube for Caustic Soda.
1   Do   Ferrous Sulphate.
1   Do   Granulated Zinc.
1   Do   Sodium Sulphide.
1   Do   stock of fine glass tubes.

1 Tube of pure Vaseline.

2 Glass stoppered bottles for Hydrochloric Acid.

8 Spare tubes for testing.

1 Cleaning cloth.

1 Candlestick.

1 Removable cell containing:-

                8 Spare corks for Arsenic Test.
                1 Wire test tube support.
                1 Candle for boiling reagents.
                1 Adjustable test tube stand.
                1 Box of matches.

The tubes containing reagents fit into the spare test tubes, thus economising space.

The body of the case is adapted from a waste horseshoe-nail tin (these are obtainable at any Divisional Farriers) and divided into two compartments, one containing accessories for the Chlorination Test, and the other for the Metal Poison Test.   It is coated externally with grey enamel or paint, and internally with white enamel or paint.   A 30" equipment strap is attached, acting as a sling for carrying.   Fixed in the bottom of the case is a block of wood having a series of

wells lined with cotton wool, on which tubes containing
reagents rest in a vertical position, being held securely
by a perforated diaphragm, situated about mid-way. The cup is
inverted and rests over the neck of the bottle.

The case will carry sufficient reagents to complete 600
Chlorination tests, and 25 tests for every poison provided
against in the Metal Poison Box. A reserve stock of
reagents is always obtainable at Field Ambulances.

The accompanying photograph shews the way in which the
apparatus may be carried. By a simple contrivance the
compartments may be readily detached one from the other, or
reattached, the same strap being adapted to carry either
compartment singly or both combined suspended from the
shoulder and secured under the shoulder strap.

- Directions for using Apparatus -

Chlorination Test.

1. Place in bottle water to be tested to the level of black line (6 ozs.)

2. Add one drop of No.1 Solution (Chloride of Lime) and well shake bottle. It is advisable to shake No.1 Solution before using.

3. Now place in the bottle three drops of No.2 Solution (Potassium Iodide and Starch) and reshake bottle.

4. If water turns a definite blue, allow it to stand for ten minutes. If by this time no change in colour has taken place the test is completed, and one measure of Chloride of Lime should be placed in the body of the Water Cart.

5. If the blue colour disappears, another drop of No.1 Solution must be added, and repeated until a permanent blue colour is restored. The total number of drops of No.1 Solution placed in the bottle will indicate the number of measures of Chloride of Lime to be placed in the body of the Water Cart, to effect sterilisation. In cases where the blue colouration is only faintly discernable it will become more apparent by pouring the contents of the bottle into the white cup supplied. It is an advantage to make the test in a bottle, since it obviates the necessity of waiting at the supply to ascertain if a blue colour persists. The bottle can be replaced in the case and the result ascertained when arriving at the next supply, thus economising much valuable time.

NOTE.

All stream waters and water containing suspended matter must be clarified before making the above test.

Directions for making stock solution of Chloride of Lime.

Take one measure of Bleaching Powder from stock supplied and place in white cup. Add water sufficient to mix into a paste, and fill cup to within ½ inch of brim with pure water. Having well mixed the solution, refill No.1 Test Tube and throw the remainder away. The solution, if well corked, will retain its strength for several days.

It is important to well rinse the white cup after mixing solution.

- Directions for using Apparatus -

Chemical Tests.

1. **LEAD, COPPER, MERCURY, ARSENIC.**

   Quarter fill a test tube with the water to be examined.
   Add No. 8. Solution (Sodium Sulphide), in an amount
   occupying quarter of an inch length of test tube.
   A BROWN colour indicates the probable presence of a
   metal, but the absence of a colour does not indicate
   the absence of arsenic.
   Now add to the same test tube an amount of No. 4
   Solution (Hydrochloric Acid) to occupy half an inch
   length of tube -
   (a) If the colour remains still BLACK or BROWN, LEAD,
        COPPER, or MERCURY is present.
   (b) If a canary-yellow milky colour develops ARSENIC
        is present. (Note – Slight milkiness may be
        ignored)

   Confirmation of the above indication of the presence of

ARSENIC is obtained as follows:-

1. Place in test tube water to be examined to an amount
   occupying ½ of an inch length of tube, and add 5 pellets
   of Granulated Zinc.

2. Now prepare test tube and enamel cup according to the
   arrangement shown in the diagram:-

3. Next add ½ an inch of No. 4 Solution (Hydrochloric
   Acid); allow precisely half a minute to elapse, and
   light the gas escaping from the end of the fine glass
   tube. (A better flame can be produced by sealing the
   gas in the tube. This can be done by smearing the
   crevice between the cork and tube with pure Vaseline
   supplied). Replace the test tube in the manner
   previously shown and move the tube backwards and
   forwards until the flame just touches the enamelled
   surface of the cup.
   If no stain appears the water is ARSENIC FREE. A
   black or brown stain on the enamel indicates the
   presence of ARSENIC.

IMPORTANT NOTE.

The stain may be due to a deposit of Metalic Zinc in
which case it is quickly soluble in dilute Hydro-
-chloric Acid. Whereas Arsenic stain will remain un-
-dissolved after contact with Hydrochloric Acid of the
Test Case.
The typical Arsenic stain usually assumes a bronzed-
-mirror appearance.

N.B. A fresh cork must be used for every test, but the
fine glass tube is suitable for use again after having
been boiled in clean water. It is sufficient to care-
-fully wash and well rinse the test tube in clear water
before returning to the case.

CYANIDE.

Quarter fill the test tube with the sample. Add quarter of an inch depth of No 5 solution(Caustic Soda) and three drops of No 6 solution(Ferrous Sulphate). Boil very thoroughly. Add No 4 solution(Hydrochloric Acid) until the contents of the test tube are clear.
A Blue colour indicates the presence of CYANIDE. This colour is more pronounced if the test tube is allowed to stand for thirty minutes.

NOTE.

The water cannot certainly be regarded as free from poisons until the above tests have been repeated with negative results, in two consecutive examinations.

- Advantages of Apparatus. -

Apparatus present in use.	"Southgate's Combined Test Case"
Weight:-	Weight:-
"Horrocks' Box" 6lbs.	4lbs Complete.
Metal poison Box 14lbs.	

Dimensions:-

"Horrocks' Box"
  13" x 6" x 6".
Metal Poison Box.
  12" x 8½" x 6".

The "Horrocks'" and Metal Poison Box are rather too bulky to be carried about by Water Inspectors when going on in advance to open up supplies in a wide area, both hands are necessarily engaged when carrying these apparatus. Whereas "SOUTHGATE'S COMBINED TEST CASE" in no way incommodes. Being strapped to the shoulder it leaves the arms free of action, enabling the Inspector to ride a horse or bicycle as the case may be. This is an important point when inspecting Water Supplies in the trenches.

- CHLORINATION COMPARTMENT. -

The manipulation of the "Horrocks'" apparatus is lengthy, and, under Active Service conditions, somewhat unweildy. "Southgate's" apparatus is specially designed to facilitate Tests in all weather conditions. Rain, dust, wind, or absence of cover, do not disturb examinations as in the former case. In practice 40 different sources have been tested in a day, as against not more than 12 with the apparatus at present supplied, the testing of one source is going on in the bottle while the next source is being found. "Horrocks'" proceedure is perhaps not as fool-proof as is urged, the 7 cups used complicate the Test by introducing different shades of blue, causing confusion as to which cup should indicate the number of scoopfuls of Bleaching Powder required, and errors in the chlorination of water carts often arise therefrom. Whereas only one cup is used with the new Test Case, and there is only one shade of blue to decide from. Thus the requisite number of scoopfuls is directly indicated by the minimum number of drops of Chlorine solution placed in the cup to obtain a persistant blue colouration. In the "Horrocks'" Test two stirring rods are required, one for mixing the Chlorine solution, the other for stirring the samples of water under examination in the six white cups. In testing it is easy to interchange these rods accidentally with the result that an under-estimation of the chlorination is arrived at, and bad water may pass as good through an error of this kind. Even when the proper rod is used the test may be vitiated by stirring the cups in the wrong order. I.E.- Commencing from left to right, the cups are laid out numbering 1,2,3,4,5,6, and water requiring 1½ scoops per water cart is placed in them for examination. Chloride of Lime equal to 1,2,3,4,5&6 scoops respectively per water cart is added, and after the addition of Potassium Iodide & Starch No1 cup should remain white, and the remainder shew a blue colouration. If No 1 sample is stirred subsequent to No 6, the probable result is that No 1 sample will become sufficiently vitiated to shew a blue colouration, and the water would appear to require one, instead of one and a half scoops. "Southgate's" proceedure simplifies the process to three actions, instead of fifteen, as with the "Horrocks'," thus obviating possible errors such as those discussed.

METAL POISON TEST.

The proceedure with the Metal Poison Test is almost identical with the one at present adopted. The exceptions are as follows:-

1. A Test is added to distinguish between a Real and False Arsenic Mirror. In the present campaign water quite free from Arsenic has been condemned when using the present apparatus. This matter is dealt with above under "IMPORTANT NOTE".

2. ARSENIC TEST. Vaseline is provided for sealing the gas in the tube. This prevents wastage of the gas, and will often increase the diameter of a flame as much as six times.

3. The expenditure of reagents is reduced by one half, being Arsenic free they are expensive, and difficult to procure, which makes this an important feature.

This apparatus has been used at the Front by the 56th Sanitary Section, 79th Division, for the past six months.

S

19th Division

36th Sany. Section

July 1916

COMMITTEE FOR THE
MEDICAL HISTORY OF THE WAR
Date 31 AUG 1916

To A.A. & Q.M.G. 19th Div.

Herewith War Diaries for
Month of July for

57 Field Amb
58 Field Amb
59 Field Amb
H Sanitary Section

J.W. Kendrick
Capt R.A.M.C.
for

.... COL, A.M.S.
A.D.M.S. 19th DIVISION.

To ADMS
   19 Division

I beg to forward herewith War
Diary of this Unit for July last

                    Lloyd Capt RAMC
          OC 19 Divisional Sanitary Section

   2
   AA & QMG   Confidential
      19 Div

   Forwarded

                Hawkins Col
                   ADMS
                     19 Div
1/8/16.

WAR DIARY
~~or~~
INTELLIGENCE SUMMARY

Army Form C. 2118

19 36 Son See

Vol 13

Confidential

War Diary

19th Divisional Sanitary Section

from 1st July to 31st July 1916.

Vol 13

WAR DIARY
or
INTELLIGENCE SUMMARY
(Erase heading not required.)

Army Form C. 2118

Instructions regarding War Diaries and Intelligence Summaries are contained in F. S. Regs., Part II. and the Staff Manual respectively. Title Pages will be prepared in manuscript.

Place	Date	Hour	Summary of Events and Information	Remarks and references to Appendices
MILLENCOURT	1st July.		Boar at MILLENCOURT cleaned and sanitary arrangements carried out. The opener of temporary attached men engaged in cleaning up town. Men of section assisting with Ambulance at MILLENCOURT. OWP	
MILLENCOURT	2nd July.		Squad of temporary attached men engaged in cleaning up town and sanitation arrangements. Section duty with three men evacuated wounded from Ambulance at LAVIEVILLE. Men of Section assisting with Ambulance at MILLENCOURT. One man with stores dumped at FRECHENCOURT. OWP	
MILLENCOURT	3rd July.		Squad of temporary attached men engaged in cleaning up town. Sanitation of town superintended. Men of Section assisting with Ambulance at MILLENCOURT. Two men and store dumper at FRECHENCOURT. Blankets from Ambulance disinfected. Two men engaged in Water Lorry Disinfector. Section lorry and two men stand by for return to evacuate wounded. The men of Section making cases for new Nolan & Poison Testing Apparatus. OWP	

WAR DIARY
or
INTELLIGENCE SUMMARY
(Erase heading not required.)

Army Form C. 2118

Place	Date	Hour	Summary of Events and Information	Remarks and references to Appendices
MILLENCOURT	4th July.		Sanitation of MILLENCOURT superintended and latrines inspected. Fatigue squads of temporarily attached men engaged in cleaning up town and billets. Two men with others encamped at FRECHENCOURT. Blankets from Field Ambulance disinfected. Two men engaged in Frozen Rum Disinfector. One man of Section making cases for new Wash and Poison testing Apparatus. Admin Room and two men standing by for orders to evacuate wounded.	OMP
MILLENCOURT	5th July.		Sanitation of MILLENCOURT superintended and billets inspected. Fatigue squads of temporarily attached men engaged in cleaning up town and billets. Two men with others encamped at FRECHENCOURT. Blankets from Field Ambulance disinfected. Two men engaged in Frozen Rum Disinfector. Admin Room and two men standing by for orders to evacuate wounded. One man of Section engaged in making cases for new Wash and Poison Testing Apparatus.	OMP
MILLENCOURT	6th July.		Fatigue squads of temporarily attached men engaged in cleaning up town and billets and sanitation of MILLENCOURT superintended. Two men with others encamped at FRECHENCOURT. Blankets from Field Ambulance disinfected and two men engaged.	

WAR DIARY
or
INTELLIGENCE SUMMARY

(Erase heading not required.)

Army Form C. 2118

Instructions regarding War Diaries and Intelligence Summaries are contained in F. S. Regs., Part II. and the Staff Manual respectively. Title Pages will be prepared in manuscript.

Place	Date	Hour	Summary of Events and Information	Remarks and references to Appendices
MILLENCOURT	7th July		On Extra Lorry Disinfector. Lechne Lorry and squad standing by to return to Evacuate wounded. One man of Lechne making cases for new Nails and Person Testing Apparatus.	OMP
MILLENCOURT	8th July		Mannlation of MILLENCOURT superintended and squad of Employers attached men engaged on clearing up Farm and Fields. One man of Lechne making cases for new Nails and Person Testing Apparatus. M.O. and 28 men assisting in Cleaning wounded from Advanced Dressing Station at BECOURT. Two men with skin dumped at FRECHENCOURT. 8 T.U. men temporary attached to Lechne Company.	OMP
MILLENCOURT	8th July		Mannlation of MILLENCOURT superintended and squad of Employers attached men engaged on clearing up Farm and Fields. M.O. and 28 men assisting in Clearing wounded from Advanced Dressing Station at BECOURT. One man of Lechne making cases for new Nails and Person Testing Apparatus. One man with skins dumped at FRECHENCOURT. Lorry attached from Supply Column and two men of Lechne proceeded to BOVES with collected clean underclothing.	OMP

WAR DIARY
INTELLIGENCE SUMMARY
(Erase heading not required.)

Army Form C. 2118

Instructions regarding War Diaries and Intelligence Summaries are contained in F. S. Regs., Part II. and the Staff Manual respectively. Title Pages will be prepared in manuscript.

Place	Date	Hour	Summary of Events and Information	Remarks and references to Appendices
MILLENCOURT	9th July		Sanitation of MILLENCOURT superintended and squads of temporary attached men cleaning up town and billets. One man of section making cases for new Water and Poison Testing Apparatus. Rest unaerclothing disinfected and squad of men engaged with Justin Lorry Disinfector. Section lorry and 2 trailers for repairs billed. Underclothing brought from ALBERT to MILLENCOURT. Lorry from Divisional Supply Column detailed to Section and proceeded with load of soiled underclothing to BOVES. Two men with lorry dumped at FRECHENCOURT.	O/VP
MILLENCOURT	10th July		Sanitation of MILLENCOURT superintended and squads of temporary attached men engaged in cleaning up town and billets. Soiled underclothing disinfected. Two men engaged in Justin Lorry Disinfector. One man of section making cases for new Water and Poison Testing Apparatus. One squad in Bath Drier. Two men with lorry dumped at FRECHENCOURT. Spray Baths at MILLENCOURT - one squad of new erected of men. Erected Spray Baths at BAIZIEUX - one squad of section morning baths. Signed & O visited 9th Cheshire Regt. 6th Wiltshire Regt. 9th Welsh Regt. and 9th Royal Welsh Fusiliers Regt. and superintended erection of baths at BAIZIEUX and MILLENCOURT.	O/VP

WAR DIARY
or
INTELLIGENCE SUMMARY
(Erase heading not required.)

Army Form C. 2118

Instructions regarding War Diaries and Intelligence Summaries are contained in F. S. Regs., Part II. and the Staff Manual respectively. Title Pages will be prepared in manuscript.

Place	Date	Hour	Summary of Events and Information	Remarks and references to Appendices
MILLENCOURT	11th July		Sanitation of MILLENCOURT superintended and squad of temporary attached men engaged cleaning up town and billets. Soiled underclothing collected from Baths and disinfected - two men engaged in Steam Laundry. Water supplies in area about to be inspected by Division Motor. One squad at Baths MILLENCOURT and one squad at Baths BAIZIEUX. Units of Division inspected as to sanitary arrangements and reports received from Inspectors. Bathing with two men & 1 section proceeded to BOVES with load of soiled underclothing and collected clean washing. L.O. visited dump at FRECHENCOURT - two men with other dumped at FRECHENCOURT. L.O. visited BAIZIEUX Baths.	ONP
MILLENCOURT HENENCOURT	12th July		Section office and Equipment removed from MILLENCOURT to HENENCOURT. Billets cleaned and made sanitary. Soiled underclothing and blankets from Field Ambulance transported - two men temporarily attached engaged in Steam Laundry. Units of Division inspected as to sanitary arrangements and reports received from Inspectors. One squad at Baths MILLENCOURT and one squad at Baths BAIZIEUX. Baths at HENENCOURT taken over by section from 23rd Division and squad and working same. Lorry with two men & 1 section proceeded to BOVES with load of soiled underclothing and collected clean washing from civilians.	ONP

WAR DIARY or INTELLIGENCE SUMMARY

Army Form C. 2118.

Place	Date	Hour	Summary of Events and Information	Remarks and references to Appendices
HENENCOURT	13th July.		One squad on Walk duties. Sanitation of HENENCOURT superintended. North of Division inspected as to sanitary arrangements and reports received from Inspection. Soiled underclothing received from units and disinfected. Two temporarily attached men engaged in Stolen Lorry Dumpcar. One squad at HENENCOURT Baths. Squad at BAIZIEUX Baths and MILLENCOURT Baths. Squad at BOVES and issued underclothing and collected clean underclothing from Civilians. L.O. inspected 10th Royal Warwickshire Regt. Visited Inter Lorry Dumpcar and Baths at MILLENCOURT. Inspected 7th Royal Hants. Lancashire Regt 7th Loyal Lancashire Regt and 7th South Lancashire Regt at HENENCOURT area.	O.L.P
HENENCOURT	14th July.		One squad on Walk duties. Sanitation of HENENCOURT superintended. North of Division inspected as to sanitary arrangements and report received from Inspection. Soiled underclothing received from Units and disinfected — two temporarily attached men engaged in Stolen Lorry Dumpcar. The Inspects superintending cleaning out of Baths at MILLENCOURT. Squads at HENENCOURT, BAIZIEUX and MILLENCOURT Baths. Lorry proceeded to MILLENCOURT with clean underclothing. Lorry proceeded to Workshops for repairs. L.O. inspected LAVIEVILLE including 10th Worcestershire Regt and Bros line of 34th Divisional Train, also Transfer Valley near MILLENCOURT including transport of 8th, 83rd and 9th Field Companies, Royal Engineers. Heavy Battery Supt Troops and transport of 57th Infantry Brigade and 8th Bork	

2449 Wt. W14957/M90 750,000 1/16 J.B.C. & A. Forms/C.2118/12.

WAR DIARY or INTELLIGENCE SUMMARY

Army Form C. 2118.

Place	Date	Hour	Summary of Events and Information	Remarks and references to Appendices
			Sheffordshire Regt. & Worcestershire Regt. also three lorries of 12th Divisional Artillery at HENENCOURT. Also inspected sanitary arrangements at HENENCOURT. OMP	
HENENCOURT	15th July		One opened on Wash Bath. Sanitation of HENENCOURT superintended and opening of temporary attached men clearing up town. Work of Divison inspected as to sanitary arrangement and refuse removed from hospital. Soiled underclothing removed from Units and clean underclothing issued. Soiled underclothing disinfected. No new temporary attached men engaged in today. Army Branspech. Igava washing baths at HENENCOURT, BAIZIEUX and MILLENCOURT. Army personnel with loan of soiled underclothing & BOVES and collected clean washing from civilians. Lorry proceeded to MILLENCOURT with clean clothing. 80 inspected 39 Divisional Train and continued clearing up of HENEN COURT WOOD by fatigue of men of S.O men for 57 Field Ambulance. OMP	
HENENCOURT	16th July		One opened on Wash Baths. Sanitation of HENENCOURT superintended and opening of temporary attached men clearing up town. Work of Branam inspected as to sanitary arrangements and refuse removal from hospitals. Soiled underclothing and Harwich from Field Ambulance disinfected. Two temporary attached men engaged in today Army Branspech. Two men with other dumps at FRECHENCOURT. Squads working baths at HENENCOURT, BAIZIEUX and MILLENCOURT. Lorry proceeded	

WAR DIARY or INTELLIGENCE SUMMARY

Army Form C. 2118.

Place	Date	Hour	Summary of Events and Information	Remarks and references to Appendices
HENENCOURT	17th July		and clean underclothing to MILLENCOURT Bath. Two lorries and two men of Section proceeded to BOVES with soiled underclothing and collected clean underclothing from canteen. Divn carpenter & pioneer party attached, making latrines for incineration in HENENCOURT and fatigue groups of 25 men from 37th Field Ambulance cleaning up HENENCOURT WOOD. CAP	
			Bce agreed on Water Duties. Squads working Divisional Baths at HENENCOURT, BAIZIEUX and MILLENCOURT. Park of Divisional inspected as to carrying arrangements and refuse removal from trenches. Two men and other attached at FRECHENCOURT. Soiled underclothing and blankets disinfected — two temporary attached men engaged in Divisional Laundry disinfector which proceeded to billets of 9th Cheshire Regiment and carried out disinfection. Divn carpenter & pioneer party attached engaged in making latrine structures and one squad of temporary attached men front some in HENENCOURT WOOD. Army Lorries with load of clean clothing to MILLENCOURT Baths. E.O. visited CORBIE reference apparatus for Water Testing; also visited Baths at BAIZIEUX. CAP	
HENENCOURT	18th July		Bce agreed on Water Duties. Work of Section inspected as to sanitary arrangements and refuse removal from trenches. Two men with other attached at FRECHENCOURT. Squads	

WAR DIARY
or
INTELLIGENCE SUMMARY

Army Form C. 2118.

(Erase heading not required.)

Instructions regarding War Diaries and Intelligence Summaries are contained in F. S. Regs., Part II. and the Staff Manual respectively. Title Pages will be prepared in manuscript.

Place	Date	Hour	Summary of Events and Information	Remarks and references to Appendices
			working Divisional Baths at HENENCOURT MILLENCOURT and BAIZIEUX. Soiled underclothing collected from Baths and disinfected. Two Companies attached men engaged in Divn. Laundry at BRONFAY. One Corporal (carpenter) attached engaged in making Latrine structures and signal at temporary attached men erecting same in HENENCOURT WOOD under supervision by S.C.O. of Sectn. Lorry with two men of Sectn. proceeded to BOVES with load of soiled underclothing and collected clean washing from civilians. S.O. marked MILLENCOURT reference Baths and sanitation.	OMP
HENENCOURT	19th July.		Work of Divisional Baths and Laundry and repairs received from Inspection Squad making Divisional Baths at HENENCOURT. BAIZIEUX and MILLENCOURT signed of Carpenters temporary attached making Latrine structures and signal at temporary attached men temporary section of same at HENENCOURT WOOD under supervision of S.C.O. of Sectn. Lorry proceeded to MILLENCOURT Baths with clean underclothing. Spray bath at BAIZIEUX dismantled and tanks and equipment brought in. Sectn. Lorry took four men of Sectn. to men of Sectn. proceeded to FRECHENCOURT and dumped underwater underclothing at Raikhead. Two men with other members at FRECHENCOURT held supplies on forward area about to be occupied by the Division inspected. S.O. moved BECOURT reference Baths and BUIRE reference camps.	OMP

2449 Wt. W14957/M90 750,000 1/16 J.B.C. & A. Forms/C.2118/12.

Army Form C. 2118.

WAR DIARY
or
INTELLIGENCE SUMMARY
(Erase heading not required.)

Instructions regarding War Diaries and Intelligence Summaries are contained in F. S. Regs, Part II. and the Staff Manual respectively. Title Pages will be prepared in manuscript.

Place	Date	Hour	Summary of Events and Information	Remarks and references to Appendices
HENENCOURT & ALBERT	20 July		One Officer and Water Duties. Work of Division and Corps inspected as to construction and repairs received from Inspection. One Officer at HENENCOURT Baths and one Officer at MILLENCOURT Baths. Baths at MILLENCOURT dismantled and Baths equipment from this Bath and BAZIEUX Baths sent on dump at BUIRE. Two men with Officer dumped at BUIRE. Wire handed from HENENCOURT to dump at BUIRE FRECHENCOURT dump transferred to BUIRE. Wire and equipment removed from HENENCOURT & Section Silent at ALBERT. Men of Section marched to new hut at ALBERT. Section's hut returned from Workshops after repair. Lorry transport attached returned to 19 Divisional Supply Column. CO crossed FRECHENCOURT and arranged for dumps at BUIRE.	W.T. Fw. T. HP
ALBERT	21st July		One Officer on Water Duties. Sections huts and sites cleaned and put in order. Condition Fatigue squads of temporary attached men cleaning up Billet in ALBERT. I.O. investigated Water Supplies in forward area and FRICOURT, MAMETZ, MAMETZ WOOD and BAZENTIN LE PETIT. One carpenter (temporary) attached engaged on making Latrine structures. Two men with Officer dumped at BUIRE. One man of Section making cases for new Water Testing Apparatus.	W.T. Fw. T. HP

WAR DIARY
INTELLIGENCE SUMMARY

Place	Date	Hour	Summary of Events and Information	Remarks and references to Appendices
ALBERT	22nd	a.m.	One squad on Water duties. Four carpenters temporary attached making Latrine structures. Reports received from Inspection as to sanitary condition of ALBERT. Bedding lorry and two men proceeded to BOVES and collected clean underclothing from Divisional C.O. Inspected Kinopital lines of 58th, 67th and 58th Infantry Brigades. Also visited Town Major of ALBERT and arranged as to sizes of latrines & to make over arrangements for flushing with same. Two men with other transport at BUIRE. Fatigue 1 squads 1 temporary attached men cleaning up billets of ALBERT. One man of section mechanic cases for new Water Testing Apparatus.	W.I. for MHP
ALBERT	23rd	a.m.	One squad on Water duties. Report received from Inspection as to sanitary condition of ALBERT. Fatigue squads 1 temporary attached men engaged in cleaning up billets and burning refuse etc at ALBERT. Temporary troops men attached to section medicals examined by A.D.M.S. of Division. Two men with other transport at BUIRE. One man of section making cases for new Water Testing Apparatus. Sr. notes from A.D.M.S. of Division Section Lorry with squad of five men referred to U/C Beacon Division. 58th Field Ambulance for conveyance of wounded but lorry not required. Three carpenters and one man of Section constructing dugouts at BOTTOM WOOD for 58th Field Ambulance. 1 O.R. inspected from sanitation.	W.I. for MHP

WAR DIARY
or
INTELLIGENCE SUMMARY
(Erase heading not required.)

Army Form C. 2118.

Place	Date	Hour	Summary of Events and Information	Remarks and references to Appendices
ALBERT	24th July		One squad in Nalu Boshi. Reports received from Inspector as to sanitary condition of ALBERT. Fatigue squads of temporary attached men cleaning up billets and turning refuse etc in ALBERT. Two men with other dumped at BUIRE. Section party with two men proceeded to BOVES area collected clean washing. Underclothing issued to and received from Units. The men of section making cases for new Water Testing Apparatus. Carpenters temporary attached to section making latrine structures. N.C.O. Inspector from Sanitation.	
ALBERT	25th July		One squad in Nalu Boshi. Reports received from Inspector as to sanitary condition of ALBERT. Fatigue squads of temporary attached men cleaning up billets and turning refuse etc in ALBERT. Two men with other dumped at BUIRE. Section party however to workshops to the religion Army Hutho erected at ALBERT. A squad of temporary attached carpenters erecting same. Section party Drompton in instruction from R.A.M.C. of Divisions proceeded to workshops for repairs. The men of section making cases for new Water Testing Apparatus. Underclothing issued to and received from	

Army Form C. 2118.

WAR DIARY
or
INTELLIGENCE SUMMARY
(Erase heading not required.)

Place	Date	Hour	Summary of Events and Information	Remarks and references to Appendices
ALBERT	26th July.		units of Divisions. OC attended conference of Divisional Officers at Town Major's Office, ALBERT. One squad on Water Duties. Reports received from Inspector of working baths at ALBERT. One squad working baths at ALBERT. One squad of Companies engaged at ALBERT Baths. Fatigue squads of Companies engaged in clearing up billets and running refuse etc in ALBERT. Two men with other exempted at BOIRE. One man of Section making cases for new Notin Testing Apparatus. Army Headquarters attached to Section from Supply Column. Lorry with this men proceeded to BOUVES with soiled underclothing and collected clean washing. Clean clothing issued to Units and soiled clothing received. C.O. inspected men on return.	10L/76 CHP
ALBERT	27th July.		One squad on Water Duties. One squad working baths at ALBERT. Reports received from Inspector as to results of inspections of Units. Fatigue squads of Companies attached men engaged in clearing up billets and running refuse etc in ALBERT and work superivised. Two men at dump at BOIRE. One man of Section making cases for new Notin Testing Apparatus. Section lorry returned after being repaired. Two men of Section proceeded to BOUVES.	10L/76 CHP

2449 Wt. W14957/M90 750,000 1/16 J.B.C. & A. Form/C.2118/12/

WAR DIARY
INTELLIGENCE SUMMARY
(Erase heading not required.)

Army Form C. 2118.

Place	Date	Hour	Summary of Events and Information	Remarks and references to Appendices
			Unit sorted washclothing and collected clean washing from sundries. Attached lorry returned to Supply Column. O.C. (Capt PETERS O.H.) of Unit nominated in ALBERT about 10 a.m. and transferred to Field Ambulance. Capt POLE L.W. R.A.M.C. Medical Officer, nominated Royal Engineers in command of Unit.	*[initial]*
ALBERT	28th July		O/C opened in Natts Butts. Reports received from Inspector of Works. One opened working baths at ALBERT. Anti-gas machine prepared for use in trenches. Section LW, and two men proceeded to BOVES unit order washclothing for machine to ensure. Fatigue squads of Renforming attached men engaged in cleaning up traile and tramway refuse in ALBERT. Two men at section dump at BUIRE. O/C men of section making gear for new water Testing Apparatus. Distribution of aerated water advertising to Units of Division carried out. 60 advanced sanitary officer of ALBERT when no man arrange that then Unit should erect a public latrine.	*[initial]*
ALBERT	29th July		O/C opened in Natts Butts. Work of Division inspected and reports received as to sanitary condition prevailing. One squad working Spray Baths at ALBERT.	

2449 Wt. W14957/Mg9 750,000 1/16 J.B.C. & A. Forms/C.2118/12.

WAR DIARY
-or-
INTELLIGENCE SUMMARY
(Erase heading not required.)

Army Form C. 2118.

Place	Date	Hour	Summary of Events and Information	Remarks and references to Appendices
			Squad of carpenters (temporary) attached erecting Portic latrine at ALBERT. Fatigue squad of temporary attached men cleaning up billets and attending incinerator at ALBERT. Two men at latrine dump, BUIRE. One man at latrine making cases for new Waller Testing Apparatus. Tender to for Public latrines drawn from temporary dump. Section horse and two men proceeded to BOVES with extra undercloth and collected clean undercloth from civilian. Distribution of clean clothing to horse of horses carried out.	
ALBERT	30 July		One squad on Water Duties. All horse of Division concerned with loss of water supplies in area about to be occupied by Division (after hostile attack). One squad in anything Gray baths at ALBERT. Distribution of clean undercloth to horse of Division carried out. Section horse and two men proceeded to BOVES with extra undercloth. Section horse equipment and extra squad of carpenters temporary part of Section equipment and extra squad of carpenters temporary proceeded to BAIZIEUX with	1/6/24

attacked completed inoculum of Battle Positive at ALBERT. Symptoms of temporary
attached men engaged in cleaning up billets and training when we at ALBERT.
Two men at Section dump BOIRE. One man of Section making case for
new Kata Testing Apparatus. Unit of Division inspected and report
received as to sanitary condition forwarded. C.O. proceeded to new
Divisional Area and arranged as to Section of Baths at FRANVILLERS.
Seven from Brimfield opened for units after having been refreshed. [signature]

Place	Date	Hour	Summary of Events and Information
ALBERT / BAIZIEUX	31st July		One squad on Kati Kacha. Units of Division inspected as to condition of camps after move and report received. Shower bath at ALBERT dismantled and transported in sections from FRANVILLERS and re-erected by squad. Seven from Brimfield provided at BAIZIEUX, and in addition water succession, bathing arrangement at new premises. Two men at Section dump BOIRE. C.O. made all necessary arrangements for the bathing of Units of Division. Remainder of Section equipment and other transferred on lorry to BAIZIEUX. [signature]

30th July 1916.

List of Main Water Supplies. Baizieux and District

No		Source of Supply and Locality	Treatment
1	Franvillers	Piped Supply at Church.	2 Scoop.
2	"	Piped Supply on Albert Rd. Between Franvillers & Hielles	1. Scoop.
3	Hielles.	Running Stream. (After Clarification)	1. Scoop.
4	"	Piped Supply in Main Corbie Rd	½ Scoop.
5	Ribemont	Running Stream. (After Clarification)	1. Scoop.
6	Buire	Running Stream. (Draw from Tank near Railway)	½ Scoop.
7	Ville	Pump in YMCA yard Queen Street.	1. Scoop.
8	"	Pumped Supply at Cross Rds. ½ mile East of Village.	1. Scoop.
9	Dernancourt	Running Stream. (After Clarification)	1. Scoop.
10	Albert.	Large Piped Supply. Near Square	½ Scoop.
11	"	" " " (Southern)	½ Scoop.
12	Boozincourt.	Piped Supply on Boozincourt Rd.	1. Scoop.
13	"	" " On Bridge. Opposite Church.	2 Scoop.
14	Martinsart.	" " Off Main Rd.	1. Scoop.
15	Millencourt.	Stand Pipe Near Bath House. Rue d'Albert	1. Scoop.
16	"	" " North Side of Church.	1. Scoop.
17	"	Well at Corner of Rue de Senlis and Rue d'en Haut.	1. Scoop.
18	"	Well in Rue d'Albert.	1. Scoop.
19	"	Well in Rue Bastien.	1. Scoop.
20	Lavieville.	Piped Supply on Main Rd.	2. Scoop.
21	"	Communal Well in Main Rd.	1. Scoop.
22	Bresles.	Piped Supply.	2. Scoop.
23	Frechencourt.	Piped Supply on Main Rd. near C.T. Man.	1. Scoop.
24	Hénencourt.	" " in road, next to Chateau.	1. Scoop.
25	Senlis	" " in Hénencourt Rd.	1. Scoop.
26	Warloy.	" " in Rue de la Croix.	1. Scoop.
27	Frechencourt.	" " At T Rds. near Railway	1. Scoop.
28	"	Running Stream Near Railway (after Clarification)	1. Scoop.
29	"	" " near Mill "	1. Scoop.
30	Béhencourt	Running Stream	1. Scoop.
31	Pont Noyelles.	" " Side of Bridge St.	1. Scoop.
32	Mirvaux	Piped Supply Near Church.	½ Scoop.

3	Bajgura	Piped Supply at Mairi	1. sc.op.
4	"	Well in Shield St. at T Road	2. scoops
5	"	Well in Church St. (after Chlorination)	1. scoop

Note :-

Owing to the difference in the strength of the Chloride of Lime supplied to units, and the variation in quality of small water supplies from time to time, the above figures for chlorination are only suggestive. Standards should be re-adjusted with the sample of Lime to be used.

W. ... Capt.
O.C. 19th Divisional Sanitary Sec.

Army Form C. 2118

WAR DIARY
INTELLIGENCE SUMMARY
(Erase heading not required.)

Instructions regarding War Diaries and Intelligence Summaries are contained in F.S. Regs., Part II. and the Staff Manual respectively. Title Pages will be prepared in manuscript.

Place	Date	Hour	Summary of Events and Information	Remarks and references to Appendices
	August 1916		(No 36) 19th Divisional Sanitary Section War Diary of from 1st August to 31st August 1916 Vol 14	

COMMITTEE FOR THE MEDICAL HISTORY OF THE WAR
Date -9 OCT. 1916

New Water Station

Map Ref	Locality	Treatment
M 9 c. 8. 2.	In main Rd. Outside DHQ.	2 scoops

The chlorinating figure will be posted daily at this supply.

18/8/16. GM Anderson Capt RAMC.
O6 19th Div'n Sanitary Section.

List of Main Water Stations in 19th Divisional Area

Map Reference	Locality	Treatment
(1) M.24.c.2.5	Ouderdom–Bailleul Rd.	} 1 to 2 teas- spoons of chloride of lime per water cart
(2) M.13.c.9.0	La Clytte–Kemmel Rd.	
(3) M.12.d.2.3	La Clytte Rd.	
(4) M.13.a.6.4	Bodeenge Rd.	
(5) M.36.b.4.6	Kemmel Wells	
(6) M.31.c.0.3 (approx)		
(7) M.35.a.8.8	Dranouter Rd.	

NOTE:—

(1) The chlorinating figures of the above supplies varies from time to time. Standards should be re-adjusted with the sample of lime to be used.

(2) A supplementary list of emergency water supplies will be issued later.

J.R. Anderson.
Capt.
O.C. 19th Divisional Sanitary Section

WAR DIARY or INTELLIGENCE SUMMARY

Army Form C. 2118.

Place	Date	Hour	Summary of Events and Information	Remarks and references to Appendices
BAIZIEUX	1st August		The squad in Khaki Drills. Transport lines of Units inspected on 15 emptium of the moving and refuse received from Inspection. Sanitary arrangements at BAIZIEUX inspected. Billets of 51st Brigade Machine Guns at FRANVILLERS disinfected. Squad of men engaged making spray Bath at BRESLE. The squad working spray bath at FRANVILLERS. Fallen Army Disinfector at FRANVILLERS disinfecting civilian manufacturing from Baths and clothing of Units. Clean manufacturing distributed to Units from baths at FRANVILLERS. Squad of Company attached men cleaning up premises occupied by Section. Section Army Furnaces & Transports for repair & firing. Army Company attached from Supply Column with one man of Section proceeded to BOVES with order manufacturing and collected clean manufacturing. Capt. ANDERSON, G. N., R.A.M.C. (T.F.) took up duties as commanding officer of Section. C.O. investigated generally the working of the Section and proceeded to FRANVILLERS and inspected Baths	
BAIZIEUX	2nd August		The squad in Khaki Drills. Units inspected as to cleanness of camps and billets and reports received from Inspection. Sanitary arrangements at BAIZIEUX inspected.	

WAR DIARY or INTELLIGENCE SUMMARY

Army Form C. 2118.

Place	Date	Hour	Summary of Events and Information	Remarks and references to Appendices
			Arrived at BRESLE Ricks and FRANVILLERS Ricks. Two men at Return dump BOIRE - one at the dump. Transport to BRESLE and marque handed over to A.D.O.S. 3rd Corps. John Lorry Transport at FRANVILLERS transporting coal and ammunition from BOVES to 2nd inches Baronial Pooks and John Lorry Transport. All march BOVES and made arrangement for all ammunition found not to civilians to be collected and put in rail at LONGEAU for removal to BAIZIEUX. Return Lorry with two men proceed to BRESSE and transported ammunition to LONGEAU.	hull.
BAIZIEUX	3rd August		As again on new ricks. Extra officers on return when mounted and horses cleaned up from R Return expense. Work of Return inspection as to mounting of teams after service of FRANVILLERS ammunition sent for to dump at BRESLE. Two men left in charge of dump. All motor lorries taken and special lorries received. 6.6. Inspected Ticken sheeter 57 Infantry Brigade. 6.6. Returns Lorry transports and inspected the dump to remain at FRANVILLERS until dump has been cleared. Return lorry with two men proceed to BOVES and collected rounds and extra ammunition and put same on rail at LONGEAU. All of return dump cleared.	

WAR DIARY
INTELLIGENCE SUMMARY
(Erase heading not required.)

Army Form C. 2118.

Instructions regarding War Diaries and Intelligence Summaries are contained in F. S. Regs., Part II. and the Staff Manual respectively. Title Pages will be prepared in manuscript.

Place	Date	Hour	Summary of Events and Information	Remarks and references to Appendices
			Arrived and marched to FRESNENCOURT and entrained for LONGPRE, a party m/o proceeded to LONG by 2nd Ambulance and made arrangements as to decan: dechem lines, arch drive of other personnel to dechems new lives at LONG. [signature]	
LONG	4th August		C.O. passed Infection file and arrangement methods of dealing with infectious disease. Units of Division inspected as to sanitary arrangements on new area. Area report received from Inspection. The original in Falk. Lulin. Men of dechem and temporary attached men unwashed at LONGPRE Station at 2 a.m. and marched to new billet at LONG. dechem Hory arrived at LONG with stores and equipment. Sanitary arrangements and improvements carried out as Divisional Headquarters and dechems billets. Two men at dechems camp. BRESLE. [signature]	
LONG	5 August		C.O. visited O.C. Chakhai Regiment reference scabies in horses recently received by them. The original in North Punta. Units of Division inspected and reports	

WAR DIARY or INTELLIGENCE SUMMARY

Army Form C. 2118.

Place	Date	Hour	Summary of Events and Information	Remarks and references to Appendices
LONG	6th August		Received from Inspector Ord man of Section overhauling cases for new water testing apparatus. Two men with store started at BOSCKE. Various arrangements at Divisional Headquarters inspected and fatigue of men of transport attached men engaged in cleaning up town. One again on Water Cart. Work of Divisional inspector and refuse section from Inspector. Two men with store at LONGPRE. O.C. visited LONGPRE afternoon & on to be removed by rail.	[signature]
LONG	7th August		Men of Section together with temporary attached men marched from LONG and entrained at PONT REMY at 11am to proceed to BAILLEUL. O.C. proceeded with section lorry and stores to St JANS CAPPEL. Section Billet at LONG cleaned and refuse burnt before section arrived.	[signature]
WESTOUTRE	8th August		O.C. took Section lorry and stores and equipment procured from St JANS CAPPEL to WESTOUTRE. Men of Section and temporary attached men arrived at BAILLEUL at 6pm; retirement and marched to new billets	

WAR DIARY or INTELLIGENCE SUMMARY

Army Form C. 2118.

Place	Date	Hour	Summary of Events and Information	Remarks and references to Appendices
at WESTOUTRE			Sanitary arrangements at new areas to Baths at LOCRE and DRANOUTRE. Baths and laundry at WESTOUTRE together with Water tray Disinfector and Guest Disinfector taken over from 50th Divisional Sanitary Section. Water Station on Divisional area visited and samples of water tested. C.O. visited all Divisional Baths and arranged as to procedure for baths. M.O.	
WESTOUTRE	9th August		Work of Division inspection as to sanitary arrangements in new area. Sanitary Inspectors placed in Brigade areas. Divisional Baths at WESTOUTRE, LOCRE and DRANOUTRE supervision and spraying attached men at each Bath. Section lorry with 3 men proceeded to WIPPENHOEK and cleared railway truck of rubbish - five journeys. Arrangements made for working Divisional Laundry. C.O. visited Water Station in Divisional area and made arrangements for supplying treated water for same. C.O. also arranged for additional fatigue men to be attached to assist in the working of Divisional Baths. Also Water Station in new area inspected and provision to Regimental Medical Officers (copy attached). M.O.	

WAR DIARY or INTELLIGENCE SUMMARY

Army Form C. 2118.

Place	Date	Hour	Summary of Events and Information	Remarks and references to Appendices
WESTOUTRE	10th August		Six squad on Water Duties and guards of transport attacked men placed on east of the main Station in Divisional Area. C.O. arranged supervision of bath supplies. C.O. interior cleaning up of WESTOUTRE - fatigue against from Field Ambulance supplied. Divisional Baths organised and squads of transport attacked men at WESTOUTRE, LOCRE and DRANOUTRE Baths. Divisional Laundry at WESTOUTRE in permanence and the distribution of clean clothing to units of Division cannot act. Two men another from from Dranoutre carried men'sclothing disinfected. Unit of Division improves as is sanitary arrangements. Fatigue squad with civilian brat arms out engaged in carting refuse etc to incinerate - one temporarily attached men attending incinerate. C.O. arranged for fatigue squads to be supplied for sanitary duties at WESTOUTRE LOCRE and DRANOUTRE. Our G.S. wagon engaged in carting clean clothing to Divisional Baths and collecting soiled unwashed clothing.	

WAR DIARY or INTELLIGENCE SUMMARY

Army Form C. 2118.

Place	Date	Hour	Summary of Events and Information	Remarks and references to Appendices
WESTOUTRE	1st August		M.O. inspected Divisional Baths at LOCRE and DRANOUTRE. 57th Infantry Brigade Headquarters, 1st Royal Warwickshire Regiment and 82nd Field Company Royal Engineers reference cantonments. The hours of Divisional Baths are arranged by Inspection on sanitary arrangements. O.C. made arrangements with Infantry Brigades & Division for fatigue squads to be supplied for cleaning at villages of LOCRE and DRANOUTRE under the supervision of N.C.O. of Section. 80 workers from Westoutre, Divisional Brie, and assisted with Inspection on each Station. About 9 Temporary attached men at Main Station. Men there at platoon standdown. 1 Headquarters train complete... temporary attached men work... civilian horse and boat cleaning, carry refuse — one man attending Sprinters laths and Infirmary attached to Section for sanitary duties. Pioneers working Divisional Baths at WESTOUTRE, LOCRE and DRANOUTRE. Divisional Laundry at WESTOUTRE superintendent and the disinfection of clean underclothing at hands of Division carried out. Two men working Laundry Disinfector. G.S. Wagon engaged in carrying clean underclothing to Divisional Baths and collecting soiled clothing. W.A.	

WAR DIARY or INTELLIGENCE SUMMARY

Army Form C. 2118.

Place	Date	Hour	Summary of Events and Information	Remarks and references to Appendices
WESTOUTRE	10th August		C.O. visited Headquarters of Infantry Brigade re-fixing arrangements for baths. Fatigue parties of 30 men and 2 N.C.O.'s from 57th and 59th Field Ambulances cleaning up vacant camps in Locre district under the supervision of A.C.O. 1 section. O.C. section personnel Baths and Laundry. (Squads of Personnel attached men engaged in cleaning up WESTOUTRE, LOCRE and DRANOUTRE under supervision of N.C.O. of 1 section. Two men with civilian hose and shirt cleaning refuse passages at WESTOUTRE & Dranoutre - one man attending Incinerator, Personnel Laundry superintendent and the distribution of clean underclothing. A truck of Divisional men attached. Troops carried out squads of Personnel attached men running Personnel Baths at WESTOUTRE, LOCRE and DRANOUTRE. O.C. Wagon delivered clean underclothing, &c. Personnel Baths and collected soiled clothing. Two men employed John Army Disinfector. Stewards of Personnel attacked men employed Supervision 1 N.C.O. 1 section at Water Station and Motor 2.O. visited LA CLYTTE and arrangements with Staff Major of Canadian Contingent that Sanitary arrangements of Two Divns be in their charge. Area	

WAR DIARY
or
INTELLIGENCE SUMMARY

Army Form C. 2118.

(Erase heading not required.)

Instructions regarding War Diaries and Intelligence Summaries are contained in F.S. Regs., Part II. and the Staff Manual respectively. Title Pages will be prepared in manuscript.

Place	Date	Hour	Summary of Events and Information	Remarks and references to Appendices
WESTOUTRE	13th August		M.O. moved KEMMEL SHELTERS and had ground adjacent to wells cleared so as to prevent pollution of water. Fatigue squad of 15 men and 1 N.C.O. from Field Ambulance cleaning up LOCRE under supervision of N.C.O. of Section. Unit of Division inspected as to sanitary arrangements and reports received from Inspector. Main supply at WESTOUTRE opened and Regimental Medical Officers notified (copy attached) Guards at Water Stations in Divisional Area and tanks at LACLYTTE - KEMMEL Road cleaned. Water Stations visited by Inspector and samples taken and tests made. Fatigue squads of temporary attached men under supervision of N.C.O.: 1 Section engaged in sanitary work at WESTOUTRE, LOCRE and DRANOUTRE. Squads of temporary attached men working Divisional Baths at WESTOUTRE, LOCRE and DRANOUTRE. Divisional Laundry at WESTOUTRE supervised and the distribution of clean underclothing to Units of Division carried out. Two men sent from Army Brickfields. One man of Section working throat disinfector.	

Army Form C. 2118.

WAR DIARY
or
INTELLIGENCE SUMMARY
(Erase heading not required.)

Place	Date	Hour	Summary of Events and Information	Remarks and references to Appendices
WESTOUTRE	14 August		A.D.M.S. accompanied A.D.M.S. of Division on tour of inspection to KEMMEL SHELTERS and DRANOUTRE Water Supply. Further group of temporary attached men placed at KEMMEL Wells. Water Wagon visited, samples taken and noted. Guards at all Divisional Water Wagons. Units of Division inspected as to sanitary arrangements and reports received from Inspection. Fatigue Squads of temporary attached men inown the supervision of N.C.O. of section engaged in sanitary duties at LOCRE, WESTOUTRE and DRANOUTRE. Squad of men preparing anti-gas ointment. Squads of temporary attached men working Divisional Baths at WESTOUTRE, LOCRE and DRANOUTRE. Divisional Laundry at WESTOUTRE supervised and the distribution of clean underclothing to Units of Division carried out. Two men working pro tem from Disinfector at WESTOUTRE Laundry. One man of section engaged on Unit Disinfector.	[signature]

WAR DIARY

INTELLIGENCE SUMMARY

Army Form C. 2118.

Place	Date	Hour	Summary of Events and Information	Remarks and references to Appendices
WESTOUTRE	15th August		Park of Divison inspected as to sanitary arrangements and reports received from Inspector. C.O. conferred with Inspector upon same. C.O. visited Divisional Baths in company with Capt. Forbes of 58th Field Ambulance preparatory to handing over the control of Divisional Baths and Laundry to Capt. Forbes. Squads of temporary attached men at Divisional Baths at WESTOUTRE, LOCRE and DRANOUTRE. Divisional Laundry at WESTOUTRE supervised and the distribution of clean underclothing to Units of Division carried out. N.S. wagon engaged in Battery clean underclothing to Divisional Baths and collection soiled clothes. Two men with Fodder Lorry Disinfector at Laundry. One man with threak Disinfector. Squads of temporary attached men engaged on sanitary work under supervision of N.C.O. of Section at WESTOUTRE, LOCRE and DRANOUTRE. Guards of temporary attached men at air walk station in Divisional Area — samples taken and tests made.	Vic.

WAR DIARY
or
INTELLIGENCE SUMMARY
(Erase heading not required.)

Army Form C. 2118.

Place	Date	Hour	Summary of Events and Information	Remarks and references to Appendices
WESTOUTRE	11th August		Units of Division inspected as to sanitary condition and arrangement and reports received from Inspectors. Fatigue squads of Kempenars attached men engaged under supervision of N.C.O. of Section, in sanitary duties at WESTOUTRE, LOCRE and DRANOUTRE. Squads of Kempenars attached men at Divisional Baths at WESTOUTRE, LOCRE and DRANOUTRE. Divisional Laundry at WESTOUTRE superintended and the distribution of clean underclothing to Units of Division carried out. Two men working Order Room Disinfector. One man working Threst Disinfector. Wagons at all Water Stations in Divisional Area. Samples of water taken and tests made. US wagon delivered clean clothing to Divisional Baths and collected soiled clothes. On instruction from Divisional Headquarters the Laundry at WESTOUTRE and Baths at WESTOUTRE, LOCRE and DRANOUTRE handed over to Capt C.C. Finlake R.A.M.C. together with personnel of attached men. CO Hilarion working. I came to Capt Finlake.	G.M.C.

Place	Date	Hour	Summary of Events and Information	Remarks and references to Appendices
WESTOUTRE	17 August		Work of Divison inspected and reports received from Inspection as to sanitary arrangements. Fatigue squads of Regiments attached were under supervision of A.C.D. of Division. Inspected sanitary duties at WESTOUTRE, LOCRE and DRANOUTRE. Inspected carpenters erecting latrine at Officers Club, LOCRE. Arranged for re-construction of Public Latrine by Divisional Engineers at DRANOUTRE. C.O. inspected 7th East Lancashire Regiment and Transport Lines of 57th Infantry Brigade. C.O. in company with O.C. Works Patrol & Corps Inspector Alkinson [?] Kennedy [?] at Doncaster Huts and Wakefield Huts, have watering troughs at Doncaster Huts, LACLYTTE - KEMMEL Water Supply, Supplies at LOCRE, LINDENHOEK Huts, KEMMEL WELLS and KEMMEL SHELTERS, and arranged for opening quarry. Investigated Water supply at DRANOUTRE when OC Patrol stated he could detect this supply was in the Divisional area in the 34th Division. Conferred with OC Patrol as to drainage of camps in Kemmel and as to getting the assistance of Lieut Brown of South Wales Boro [?] Guards and Inspectors at all North Sections in Divisional area - complete taken and received. One man sent Mental Compton in the man at DRANOUTRE Baths and two at Divisional Laundry.	

WAR DIARY
INTELLIGENCE SUMMARY
(Erase heading not required.)

Army Form C. 2118.

Place	Date	Hour	Summary of Events and Information	Remarks and references to Appendices
WESTOUTRE	18th August		Work of Division inspected as to sanitary arrangements and reports received from Inspectors. C.O. in company with A.D.M.S. of Division inspected transport lines of 8th Gloucestershire Regiment. 8th South Staffordshire Regiment 1914 Section, Divisional Ammunition Column. Headquarters 86 Brigade Royal Field Artillery and Motor Veterinary Column. Also visited 59 Field Ambulance and Advanced Dressing Station at KEMMEL. Approach of transport attached now under inspection, 1 N.C.O. of Section engaged in sanitary duties at WESTOUTRE, LOCRE and DRANOUTRE. Kind of transport attached men at all Wash Stations in Divisional Area. Inspection of Station at Wash Stations. All Wash Station marked completed Wash taken and fixed. Tea mess with Field Transport Division at DRANOUTRE Baths and tea mess at Divisional Laundry, WESTOUTRE.	Sgd
WESTOUTRE	19th August		Work of Division inspected as to sanitary arrangements and reports received from Inspectors. C.O. inspected 1911 2 and 3 Section Divisional Ammunition Column A/67 and C/55 Royal Field Artillery. Co in company	Sgd

WAR DIARY
INTELLIGENCE SUMMARY
(Erase heading not required.)

Army Form C. 2118.

Instructions regarding War Diaries and Intelligence Summaries are contained in F. S. Regs., Part II. and the Staff Manual respectively. Title Pages will be prepared in manuscript.

Place	Date	Hour	Summary of Events and Information	Remarks and references to Appendices
WESTOUTRE	20th August		The Divisional Baths visited LOCRE Baths afternoon,. Pumps and improvement of classification of baths; proceeded to DRANOUTRE and took over Laundry Scheme & Laundry. Proceeded to BAILLEUL with samples of water from WESTOUTRE Laundry before classification and after classification for examination. Interview with O.C. Canadian Mobile Laboratory. Improved manner arrangement at WESTOUTRE and made arrangements for this in manner as to assist the morning service. Issued of temporary attached men at our main Laundries at Divisional Oven and Kopfenes at each station all Sections visited samples taken and tested. Our men with their Kicopers. Our men at DRANOUTRE Baths and two men at Laundry. WESTOUTRE. (Signed) 1. R.C.Es & Section engaged in sanitary duties at WESTOUTRE, LOCRE and DRANOUTRE. Squad of Carpenter engaged in erecting Divine service at WESTOUTRE. GM.	
WESTOUTRE	20th August		Men of Division inspected as to sanitary arrangement and refuse removal two Inspectors. O.C. proceeded to BAILLEUL and met Capt Wheeler, V.S.	

WAR DIARY
or
INTELLIGENCE SUMMARY

(Erase heading not required.)

Army Form C. 2118.

Place	Date	Hour	Summary of Events and Information	Remarks and references to Appendices

Major Pollard and Capt Arthur R.E. IX Corps interviewed O.C. Canadian Motor Laboratory and discussed the question of Working wash samples from the Divisional trenches baths by the Canadian Army Medical Corps. Proceeded to 3rd Divisional Headquarters and discussed question of removal of manure so as not to pollute BAILLEUL Water Supply. Proceeded to KEMMEL and inspected tanks under process of construction for supplying wash to advanced area, also collecting tanks and pumping station. Inspected pumping station and tanks at KEMMEL SHELTERS. Squads of Pontoneers attached men as guard at all works working in Divisional area under supervision of N.C.O. of section. Wash samples taken and noted. On way met Staff Champlain and men at DRANOUTRE Baths. Two men at Divisional Laundry WESTOUTRE. Squad of carpenters completed section of Public Latrine at WESTOUTRE. Squad of Pontoneers attached men engaged in sanitary works under supervision of N.C.O. of Section at WESTOUTRE, LOCRE and DRANOUTRE.

hrs.

WAR DIARY
INTELLIGENCE SUMMARY

Army Form C. 2118.

Place	Date	Hour	Summary of Events and Information	Remarks and references to Appendices
WESTOUTRE	21st August		Work of Division inspected and reports received from Inspectors as to Sanitary arrangements and cleanliness. C.O. inspected "B" Battery 80th Brigade R.F.A. "D" Battery and Headquarters 81st Brigade R.F.A. "B" and "D" Batteries 82nd Brigade R.F.A. and "A" Battery 89th Brigade R.F.A. Transport Horse Lines of 58th Infantry Brigade, Divisional School and 57th Field Ambulance. He later in company with the O.C. Ambulance Fatigue squads of Temporary attached men, under supervision of N.C.O.s of Section, engaged in sanitary duties in WESTOUTRE, LOCRE and DRANOUTRE. Saw men with Street Disinfector. Also men at DRANOUTRE Baths and two men at Divisional Laundry, WESTOUTRE. Groups of Temporary attached men in all North Section in Divisional Area under supervision of N.C.O.s of Section. All Water Stations noted - Samples taken and tested. Hra.	
WESTOUTRE	22nd August		Work of Division inspected as to sanitary arrangements and reports received from Inspectors. C.O. inspected WESTOUTRE reference countdown	

WAR DIARY or INTELLIGENCE SUMMARY

Army Form C. 2118.

Place	Date	Hour	Summary of Events and Information	Remarks and references to Appendices
WESTOUTRE	23 August		Generally. M.O. visited MONT DES CATS Reservoir and BOESCHEPE Water supplies. Proceeded to No 1 Reservoir with O.C. Water Patrol II Corps and worked there this morning. Unit of temporary attached men under supervision of N.C.O. of Section, as all Water Patrol ni Personnel area. All Water Patrol worked and samples taken and tested. Fatigue squads of temporary attached men, under supervision of N.C.O. of Section, engaged in sanitary duties at WESTOUTRE, LOCRE and DRANOUTRE. One man at DRANOUTRE Baths. Two men with Troops Disinfector. Two men at Divisional Laundry, WESTOUTRE.	[signature]
			O.C. Water Patrol II Corps afternoon returned at MONT DES CATS. Proceeded to Montignation Canadian Corps and interviewed Officer-in-charge Water Patrol. Patrols returned at MONT DES CATS and work Mechanic [?]	

2449 Wt. W14957/M90 750,000 1/16 J.B.C. & A. Forms/C.2118/12.

WAR DIARY
or
INTELLIGENCE SUMMARY

Army Form C. 2118.

Place	Date	Hour	Summary of Events and Information	Remarks and references to Appendices
WESTOUTRE	7th April		Steaming Station. C.O. in company with A.D.M.S. inspected WESTOUTRE with special reference to reconnaissance. Lieut. ? Henderson attached men under supervision of N.C.O. ? Section at all Water Stations in Divisional area. Water Stations various samples taken and taken in vain to prevent pollution of Water Stations. Orders at M 24 & M 2/8 (Map Sheet 28 Belgium and France) tested and places went over. Lieut. ? inspected men engaged in erecting permanent latrine at WESTOUTRE. Lieut. ? Henderson attached men under supervision of N.C.O. ? Section. Engaged in sanitary duties at WESTOUTRE, LOCRE and DRANOUTRE. Six men at DRANOUTRE Baths and two men at Divisional Laundry. Two men engaged in Wheat Steamfoot. LWA	
WESTOUTRE	8th April		Work of Divisn. inspected as to sanitary condition and arrangement and work received from Inspector. C.O. in company with Major FINLATOR of Divisional Baths, visited WESTOUTRE Laundry reference accommodation.	

WAR DIARY
or
INTELLIGENCE SUMMARY

(Erase heading not required.)

Army Form C. 2118.

Place	Date	Hour	Summary of Events and Information	Remarks and references to Appendices
			of Staff moved in output of January and reporting officer. C.O. interviewed DR DEWULF of the Belgian Public Health Service reference sanitation at WESTOUTRE. Fatigue squads of temporary attached men, now supervision of N.C.Os of Section engaged in sanitary duties at WESTOUTRE, LOCRE and DRANOUTRE. Issued of temporary attached men under supervision of N.C.B. of Section at all Water Points in Divisional Area. All Antoni rooms and sample bathes and hotels horseshoes given to N.C.O of 18th Durge Battery, R.G.A. in one of Water Cart. Two men at Divisional Laundry, WESTOUTRE and two men with Threat Divisional.	
WESTOUTRE	25th August		Unit of Division inspected as to sanitary conditions and reports received from Inspector. C.O. in company with A.D.M.S. of Division inspected lines of 7th King's Own Royal Lancaster Regiment, KEMMEL SHELTERS and WAKEFIELD HUTS. Also camp of 82nd Field Company	

WAR DIARY
or
INTELLIGENCE SUMMARY
(Erase heading not required.)

Army Form C. 2118

Place	Date	Hour	Summary of Events and Information	Remarks and references to Appendices
			Royal Engineer and 5th Infantry Brigade Transport lines. S.O. inspected WESTOUTRE refuse pound corroboration and method of manurine. Fatigue squads of Engineers attached men under supervision of N.C.O. of Section engaged in sanitary duties at WESTOUTRE, LOCRE and DRANOUTRE. Squad of Engineers attached men at all Water Points in Divisional Area. Water Inspector at each Station. All Stations visited and samples taken and tested. Two men at Divisional Laundry, WESTOUTRE and two men engaged in Bread Preparation. [signature]	
WESTOUTRE	26th August		Units of Division inspected as to sanitary arrangements and reports received from Inspectors. S.O. inspected Transport lines of Royal Welsh Fusilier Regt, 9th Cheshire, 9th Welsh Regt and 6th Wiltshire Regt. S.O. also inspected 10th Lincoln Regt, 57th Infantry Brigade Headquarters, 86th Brigade R.F.A. Headquarters, 57th Infantry Brigade Headquarters Transport, 82nd Field Co. R.E. (Wire Carrier) 57th Trench Mortar Battery, 8th Gloucester	

WAR DIARY
INTELLIGENCE SUMMARY

Army Form C. 2118

Place	Date	Hour	Summary of Events and Information	Remarks and references to Appendices
WESTOUTRE	27 August		Regimental Aircraft Park and Daylight Comn. Fatigue squads of Company attached men engaged under supervision of NCO of Section on sanitary duties at WESTOUTRE, LOCRE and DRANOUTRE. Means of Company attached men under supervision of Inspector of Section on all Walk Station in Divisional Area. All Walk Station visited. Samples taken and tested. Two men at Divisional Laundry. WESTOUTRE and two men at DRANOUTRE with Field Disinfector.

ENE.

Short of Division inspected as to sanitary condition and arrangements and reports received from Inspector. O.O. accompanied A.D.M.S. of Divn. in tour of inspection of Camp Area around DRANOUTRE. I.O. inspected new incinerators at WESTOUTRE. Fatigue squads of Company attached men, under supervision of N. CO of Section engaged on sanitary duties at WESTOUTRE, LOCRE and DRANOUTRE. Two men at Divisional Laundry, WESTOUTRE and | |

WAR DIARY
INTELLIGENCE SUMMARY

Army Form C. 2118

Place	Date	Hour	Summary of Events and Information	Remarks and references to Appendices
			Two men engaged working Sheet Sheepskin. Guard of Temporary attached men and Inspector of Section as well as Bath Station in Armoured area. All Stations would sample taken and tested. Ems.	
WESTOUTRE	28th August		Work of Division inspected as to sanitary arrangement and condition and units relieved from Inspection. Fatigue squads of Temporary attached men under supervision of N.C.Os of Section engaged on sanitary duties at WESTOUTRE, LOCRE and DRANOUTRE. Two men as laundry WESTOUTRE and two men engaged working Sheet Sheepskin. Guard of Temporary attacked men under supervision of D.C.O. of Section as all Water Stations on Armoured Area. All Stations visited and samples taken and tested. N.O. in company with Capt Dunlop. O.C. Baths proceeded KBANHEOL and interviewed O.C. Main Baths 13 Corps re future location of bath outfit for proposed new bath near LOCRE. N.O. proceeded to Advanced Dressing Station at KEMMEL and in	

Army Form C. 2118

WAR DIARY
or
INTELLIGENCE SUMMARY
(Erase heading not required.)

Place	Date	Hour	Summary of Events and Information	Remarks and references to Appendices
			Company with O.C. inspected the village in view to advise measures to be taken to ensure efficient sanitation. Proceeded to 250 Tunnelling Co. R.E. camp at KEMMEL DUGOUTS and inspected same. Also inspected bath tanks at KEMMEL SHELTERS.	
				Y.N.A.
WESTOUTRE	19th August		Units of Division inspected as to cleanliness of camps and billets received from Inspection. S.O. inspected "B" Battery 89th Brigade R.F.A. and Divisional Signal Company at WESTOUTRE. Transport lines of 9th Royal Welsh Regiment and 9th Cheshire Regiment. C.O. in company with N.C.O's. of Division inspected method of incineration at WESTOUTRE. Agreed of temporary engaged in sanitary duties at WESTOUTRE, of N.CO. of Section engaged in sanitary duties at WESTOUTRE, LOCRE and DRANOUTRE. Two men with Thresh Disinfector at DRANOUTRE and one at Divisional Laundry at WESTOUTRE.	

WAR DIARY
or
INTELLIGENCE SUMMARY
(Erase heading not required.)

Army Form C. 2118

Instructions regarding War Diaries and Intelligence Summaries are contained in F. S. Regs., Part II. and the Staff Manual respectively. Title Pages will be prepared in manuscript.

Place	Date	Hour	Summary of Events and Information	Remarks and references to Appendices
			Squads of temporary attached men as guards at all Divisional Water Stations under supervision of NCOs, 1 Section. All Water Washing water samples taken and tested. Engr.	
WESTOUTRE	30 Myns		Units of Division inspected as to condition of camps and billets and work received from hospitals. C.O. superintended carrying out of Divisional methods of treatment of scabies at WESTOUTRE. CO made detailed inspection of Divisional baths regarding sanitation; prepared monthly refuse influence sanitation and conferred with Sanitary Inspector. Squads of temporary attached men under supervision of NCOs, 1 Section engaged on sanitary duties at WESTOUTRE, LOCRE and DRANOUTRE. Two men with Street Sweepers and one man at Divisional	

1875. Wt. W593/826 1,000,000 4/15 T.B.C. & A. A.D.S.S./Forms/C. 2118.

WAR DIARY
or
INTELLIGENCE SUMMARY
(Erase heading not required.)

Army Form C. 2118

Place	Date	Hour	Summary of Events and Information	Remarks and references to Appendices
			Gunnery. WESTOUTRE. Guards of Honorary attached men at all Motor Stations under supervision of N.C.O. of Section. All Motor Stations visited - samples taken and tested. *Ina*	
WESTOUTRE	3/5/1918		Visit of Division inspected on its condition of camps and billets and which demand from Inspector. N.O. arrangement area of Infection. Disease in Advanced Dressing Station. KEMMEL, D Battery 86th Brigade R.F.A. and 115th Siege Battery R.G.A. at LA CLYTTE. C.O. accompanied Capt Smith to LOCRE and superintended filling of new pump at Baths; inspected men killed at LOCRE. Square of temporarily attached men, under supervision of NCO of Section engaged on sanitary duties at WESTOUTRE, LOCRE and DRANOUTRE. Two men sent about trumpets at DRANOUTRE and one man at Divisional founders. WESTOUTRE. Guards of Honorary attached men at all	

Army Form C. 2118

WAR DIARY
INTELLIGENCE SUMMARY
(Erase heading not required.)

Instructions regarding War Diaries and Intelligence Summaries are contained in F. S. Regs., Part II. and the Staff Manual respectively. Title Pages will be prepared in manuscript.

Place	Date	Hour	Summary of Events and Information	Remarks and references to Appendices
			Baths Station in Divisional Area, under supervision of N.C.O. of Section. All Baths Stations visited - Samples taken and tested.	

M Anderson
Capt R.A.M.C.
OC 19th Divisional San. Section

Army Form C. 2118

WAR DIARY
INTELLIGENCE SUMMARY
(Erase heading not required.)

140/1754

War Diary
of
19th Divisional Sanitary Section
from 1st to 30th September 1916
Vol 15

(No. 36)

COMMITTEE FOR THE
MEDICAL HISTORY OF THE WAR
Date 30 OCT. 1915

List of R.E. Water Supplies in 19th Divisional Area.

N°.	MAP REF.	Source of Supply and Locality.	Treatment.
58.	F/d.0.4	Merris. Communal Pump. Opposite Church.	1. Scoop.
59.	F/d.3.3.	" Pump opposite Estaminet "Au Soleil."	1. Scoop.
68.	W29a 5.6	Strazeele. Pump in main Rd. South of Village	1. Scoop.
69.	W21d 10.8	" Farmhouse Pump.	1½ Scoops.
70.	W27d 5.4	" Roadside Pump.	1. Scoop
91.	W21c 7.7	Pradelles. Communal Pump. Opposite Church.	1. Scoop.
92.	"	" Pump Opposite Above	1½ Scoops.
93.	W19d 4.9	Borre. Farmhouse Pump.	1½ Scoops.
102.	W19 2.9	" Communal Pump. On Green. Opposite Church.	1. Scoop.
94.	E3a 8.8	Le Bois. Pump at Estaminet "Debit de Boisson"	1. Scoop.
98.		" " " "Au Petit Sec Bois"	1. Scoop.
99.		Au Sauveur. Roadside Pump near Canal.	1. Scoop.
71.	F9a 2.1	Outtersteene. Roadside Pump.	1. Scoop.
72.	F9a 3.6	" Pump Opposite Estaminet du Bureau des Douanes	1. Scoop
73.	F3c 2.1	" Pump outside Estaminet du Soleil.	1. Scoop.
74.	F9a 0.7	" Roadside Pump. near Church.	1½ Scoop.
75.	F9a 7.7	" Open Well at Estaminet "A St Gregoire"	1. Scoop
76.	F8c 6.0	Noote Boom. Pump in Field. Not Recommended	3½ Scoops.
77.	F12a 9.7	Meteren. Pump in Square.	1. Scoop.
78.	F23c 6.2	" Roadside Pump Near Estaminet "Au Pont Wemaers"	2. Scoops.
79.	F21a 7.6	" " " " du Bon Labourers (not recommended)	2½ Scoops
80.	E24c 3.8	Vieux Berquin. Pump in Yard First to left Main Post Street Not recommended	2½ Scoops
81.	E24a 0.6	" Pump at Estaminet au Champ de ?	1. Scoop.

Note:-

Out of Bounds for all purposes.
   Roadside Pump at Estaminet "A La Triple Entente"
   Sec Bois Water very bad (20 Sc...)

                           G. R. Anderson Capt.
                           O.C. 19th Divisional Sanitary Section

25.9/16

WAR DIARY
or
INTELLIGENCE SUMMARY

Army Form C. 2118

(Erase heading not required.)

Place	Date	Hour	Summary of Events and Information	Remarks and references to Appendices
WESTOUTRE	1st September		S.O. interviewed Sanitary Officer 1st Canadian Division as to sanitary work in this Divison mining farm area. M.O. in charge LOCRE and area about to be occupied by Division. Two men with trench showers at DRANOUTRE and six men at Divisional Laundry. One N.C.O. of Section and one temporary attached men at LACLYTTE – KEMMEL ROAD, LACLYTTE Road and BRULOOS Road train Station. One N.C.O. of Section and three temporary attached men at KEMMEL WELLS and LINDENHOEK train Station. One N.C.O. of Section and three temporary attached men at LOCRE train Station. The N.C.O. of Section and five temporary attached men at KEMMEL SHELTERS train Station. Two temporary attached men at WESTOUTRE train Station. The following train Stations inspected and samples taken and tested – LA CLYTTE, KEMMEL, KEMMEL SHELTERS, WESTOUTRE, LOCRE and KEMMEL WELLS. Reports to date have received. The following Units of Division inspected as to sanitary condition:– 8th North Staffordshire Regt. Transport, 8th Cheshire Regt Transport, 10th Lincoln Regt Transport, 10th Royal Warwickshire Regt Transport, 5th South Wales Borderers Headquarters and Transport, 87 Brigade R.F.A. "B" Battery and Headquarters.	

WAR DIARY
INTELLIGENCE SUMMARY

(Erase heading not required.)

Army Form C. 2118

Place	Date	Hour	Summary of Events and Information	Remarks and references to Appendices
WESTOUTRE / LOCRE	2nd Apr.		198th Army Troops R.E., 58th Machine Gun Coy, 58th Brigade Headquarter Transport, 7th East Lancashire Regt. Transport, 7th South Lancashire Regt. Transport, 115th Siege Battery R.G.A., 6th Wiltshire Regt. 1st Entrenching Batt. O'Cherie Regt. and O'Ryan Wield Amb. Reft. Transport. Inn huts as 57th Brigade Transport Headquarters. Fatigue squads of Coy attached men engaged in sanitary duties at WESTOUTRE, LOCRE and DRANOUTRE. / hua.- / C.O. interviewed Sanitary Officer of 23rd Division and inspected baths at PONT DE NIEPPE. C.O. inspected Divisional Baths and surrounding area. Latrine Office and equipment removed to new billets at LOCRE. Men of section and attached men marched to LOCRE. New billets cleaned and squad of attached men put on sanitary work. Sister from Divisional Successor to DRANOUTRE Thresh Disinfector on motorlorry received from Divisional Headquarters. Handed over to H. Tarrance Divisional As N.C.O. of Section and	

WAR DIARY
of
INTELLIGENCE SUMMARY
(Erase heading not required.)

Army Form C. 2118

Place	Date	Hour	Summary of Events and Information	Remarks and references to Appendices
			One Company attached men as guards at Water Station at LA CLYTTE – KEMMEL Road, LA CLYTTE Road, & BRULOOGE Road. The N.C.O. of Section and three Company attached men at KEMMEL WELLS and LINDEN HOEK Water Station. One N.C.O. and three Company attached men at LOCRE Water Station. One N.C.O. and two Company attached men at KEMMEL SHELTERS Water Station. Two Company attached men at WESTOUTRE Supply. All the Regtl. machine Water Station visited, samples taken and tested. On arrival at LOCRE the following visits etc. made as to sanitary arrangements IX Corps Cavalry. Y.M.C.A. Hut. A.D.M.S. Office. D.A.D.S. Mounted Military Police. Officers' Club. Divisional Bread and 9th Corps Cyclists. The following Units of Divisions inspected – 7th South Lancashire Regt. 7th Kings Own Royal Lancashire Regt. 12th Kings Labour Battn. 11th Labour Battn. R.E., B. & C. Batteries of 88th Brigade R.F.A.	

WAR DIARY
or
INTELLIGENCE SUMMARY

(Erase heading not required.)

Army Form C. 2118

Place	Date	Hour	Summary of Events and Information	Remarks and references to Appendices
			Marguerite and "A" "B" "C" and "D" Batteries of 87th Brigade R.F.A. Squads of temporary attached men engaged in sanitary duties at WESTOUTRE, LOCRE and DRANOUTRE. The NCO of section at Divisional Laundry, DRANOUTRE. Billets at WESTOUTRE inspected after being vacated by units. Lamps and killers of No 2 Kitt Bastion Section, 82nd Field Company R.E. 8th Minnesota Regt + 57th Brigade Transport.	
LOCRE	3rd Sept		to Inspected "C" and "D" Companies 7th North Lancashire Regt. Y.M.C.A. Hut at KEMMEL SHELTERS, "B" Battery 87th Brigade R.F.A. and 5th South Wales Borden Regt. Transport lines. The following Units inspected as to sanitary arrangements – 19th Divisional Salvage Co. 9th Royal Welsh Fusilier Regt. Transport. 9th Cheshire Regt Transport and "D" Battery, 87th Brigade R.F.A. One N.C.O of Section and one temporary attached men as guards at main Stationary	

WAR DIARY or INTELLIGENCE SUMMARY

Army Form C. 2118

Place	Date	Hour	Summary of Events and Information	Remarks and references to Appendices
			LA CLYTTE – KEMMEL Road, LA CLYTTE Road and BRULOOGE Road. One N.C.O. of Section and three temporary attached men as guard at KEMMEL WELLS and LINDENHOEK Water Station. One N.C.O. and three temporary attached men as guard at LOCRE Water Station. One N.C.O. and five temporary attached men as guard at KEMMEL SHELTERS Water Station. One N.C.O. of Section at Divisional Laundry Squads. 1 temporary attached men engaged in sanitary fatigues at LOCRE and DRANOUTRE. EWA.	
LOCRE	4ᵗʰ Sept		C.O. inspected new Divisional Area – namely PONT DE NIEPPE, NIEPPE and PONT D'ACHELLES with Sanitary Officer 23ʳᵈ Division and arranged for posting of Water Patrols. The following Units inspected as to sanitary arrangements – 9ᵗʰ Field Co R.E. and transport, 58ᵗʰ Brigade Headquarters, 9ᵗʰ Royal Welsh Fusiliers Regt. transport, 9ᵗʰ Cheshire Regt. transport, 9ᵗʰ Welsh Regt. transport, 6ᵗʰ Wiltshire Regt. 5ᵗʰ South Wales Borders Regt. transport. Bakefours Huts (lately occupied by	

WAR DIARY
INTELLIGENCE SUMMARY
(Erase heading not required.)

Army Form C. 2118

Instructions regarding War Diaries and Intelligence Summaries are contained in F.S. Regs., Part II. and the Staff Manual respectively. Title Pages will be prepared in manuscript.

Place	Date	Hour	Summary of Events and Information	Remarks and references to Appendices
			7 Kings Own Royal Lancaster Regt) Kemmel Shelters (partly occupied by 7 North Lancashire Regt) 55th Brigade Headquarters and Transport, 55th Trench Mortar Battery, 55th Machine Gun Corps and Transport and Sgt Head to R.E. LOCRE and district inspected. Main trams at LA CLYTTE – KIMMEL Road, LA CLYTTE Road, BRULOOGE Road, LOCRE, KEMMEL SHELTERS and MONT DE CATS unknown. Gen JCO at Divisional Laundry. Fatigue squads of Infantry attached men engage in sanitary duties at LOCRE and DRANOUTRE. Guard of Infantry attached men at KEMMEL WELLS and LINDENHOEK Main Nations and provide fixed or Station in new area. JWA	
LOCRE	5th Sept.		G.O. attended Divisional Cohort for purpose of receiving instruction in use of new Box Respirator. Guards of Infantry attached men at KEMMEL WELLS and LINDENHOEK Main Nations. Fatigue squads of Infantry attached men engaged in sanitary duties at LOCRE and DRANOUTRE. The following Units of Division inspected –	

WAR DIARY / INTELLIGENCE SUMMARY

Army Form C. 2118

Place	Date	Hour	Summary of Events and Information	Remarks and references to Appendices
			58th French Mortar Battery, 58th Machine Gun Corps, 6th Wiltshire Regt. Staff in 85th Brigade R.F.A., 7th East Lancashire Regt, 7th Kings Own Royal Lancaster Regt transport, 7th Loyal North Lancashire Regt transport, 7th South Lancashire Regt transport and Divisional Sanitary Section. Strand of 1 N.C.O + 2 men at WATERLANDS Horse Supply. Guard of 1 N.C.O and three men at each of the following Water Stations :- RABOT (Drinking Supply) LE VEAU (Horse Supply) PAPOT (Drinking Supply) PAPOT (Horse Supply). All Stations proved and samples taken and tested.	
LOCRE (PONT DACHELLES)	26 Sept/17	6.0	60 horses from LOCRE & new billets at PONT DACHELLES. Men and equipment of Section transported in motor lorry from LOCRE to PONT D'ACHELLES. Men of Section and temporary attached men marched to new billets. Billets cleaned up and sanitary condition improved. Billets at LOCRE after being vacated by Section inspected. Squad of eight temporary attached men engaged in cleaning up huts of LOCRE vacated	

WAR DIARY
INTELLIGENCE SUMMARY
(Erase heading not required.)

Army Form C. 2118.

Place	Date	Hour	Summary of Events and Information	Remarks and references to Appendices
			Supervision of N.C.O of section. The following Units of Command inspected :- 8' Signal R.F.A. 3rd Mobile Veterinary Section. B Battery 89' Brigade R.F.A. (Horse lines) 89' Divisional Salvage Co. Also Y.M.C.A. Huts at KEMMEL SHELTERS. Heads of S.A.A. C.O. and three men at the following Ration Stations :- RABOT (Divisional Supply), LE VEAU (Horse Supply) PAPOT (Divisional Supply) PAPOT (Horse Supply). One N.C.O. and two men at WATERLANDS Ration Supply. All Ration Stations erected. Samples taken and tested. Six N.C.O. at Divisional Laundry. Units of three given classes at PLOEGSTEERT Supply.	
PONT D'ACHELLES	7' Sept		C.O. visited area round REMMARIN Farm, DOUDOU Farm, SOYER Farm and OOSTHOVE Farm. U.C. inspected horse watering troughs at WATERLANDS. Inspected KEDNIS at BAILLEUL. Fatigue opened of horsemen attached under engaged in cleaning up NIEPPE and PONT DE NIEPPE under supervision of N.C.O. of Section. The following Units of Command inspected :- 87' Field Company, R.E., 5' South Wales Border Regt, 31' Mobile Veterinary Section.	

WAR DIARY
INTELLIGENCE SUMMARY

(Erase heading not required.)

Army Form C. 2118

Place	Date	Hour	Summary of Events and Information	Remarks and references to Appendices
PONT D'ACHELLES	8th Sept.		D.C.G. Welsh Regt. Transport & 8th Yorkshire Regt. 57 Machine Gun Co. 19 Divisional Signal Co at NIEPPE. 9th Welsh Regt. at PAPOT and Head quarters of 6th Cheshire Regt. Guards (no. 1 no. 2, 6 Co) Three men at the following train Stations. – PABOT (Remounts supply.) PAPOT (Army supply). Three men at PLOEGSTEERT Supply and at ACQ & two men at NITERANNE Supply. All Nation Stations supplies taken over. Sanitation at Divisional Laundry. Lund. CO troops NIETEREN (58 Field Ambulance) and inspected hole supply arrived at 4 am & Ranks and hotel came: Food rations went to Divisional Headquarters and A.D.M.S. interviewed O.C. 19 Divisional Train and O.C. Train Return 12 Corps reference water supply in new area. Fatigue supplied of temporary bridges & tracked men engaged in cleaning up NIEPPE and PONT DE NIEPPE	

WAR DIARY
INTELLIGENCE SUMMARY

Army Form C. 2118

Place	Date	Hour	Summary of Events and Information	Remarks and references to Appendices
			Inspection of N.C.O.'s of Return. Two men reporting daily notice for exchanging at Bath Station. One N.C.O. at Divisional Laundry. One Bath Patrol to area washed samples twice and today. Guards of one N.C.O and five men at the following Main Stations - PAPOT (Bunkering supply) LEVEAU (Divn Supply), PAPOT (Bunkering supply) PAPOT (Divn. Supply) and POPERSTREET (Divn. Supply) One N.C.O and two men at WATERLAND Supply. [signed]	
PONT DACHELLES	9th Oct 1917		E.O. proceeded to Map reference B & C 5.2 as a member of Board constituted to examine Salvaged nature. Inspected cornbarn of camp at PAPOT RUE DE SAC and Baths. E.O. proceeded to BAILLEUL to make routine visits to Q. Office and A.D.M.S., various offices of D.A.D.O.S. C.O. received instruction from Q. Office to proceed to map reference S 30. a 1·5 in order to report on motor lorries. The following units 1 Divisional inspected - Headquarters 58th Infantry Brigade. H.Q. Heavy	

WAR DIARY
or
INTELLIGENCE SUMMARY
(Erase heading not required.)

Army Form C. 2118

Place	Date	Hour	Summary of Events and Information	Remarks and references to Appendices
			Artillery Group. 58th Machine Gun Corps. Headquarters & Wiltshire Regt and B Company. Fatigue party 1 Temporary attached men under supervision of NCO of Section engaged in sanitary duties at NIEPPE and PONT DE NIEPPE. One man preparing bath service for Section. One NCO at Divisional Laundry. Lance Corporal & 2 NCO and three men at the following bath Stations. RABOT (Drinking Supply) LEVEAU (Horse Supply) PAPOT (Drinking Supply) PAPOT (Horse Supply) and PLOEGSTEERT (Drinking Supply) One NCO and two men at WATERLANDS Supply. All bath Station water samples taken and tested. Full.	
PONT D'ACHELLES	1st Sept.		C.O. inspected in company with M.O. the camp occupied by No 2 Co. Divisional Ammunition Column and made suggestion for improvement of camp. M.O. investigated case of suspected trench spread meningitis at 71st Heavy Battery R.G.A. and made necessary arrangements. Fatigue Squad of temporary attached men engaged in sanitary duties under the	

WAR DIARY
INTELLIGENCE SUMMARY

Army Form C. 2118

Place	Date	Hour	Summary of Events and Information	Remarks and references to Appendices
			supervision of NCO's section at NIEPPE and PONT DE NIEPPE. One man making water stand for Station. The NCO at Divisional Laundry. The following units of Division inspected as to sanitary arrangements 19th Divisional Training Co. 57th Machine Gun Divisional. 7th Kings Own Royal Lancaster Regt. Transport Depot. 7th Loyal North Lancashire Regt Transport, 81st Field Co RE and A and C Batteries 88th Brigade R.F.A. Guards of men NCO and three men at the following Main Station. RABOT (Sanitary Supply) LE VEAU (Horse Supply) PAPOT (Sanitary Supply) PAPOT (Horse Supply) and PLOEGSTEERT (Sanitary Supply) An N.C.O. and two men at WATERLANDS supply. All Stations visited. Samples taken and tested.	
PONT DACHELLES	11 Sept		M.O. in company with Medical Officer of inspected A.B.C. and D Batteries 87 Brigade R.F.A. Fatigue squad evening latrinesh at NIEPPE and cleaning up streets of NIEPPE and PONT DE NIEPPE under supervision	

WAR DIARY
or
INTELLIGENCE SUMMARY

(Erase heading not required.)

Army Form C. 2118

Place	Date	Hour	Summary of Events and Information	Remarks and references to Appendices
			of NCOs of Section. The men engaged in main fatigues for Baths in area. The MO at Divisional Laundry. 1 Cd. meal arrangement for sanitary personnel from Battalion to attend and form a course of instruction. The following units of Division inspected:– Headquarters and 'B' Battery 88th Brigade R.F.A. of Cheshire Regt; A, B and C Companies 1/5th South Wales Borderers; 19th Divisional Baggage Co. 19th Divisional Salvage Co. 94th Field Co. R.E. Headquarters 19th Divisional Ammunition Column, A and C Batteries, 87th Brigade R.F.A and 7th Siege Battery. One NCO and three men on guard as the following Motor Stations – RABOT (Drinking Supply) LE VEAU (Horse Supply) PAPOT (Drinking Supply) PAPOT (Horse Supply) and PLOEGSTEERT (Drinking Supply) One NCO and two men at WATERLANDS Supply. All bath stations worked, samples taken and tested.	

Ina.

WAR DIARY
—or—
INTELLIGENCE SUMMARY

(Erase heading not required.)

Army Form C. 2118

Place	Date	Hour	Summary of Events and Information	Remarks and references to Appendices
PONT DE NIEPPE	12" Sep"		S.O. proceeded to BAILLEUL and afterwards to PLOEGSTEERT main supply for the army. Advanced A.S.C. inspected Sanitary latrines at BAILLEUL. In company with main convoy inspected and noted main supplies at ARMENTIÈRES and LA BIZET. Also noted main supply of 5th Cheshire Regt, Infantry Baths and 6th Wiltshire Regt. On M.G.O. at Divisional Laundry. Saw men preparing motors for main station. Main supplies in middle and right sector unchanged. The following units inspected as to sanitary conditions and arrangements — Headquarters and camp of F.2nd Field Co. R.E., 8th North Staffordshire Regt., Transport 57th Infantry Brigade, B/6 9th Royal Irish Lancer Regt, 9th Field 6th R.E. 19 Divisional Baths, W X Y and Z Batteries of Heavy Trench Mortar Bats and Transport of 6th Wiltshire Regt. All main stations visited. Samples taken and noted. On M.G.O. and three men as guard at the following stations. RABOT (Evening Supply), LEVEAU (Shoe Supply), DEPOT (Sunken supply) PAPOT (Shoe Supply) and PLOEGSTEERT Supply. One NCO and two men at WATERLANDS Supply. [signed]	

WAR DIARY
INTELLIGENCE SUMMARY
(Erase heading not required.)

Army Form C. 2118

Place	Date	Hour	Summary of Events and Information	Remarks and references to Appendices
PONT D'ACHELLES	13 Sept.		M.O. in company with D.H. inspected Water Filtration Range at JESUSFARM. Inspected 4.9 Heavy Artillery Horse at PONT DE NIEPPE and inspected construction of water reservoirs and other sanitary appliances erected at Lytham Mills for the purpose of giving watershed to Divisional sanitary personnel. Accompanied A.D.M.S. and D.A.D.M.S. to PLOEGSTEERT. Inspected Piggeries with a view to ascertaining out in forward trench. Inspected several Rest Ranges as to whether it was a suitable gathering ground to supply PLOEGSTEERT area. The following Units inspected:— 3rd Mobile Veterinary Section, Transport of 9th Cheshire Regt, Reorganised and 5+3 Section Divisional Ammunition Column 4.9", HAY, 5", Brigade Machine Gun Corps, 8th Worcestershire Regt and 1 East Lancashire Regt. All Water Points visited, samples taken and stated. Guard of One NCO and three men at PAPOT (Drinking) and PAPOT (Horse) supplies. Guard of one NCO and two men at RAADT (Drinking) and LE VEAU (Horse) supplies and WATERLANDS (Horse supply). Two men as guard at PLOEGSTEERT Pumping Station. One NCO at Divisional guard One man marking notices for Water Stations. Antiques carried out at NIEPPE. GMA	

WAR DIARY or INTELLIGENCE SUMMARY

Army Form C. 2118

Place	Date	Hour	Summary of Events and Information	Remarks and references to Appendices
PONT DACHELLES	14th Sept		C.O. interviewed A.D. & M.S. of Division and gave notice of three train supplies in area and discussed measures to be taken to ensure prompt supply for the Division. Inspected H.Q. 19 Divisional Ammunition Column. Horses OK. Pumping Station. JESUS FARM and arranged information regarding supply to the II Corps Area. Inspected and visited train supplies at Station Relievers and Nissen Horns. The following units of Division inspected:- No 2 Section, Divisional Ammunition Column. Transport of S. Fork Notts Border Regt. Transport of 9th Welsh Regt. 19th Divisional Artillery 10th Transport of 5th Brigade Machine Gun Corps. Transport of 7th East Lancashire Regt. Transport of 7th South Lancashire Regt and 8th Field Company R.E. Visited of one N.C.O. and three men at PAPOT (Drinking Supply) PAPOT (Horse Supply) and IODINE MANOR (Cooking and Washing Supply). Guard of one NCO and two men at RABOT (Drinking) and LE VEAU (Horse) Supplies. One NCO and two men at WATERLANDS Horse Supply. Two men	

Army Form C. 2118

WAR DIARY
OF
INTELLIGENCE SUMMARY
(Erase heading not required.)

Instructions regarding War Diaries and Intelligence Summaries are contained in F. S. Regs., Part II. and the Staff Manual respectively. Title Pages will be prepared in manuscript.

Place	Date	Hour	Summary of Events and Information	Remarks and references to Appendices
			as guard at PLOEGSTEERT Pumping Station. All Naik Mahun moved complies ration and Water. One 1/60 at Dinannal Laundry. One man making clothes for Naik Mahun se. Fatigue squad 1 temporary attached men engaged in running duties at NIEPPE and PONT DE NIEPPE. Tables 1. 6. 6. from Dinannal Laundry personnel returned for three days course of instruction. Instruction from own section 1 & 6. 6.	L. N. A.
PONT D'ACHELLES	15th Sept		C.O. moved N°5 Canadian Mobile Laboratory with sample of water from PLOEGSTEERT Supply. Pour noties now to ABMS and noted AA + RMS as to Naik supplies. Gave lecture to Dinannal sanitary personnel attached for instruction. One man engaged in making notice board for Naik supplies. One 1/60 at Dinannal Laundry. Fatigue squad of temporary attached men engaged in sanitary duties at NIEPPE and PONT DE NIEPPE. All Naik Nahum in Dinannal Area moved complies ration and Water. Rivards of and	

WAR DIARY
or
INTELLIGENCE SUMMARY

Army Form C. 2118

Place	Date	Hour	Summary of Events and Information	Remarks and references to Appendices
			N.C.O. and three men at PAPOT (Drinking Supply) and APOT (Horse Supply) Guard of one + C.O. and four men at ICRINE MANOR (Working and washing supply) Guards of one N.C.O. and two men at RABOT (Drinking) LE VEAU (Horse) and WATERLANDS (Horse) Supplies. Two men as guard at PLOEGSTEERT Pumping Station. The following were inspected as to Sanitary conditions – 49 Heavy Artillery Group, N°. 2 and 4 C°. ASC Divisional Salvage C°. Divisional Drainage C°. 10th Worcestershire Regt. Headquarters 58th Infantry Brigade, Transport of 7th South Lancashire Regt. Wagon lines of D Battery, 87 Brigade R.F.A. Wagon lines of D Battery 88th Brigade R.F.A. + 2 and 4 Sections Divisional Ammunition Column. [signature]	
PONT D'ACHELLES	14 Sept 15		C.O. paid routine visit to AA+QMG and ADMS. Interviewed O.C. 1st Canadian Mobile Laboratory. Inspected buildings to be used as dump by DADOS near PONT D'ACHELLES from Sanitary standpoint	

WAR DIARY
or
INTELLIGENCE SUMMARY

(Erase heading not required.)

Army Form C. 2118

Place	Date	Hour	Summary of Events and Information	Remarks and references to Appendices
			Inspected X Heavy Trench Mortar Battery and Divisional Baths. Reports forwarded A.D.M.S. reference X Heavy Trench Mortar Battery. Inspected Public Urinals at NIEPPE and PONT DE NIEPPE. Intym agreed 1 temporary attached man engaged on sanitary duties at NIEPPE and PONT DE NIEPPE under supervision of N.C.O. of Section. One N.C.O. at Divisional Laundry. One man engaged on sanitary duties for train supplies. The following units inspected as to sanitary arrangements — 92nd Field Company R.E., D Co. 5th Irish Rifles Border Regt., G Wilts Regt. and "C" Battery 87 Brigade R.F.A. Urinals of one N.60 and three men at PAPOT (Dunking) and PAPOT (Stove) supplies. One N.6.0 and five men at TODINE MANOR (Clothing and washing supply). One N.6.0 and two men at RABOT (Dunking) LE VEAU (Stove) and WATERLANDS (Stove) supplies. Two men at P. DE GSTEERT Pumping Station. All station water samples taken and tested. G.M.a.	

WAR DIARY
INTELLIGENCE SUMMARY

Army Form C. 2118

Place	Date	Hour	Summary of Events and Information	Remarks and references to Appendices
PONT D'ACHELLES	17/Sept		A.D. inspected 83 Brigade R.F.A. and two unoccupied camps at LE VEAU. Rain water tanks and pumps at BAILLEUL. Proceeded to PONT DE NIEPPE and gave instructions for cleaning and disinfection of N.C.O. at Divisional Laundry. The men engaged in washing were warned for fresh supervision. Sanitary squad of Hampshires attended and on sanitary duties under supervision of N.C.O. of section at NIEPPE and PONT DE NIEPPE. All water Medium marked Damflies taken and tested. Teams of one N.C.O. and three men at PAPOT (Drinking) and PAPOT (Horse) supplies. One N.C.O. and five men at TOURNE MANOR cleaning and washing supply. One N.C.O. and two men at RABOT (Drinking) LE VEAU (Horse) and WATERLANDS (Horse) supplies. Two men at PLOEGSTEERT Pumping Station. The following units inspected as to sanitary arrangements:— 5th South Wales Border Regt, Transport lines of 7th Royal Lancashire Regt, Transport of 7 King's Own, Royal Lancashire Regt, Personnel Hutting B, C Battery 82 Brigade R.F.A, and Headquarters 87 Infantry Brigade.	

1875 Wt. W593/826 1,000,000 4/15 J.B.C. & A. A.D.S.S./Form/C.2118.

WAR DIARY
INTELLIGENCE SUMMARY

Army Form C. 2118

Place	Date	Hour	Summary of Events and Information	Remarks and references to Appendices
PONT D'ACHELLES	18 Sept		C.O. visited R.E. DUMP and ADMS at BAILLEUL, engaged in drawing up report for incoming A.D.M.S. and sanitary officer; proceeded to PONT DE NIEPPE and interviewed O/C. Rest and Laundry as to move. The prisoners' work inspected as to sanitary condition. Transport of 6th Wiltshire Regt. Divisional Signal Co. at NIEPPE. Transport of 9th Welsh Regt, D.Co. 5th South Wales Borderers Regt, 82nd Field Co. R.E. and R.E. Dump. One N.C.O. at Divisional Laundry. One man working stores for water supplies in Divisional Area. All Water Station crossed samples taken and tested. Shower of one N.C.O. and three men at PAPOT (Bunting) and PAPOT (Horse) supplies. One N.C.O. and five men at TODINE MANOR (Working and Washing) supply. One N.C.O. and two men at RABOT (Bunting) LE VEAU (Horse) and WATERLANDS (Horse) supplies. Two men at PLOEGSTEERT Pumping Station. Yna.	

WAR DIARY or INTELLIGENCE SUMMARY

Army Form C. 2118

Place	Date	Hour	Summary of Events and Information	Remarks and references to Appendices
PONT D'ACHELLES	19/4/9?		A.D. visited R.A.O.M.C. and A.D.M.S. at BAILLEUL. Found LE FLETRE and interviewed Sanitary Officer 7th Divn. Enteric Officer work. The following Units of Division inspected as to sanitary condition. HQrs. 9th & 10th section Divisional Ammunition Column, A. and 'D' Batteries 87 Brigade R.F.A. Headquarters 7 King's Own Royal Lancaster Regt. 'A' and 'C' 10th 5th South Wales Border Regt. 9th Rifle Bde. R.E., Sanitary & Provost Regt. 57 Brigade Machine Gun Coys. and 9 Royal Welsh Fusilier Regt. The S.F.C.O. at Divisional Laundry. See men making nets for hair supplies at Divisional area. All hair station visited, samples taken and tested. Troops of 11th N.C.O. and three men at PAPOT (Dunkirk) and PAPOT (Water) Supplies. One N.C.O. and two men at IODINE MANOR (Cooking and Washing) Supply. One N.C.O. and two men at RABOT (Drinking) Supplies. Two men at PLOEGSTEERT. LE VEAU (Water) and WATERLANDS (Water) Supplies. Pumping Station.	

Army Form C. 2118

WAR DIARY
INTELLIGENCE SUMMARY
(Erase heading not required.)

Place	Date	Hour	Summary of Events and Information	Remarks and references to Appendices
PONT D'ACHELLES	7th Sept		I.O. reported K.R.+R.M.S and ADMS at BAILLEUL. Interviewed O/c Bath as to move. Usual Ypres work. The following units of Divison inspected. B Co 9 Royal Welsh Fusiliers Regt, also transport. 8[2]ⁿᵈ Field Co R.E. N°2 and 4, 165 A.S.C. N°3 Section of Divisional Ammunition Column Headquarters and transport of 1/5 7 Infantry Brigade. 6 th Wiltshire Regt. and transport of 1/9 Cheshire Regt. All water stations in Divisional area visited. Samples taken and tested. Found 1 one NCO and three men at PAPOT (Drinking) and PAPOT (Horse) supplies. One NCO and five men at IODINE MANOR (Cooking and Washing) Supply. One NCO and two men at RABOT (Drinking) LE VEAU (Horse) and WATERLANDS (Horse) supplies. Two men at PLOEGSTEERT Pumping Station. One NCO at Divisional Laundry. One man making orders for water supplies. Advance party for 7 Divisional Sanitary Section reported and marched in. Nothing unusual.	W.A.

WAR DIARY or INTELLIGENCE SUMMARY

Army Form C. 2118

Place	Date	Hour	Summary of Events and Information	Remarks and references to Appendices
PONT D'ACHELLES	7th Sept		16.0 accompanied Sanitary Officer, 7' Division over Divisional Area: inspected IODINE MANOR, PLOEGSTEERT, and PIGGERIES. Showed baths at PAPOT and PONT DE NIEPPE, halt tanks at BRUNE-GAYE. Report on working of area handed to Sanitary Officer 7' Division. Inspected samples vacated by NCO's and 9' Royal Welsh Fusilier Regt. All water taken in Divisional Area would sample taken and tested. Guard of one NCO and three men at PAPOT (Drinking) and PAPOT (Horses). One NCO and two men at IODINE MANOR (Cooking and Washing Supply). One NCO and two men at RABOT (Drinking). LE VEAU (Horses) and WATERLANDS (Horses) supplies. Two men at PLOEGSTEERT Pumping Station. One N.CO at Divisional Laundry. One man making nitre for water Mains. The following Units: Division inspected: C Battery 87 Brigade R.F.A., Hustings Co Depot, 9th Field Co R.E., 8th Lincolns Regt and transport. 5' South Wales Borderers Regt and transport. 57' Brigade Machine Gun Corps. 57' Brigade.	

Army Form C. 2118

WAR DIARY
INTELLIGENCE SUMMARY
(Erase heading not required.)

Instructions regarding War Diaries and Intelligence Summaries are contained in F. S. Regs., Part II. and the Staff Manual respectively. Title Pages will be prepared in manuscript.

Place	Date	Hour	Summary of Events and Information	Remarks and references to Appendices
			Transport 39th Field Co. R.E. and Drainage Co. Fatigue squad & Temporary attached men engaged under supervision of N.C.O. of R.E. on Sanitary duties in MEPPE and PONT DE NIEPPE.	
			M.A.	
PONT D'ACHELLES / MERRIS	22nd Sept		The following Units of Division inspected: 2nd Cavalry 2nd and 4th Corps N.S.C. Transport of 58th Brigade Machine Gun Corp. Transports and cadres of 7th East Lancashire Regt. 7th South Lancashire Regt. 7th Royal North Lancashire Regt. and 7th King's Own Royal Lancashire Regt. kitbags & 57th Infantry Brigade Headquarters, B. Battery 57 Brigade RFA and Divisional Signal Co. (Hq.). Fatigue squad of temporary attached men cleaning up NIEPPE. C.O. in company with Sanitary Officer 7th Division visited PONT DE NIEPPE and explained method of carrying out work of same. C.O. handed over area to 7 Divisional Sanitary Officer and proceeded to MERRIS. All Motor Lorries at Divisional Motor Section observed and proceed to PONT D'ACHELLES.	

WAR DIARY
INTELLIGENCE SUMMARY
(Erase heading not required.)

Army Form C. 2118

Place	Date	Hour	Summary of Events and Information	Remarks and references to Appendices
MERRIS	23rd Sept		Men of 1st Section and attached men marched to new billets near MERRIS. Sections offrs and equipment arrived in lorry to new area. EMcA.	
		6.0	Moved Brigade Headquarters at STRAZEELE and BORRE in company with OK Parks and fixed upon site for spray bath at farm near STRAZEELE. Proceeded to HAZEBROUCK and interviewed OC No 12 (iworks) clearing station regarding washing facilities and storage of garments. Proceeded to Ellis huts and interviewed Manager and endeavoured to arrange change for washing men. Inspected premises made for A.D.Med.Serv. Signal Co. Headquarters, and arranged as to sanitation of Headquarters town. Temporarily attached men cleaning up Sections billets and area around mens' cookhouse. Village of VIEUX BERQUIN, 56th Infantry Brigade area, 57 Infantry Brigade area and 58 Infantry Brigade area inspected. EMcA.	

WAR DIARY
INTELLIGENCE SUMMARY
(Erase heading not required.)

Army Form C. 2118

Place	Date	Hour	Summary of Events and Information	Remarks and references to Appendices
MERRIS	7th Sept.		I.O. proceeded to STRAZEELE and investigated complaints by 58th Brigade H.Q. regarding drain in village. Passed HQ ASC at VIEUX BERQUIN. Passed H.Q. ASC at PONT D'ACHELLES and obtained information regarding case of Typhoid fever. Took over sanitation of MERRIS from Camp Commandant and made necessary arrangements. Squads of Company attached men engaged in cleaning up town and billets at MERRIS. One squad on Latrine duties. They now making rustics for Latrine supplies. One NCO at Divisional Laundry. The following Units of Division inspected — 56th Brigade Machine Gun Corps. Headquarters 58th Infantry Brigade, 9th Royal Welch Fusilier Regt; Headquarters 57th Infantry Brigade, 57 Brigade Machine Gun Corps, 10th Royal Warwickshire Regt and 5th South Wales Borders Regt. Incinerator erected at Division billet.	

WAR DIARY or INTELLIGENCE SUMMARY

(Erase heading not required.)

Army Form C. 2118.

Instructions regarding War Diaries and Intelligence Summaries are contained in F. S. Regs., Part II. and the Staff Manual respectively. Title Pages will be prepared in manuscript.

Place	Date	Hour	Summary of Events and Information	Remarks and references to Appendices
MERRIS.	75 Sept.		C.O. accompanied by an interpreter interviewed the Mayors of MERRIS, STRAZEELE and BORRE and made enquiries as to incidence of Typhoid disease in the village. Interviewed M.O's 10th Royal Warwickshire Regt. and advised him on question of sanitation, Water Supplies in Divisional area. All Regimental Medical Officers men messed and orderlies attached. All Regimental Medical Officers interviewed with list of men requiring supplies in Divisional area and copy (not attached). One N.C.O. at Divisional Laundry. Agents to Divisional Laundry. Two men making notices for Water Supplies. Squads of temporary attached men cleaning up billets and town of MERRIS. One squad erecting public latrines. The following Units inspected as to sanitary conditions — No.s 2 and 4 Co. A.S.C. 8th North Staffordshire Regt. Repairing Pumps of No.3 Group. 6th Wiltshire Regt and Hanover. 7th Kings Own Royal Lancaster Regt and 7th South Lancashire Regt. Squad of temporary attached men cleaning up OUTERSTEENE. Premises used as Officers Mess at 9th Cheshire Regt disinfected; also quantity of clothing at Divisional Laundry Co.	

WAR DIARY or INTELLIGENCE SUMMARY

Army Form C. 2118.

Place	Date	Hour	Summary of Events and Information	Remarks and references to Appendices
MERRIS	7th Sept		C.O. inspected YMCA premises at STRAZEELE and interviewed Mayor reference miscarriage in LA FLETRE Road. Pay Parade and C.O. gave attached men an outlying station. Iodin supplied in Drummer area marked "Iodine" and other officer was man marching notices for Iraton Supplies. The NCO at Divisional Laundry, Nguen, of Temporary attached men clearing up billets and town of MERRIS, Sant. Times from our dia. and have are down together with three attached men carting away refuse from him. The N. Co. completing rounds of sickness and inspection arrears in the Division. The following Units inspected as to Sanitary conditions: 5th South Wales Border Regt. Divisional Details. 8th Worcestershire Regt. 8th North Staffordshire Regt. 57 Machine Gun Corps. 7 Royal North Lancashire Regt, "A" Coy and Headquarters 7 South Lancashire Regt, 9 N.W.R. Regt and Transport and Divisional Shooting Co.	

Place	Date	Hour	Summary of Events and Information	Remarks and references to Appendices
MERRIS	27 Sept		Lt.Col inspected Headquarters, A B C and D Co Transport lines and depôt of Royal Welch Fusiliers Regt, and Headquarters, A B C and D Co, Transport lines and depôt 9 Welch Regt. Water supplies in Divisional area noted and notices attached. One man making notices for water supplies. One NCO at Divisional Laundry. One NCO engaged in Inspection Duties other than i/c. Fatigue squad of 1 Temporary attached men, under supervision of NCO of Section engaged in sanitary fatigue in MERRIS. The following Units inspected as to sanitary condition — Headquarters, A B C and D Co and Transport 8 Co 15th Warwickshire Regt, 7th South Lancashire Regt and 7th Loyal Lancashire Regt. Civilian cart hired for refuse carting.	
MERRIS	28 Sept		M.O. in company with ADMS inspected C. Co 5th South Wales Border Regt at VIEUX BERQUIN. Interviewed Adjutant on H.Q. all regarding supply of lime for latrines and inspected HQ 5th South Wales Border Regt.	

WAR DIARY
INTELLIGENCE SUMMARY
(Erase heading not required.)

Army Form C. 2118.

Place	Date	Hour	Summary of Events and Information	Remarks and references to Appendices
			C.O. inspected H.Q. A.B. and D. Cos. transport lines and outfits of Cheshire Regt. The following units of Division inspected as to sanitary arrangements — 7th Kings Own Royal Lancaster Regt, 68th Brigade Machine Gun Corps, 5th Brigade Trench Mortar Battery, No 2 and 4 Coy A.S.C. and 10th Royal Warwickshire Regt. Billets of 10th Royal Warwickshire Regt where cases of RUBELLA had occurred disinfected and other necessary steps taken. One squad engaged on latrine duties. One man making wires for nails through an N.C.O. at Divisional Laundry. Squads of temporary attached men engaged on sanitary fatigues in town of MERRIS. Chlorinating cart hired, and lime and chloride supplied to Mons of Divisn causing army refuse to central incinerator at MERRIS. MVA	
MERRIS	19 Sept		C.O. proceeded to BORRE and interviewed M.O. 10 Royal Warwickshire Regt. Proceeded with M.O. to farm where contacts of two Rubella cases were billeted and inspected same. Inspection A B C and D Cos together with	

WAR DIARY
INTELLIGENCE SUMMARY

Army Form C. 2118.

(Erase heading not required.)

Place	Date	Hour	Summary of Events and Information	Remarks and references to Appendices
			Transport lines of 6th Wiltshire Regt. One squad on water duties, radio cart and supplies examined. Squad of temporary attached men engaged in Divisional fatigues at MERRIS under supervision of NCO of section. One NCO at Divisional Laundry. One man making notices for water supplies. Twenty temporary attached returned to units on investigation from 19HQ. Canteen cart hired for sanitary duties. Medical check as compiled. The following units of Division inspected:- Divisional Mounting Co. (numerous recent vacancies), 94th Field Co R.E. H.Q. and H and D Co's 7th Royal North Lancashire Regt. H.Q. and C and D Co's 7th South Lancashire Regt. Supplying Point No.2 Co ASC. 5th South Wales Borders Regt and Divisional Trains. MM	
MERRIS	30th Sept		M.O. inspected Pioneers and H.Q. details of 6th Wiltshire Regt. Investigated case of Diphtheria - Pte Bailey, 16 Co 7th South Lancashire Regt - and arranged as to precautions to be taken. Investigated case of suspected Diphtheria -	

WAR DIARY
INTELLIGENCE SUMMARY
(Erase heading not required.)

Army Form C. 2118.

Place	Date	Hour	Summary of Events and Information	Remarks and references to Appendices
			Pte Lathom B Co. 7" King's Own Royal Lancasters Regt and another as I/c Pioneers to be taken. Inspected Hut Camp ASC at STRAZEELE, also carriahn of YMCA Hut and Divisional Baths. Rumours among Jews civilians at STRAZEELE in reference to what the Maire had been informed since unmasked. The following units of Division inspected — 10" Royal Manchester Regt; 57" Brigade Machine Gun Corps, (3 hrs.) 7" Royal North Lancashire Regt: 9 MMLt Regt and Nº 2, 3 and 4 & 6" Divisional Train. Nr NCO at Divisional Laundry Square of temporary character men engaged in sanitary fatigues at MERRIS work supervised. Civilian cart hired for carting away refuse to incinerator. One man making notices for water supplies, water cart and supplies tested.	

G. N. Anderson
Capt/R

140/1911

1st Div

S

No. 36. Sanitary Section.

Ork 1946

COMMITTEE FOR THE
MEDICAL HISTORY OF THE WAR
Date −9 DEC. 1916

Army Form C. 2118.

WAR DIARY
or
INTELLIGENCE SUMMARY
(Erase heading not required.)

War Diary

19th Divisional Sanitary Section — 36th Sanitary

from 1st to 31st October 1916.

Vol 16

Place	Date	Hour	Summary of Events and Information	Remarks and references to Appendices

WAR DIARY
INTELLIGENCE SUMMARY

Army Form C. 2118.

Place	Date	Hour	Summary of Events and Information	Remarks and references to Appendices
MERRIS	1st Oct		The following Units of Division inspected as to sanitary arrangements - No 4 Co Divisional Train, 57 Brigade H.Q., Refilling Point No 4 Group, Depot of 9th Royal Welch Fusiliers Regt, 58 Trench Mortar Battery and 58th Brigade H.Q. Water supplies in area tested and labelled; water cart examined and samples taken. One man making notice for water supplies. One N.C.O. at Divisional Laundry, Squad of Temporary attached men engaged on sanitary duties in MERRIS. Civilian cart hired for removal of refuse. E.O. been formed for purpose of fitting all ranks with new box respirators, all ranks fitted and drilled with new respirator.	
MERRIS	2nd Oct		E.O. made arrangements for switching Diphtheria contacts in the 7th South Lancashire Regt; also arranges for meat and new area. Weekly sanitary	

WAR DIARY
or
INTELLIGENCE SUMMARY

Place	Date	Hour	Summary of Events and Information	Remarks and references to Appendices
			report prepared. 2nd Ambulance attached to lectun previous to workshop for repair. The following Units of Division inspected - 8th North Staffordshire Regt. 9th Royal Welch Fusiliers Regt. 58th Brigade Machine Gun Corps, 7th South Lancashire Regt. 81st Field Co. R.E., 5th South Wales Borderers Regt. and No. 3 Co. Divisional Train. Water supplies in Divisional area visited and tested; water carts tested. One NCO at Divisional Laundry. Squad of temporary attached men under the supervision of NCO of lectun, engaged in sanitary duties at MERRIS. Billets at 7th South Lancashire Regt. where Case of Diphtheria occurred - Pte Chamberlain) disinfected. The S.C.O. engaged in Section Areas recorded. Ma	
MERRIS	3rd Oct		S.C. attended men reporting sick from Divisional Headquarters Units Co. visited and inspected the contacts (Diphtheria) of Pte Bailey CCo. and Pte Chamberlain A Co. 7th South Lancashire Regt. - 46 contacts swabbed; also visited and inspected contacts of Pte Wolsenholme 4/7	

WAR DIARY
or
INTELLIGENCE SUMMARY

(Erase heading not required.)

Army Form C. 2118.

Place	Date	Hour	Summary of Events and Information	Remarks and references to Appendices
			King's Own Royal Lancaster Regt – 25 contacts swabbed. Further arrangements made for men nots new area. The NCO engaged on Infection Scheme visits etc. One NCO at Divisional Laundry. Water Supplies in area tested; samples taken from Water Carts of Units and teams. Squad of temporary attached men engaged on sanitary duties at MERRIS – with supervisor. Civilian cart hired for carting away refuse. The following Units of Division inspected – 6" Wiltshire Regt, 8" Lincolnshire Regt, 57 Brigade Machine Gun Coys, 7" East Lancashire Regt and No 2 & 6 Divisional Train.	
MERRIS	4 Oct		M.O. attended sick reporting sick from Divisional Headquarters Units. Arrangements made for proposed move. Squad of temporary attached men engaged on sanitary fatigues at MERRIS under supervision of NCO of Section. One NCO at Divisional Laundry. Party of from	

Army Form C. 2118.

WAR DIARY
or
INTELLIGENCE SUMMARY
(Erase heading not required.)

Instructions regarding War Diaries and Intelligence Summaries are contained in F. S. Regs., Part II. and the Staff Manual respectively. Title Pages will be prepared in manuscript.

Place	Date	Hour	Summary of Events and Information	Remarks and references to Appendices
			entrained and proceeded to new area. The squad on route there. The following Units of Division inspected :- 10th Manchester Regt, 57 Brigade Machine Gun Coy. No. 2, 6th Divisional Train, 5th South Wales Borders Regt and 9th Cheshire, 56th Brigade Machine Gun Coy, 56th Brigade Trench Mortar Battery, 7th South Lancashire Regt, 7th Royal North Lancashire Regt and 7th East Lancashire Regt.	
MERRIS	5th Oct		G.O. allotted new sleeping accn from Divisional Headquarters Units. Routine Office work. Two sanitary inspectors instructing units reference sanitation on arrival in new area. The units inspection immediately supplies in new area. Squad of temporary attached men cleaning up MERRIS and billets hired before leaving. Men of techn. together with temporary attached men and detail from Divisional Baths and Laundry marched to BAILLEUL station for entrainment. Motor Lorry transports proceeded to new area.	M.O.

Place	Date	Hour	Summary of Events and Information	Remarks and references to Appendices
MARIEUX		11 OCT	Section lorry with stores and equipment proceeded from MERRIS to MARIEUX. Men of Section together with transport attached men and Divisional Baths and Laundry details entrained at BAILLEUL Station at 4-20 am — detrained at DOULLENS Station 1 PM next day and marched to billets at MARIEUX. Two inspection visited camps vacated in last area by following units. Head Quarters 57 Infantry Brigade, Headquarters. A B D Cos and Machine Gun Section of 8 North Staffordshire Regt, HQ. A.C.D. Co Machine Gun Section and transport of 10th Royal Warwickshire Regt. 57 Brigade Machine Gun Corps. 9th Field Co R.E., HQ. A.B.C.+ D Co Machine Gun Section. 8th Worcestershire Regt. 10th Worcestershire Regt. 82nd Field Co. R.E. 6th Wrexham Regt 9 Royal Welch Fusilier Regt 9th Cheshire Regt 9 Welsh Regt. Water supplies were [?] visited on arrival in new area as to sanitary arrangements. [signature]	
MARIEUX AUTHIE		7 OCT	Section motor lorry with stores and equipment proceeded from MARIEUX to	

WAR DIARY
or
INTELLIGENCE SUMMARY

(Erase heading not required.)

Army Form C. 2118.

Place	Date	Hour	Summary of Events and Information	Remarks and references to Appendices
AUTHIE			AUTHIE. Men of Section Supplies with temporary attached men and Divisional Baths and Laundry details marched from MARIEUX to AUTHIE. On arrival Billets cleaned and put in sanitary condition. Billets of Headquarters Units noted reference sanitary arrangements. Water supplies in Divisional area noted. Noted and labelled. EMO.	
AUTHIE	8th Oct		Water Supplies in Divisional area tested and labelled. Temporary attached men classified as T.U. attended for examination by A.D.M.S. C.O. attended men reporting sick from Divisional Headquarters. August 60. C.O. inspected new area visiting COUIN. COIGNEUX. ROSSIGNOL FARM. SAILLY-AU-BOIS, and HEBUTERNE. Blankets from 57 Field Ambulance disinfected. Temporary attached men engaged in sanitary fatigue at AUTHIE. Section lorry proceeded to workshop for repair. EMO	

WAR DIARY
or
INTELLIGENCE SUMMARY

(Erase heading not required.)

Army Form C. 2118.

Place	Date	Hour	Summary of Events and Information	Remarks and references to Appendices
AUTHIE	9 Oct		C.O. inspected sanitary arrangements at AUTHIE. C.O. moved SAILLY-au-BOIS SAILLY and COUVIN. C.O. attended men returning sick from Headquarters. Report by Sergeant of temporary attached men under supervision of N.C.O. of section erected latrines at Divisional Headquarters. These battle latrines emptied and cleaned. Two public latrines in course of construction; refuse collected and incinerated. The following units inspected as to sanitary arrangements - 58th Brigade H.Q., 9 Royal Welsh Fusiliers Regt., A.B.C. and D Batteries 87th Brigade R.F.A., A.B.C. and D Batteries 88 Brigade R.F.A. 8th North Staffordshire Regt. (A+D Companies transport) 5th Brigade H.Q. and 7 Loyal North Lancashire Regt. Blankets from 37 Field Ambulance disinfected. Water supplies in Divisional area noted. Latrines and urinals latrines. Enquiries made as to sources of contamination of AUTHIE - ST LEGER - COIGNEUX stream.	

WAR DIARY
or
INTELLIGENCE SUMMARY
(Erase heading not required.)

Army Form C. 2118.

Place	Date	Hour	Summary of Events and Information	Remarks and references to Appendices
AUTHIE	10th Oct		G.O. inspected 1st Co ADC Mess, A and Q Office, Advance GS Scheme, Divisional Headquarters Transport Lignes, Divisional Band and Public Latrine at AUTHIE. The following Units of Division inspected as to sanitary arrangements:— Transport of 7th Royal North Lancashire Regt.; 7th King's Own Royal Lancaster Regt. 10th Hampshire Regt. 5/7th Brigade Transport. No.1 H.Q. Guards ADC (refilling point) "B" and "D" Batteries 8th Brigade R.F.A. HQ 87 Brigade R.F.A. Transport of 9th Welch Regt. Transport of 9th Royal Welch Fusiliers Regt. Transport and Depôt of Cheshire Regt. and Transport of Machine Gun Regt. Fatigue squad of temporary attached men engaged in sanitary fatigue as ordered. Water supplies in Divisional Area worked. Tested and quality tabled. List of water supplies in Divisional Area prepared and forwarded to all R.M.O. (copy attached). Two carpenters engaged in construction of latrines.	

Army Form C. 2118.

WAR DIARY
or
INTELLIGENCE SUMMARY
(Erase heading not required.)

Instructions regarding War Diaries and Intelligence Summaries are contained in F. S. Regs., Part II. and the Staff Manual respectively. Title Pages will be prepared in manuscript.

Place	Date	Hour	Summary of Events and Information	Remarks and references to Appendices
AUTHIE	11th Oct		C.O. made arrangements for sanitation of COIGNEUX and interviewed Town Mayor. C.O. attended conference called by A.D.M.S. of Medical Officers at 59th Field Ambulance, COIGNEUX. Note supplies in Divisional area medical and sanitary labelled. Inspection engaged in constructing sanitary appliances. Squad of temporary attached men under supervision of N.C.O. of Section engaged in sanitary fatigue at AUTHIE. Signallers made "walking wounded" prepare for arms. The following Units of Division inspected as to sanitary arrangements :- No. 1, 2, 3 and 4 Sections of Divisional Ammunition Column. 7 East Lancashire Regt. and Transport. 6 Wiltshire Regt. 58th Brigade Machine Gun Corps. 8 Gloucestershire Regt. and Transport. Billets and clothing disinfected by Foden Disinfector. [signed] Ginn	
AUTHIE	12th Oct		C.O. proceeded to SAILLY-au-BOIS and examined water supply area arranged for supply of wash buquet. C.O. proceeded to COIGNEUX reference Disinfector contract at 7 South Lancashire Regt. Are N.C.O. not	

WAR DIARY
INTELLIGENCE SUMMARY
(Erase heading not required.)

Army Form C. 2118.

Place	Date	Hour	Summary of Events and Information	Remarks and references to Appendices

Divisional Laundry and Baths. Sgm. Brooks "Walking Wounded" prepared for A&SMS. M96 from gallon picket line delivered at trench for distribution. Squad engaged in this work. Bath supplies in area noted and suitably labelled. Squad 1 Carpenters preparing sanitary structures etc. Rocket manufacturing disinfectors by John Shreek Disinfectors. Squad 1/2 temporary attached men engaged in sanitary fatigue at AUTHIE under supervision of NCO of Section. The following units 1/Durham inspected: 1st Frocadie Regt and transport, 1st 2 and 4 Rifling Points, 9 Royal Welch Fusilier Regt. Transport and depot of Cheshire Regt. Machine of 88th Brigade R.F.A. also 4 Battery Machine Machine of 88 Brigade R.F.A. 1 Lan Lancashire Regt and transport 1/7 Royal North Lancashire Regt. Shared of one NCO and nine men (temporary attached) placed at CONNEOX Bath Supply, and guard of 4 men at SAILLY Bath Supply.

MCA.

WAR DIARY
INTELLIGENCE SUMMARY

Army Form C. 2118.

Place	Date	Hour	Summary of Events and Information	Remarks and references to Appendices
AUTHIE	13th Oct.		G.O.C. awaited to Definition contacts at 7' South Lancashire Regt. H.Q. Inspected 57th, 58th and R.A. Headquarters. 7' East Lancashire Regt. 7' South Lancashire Regt and 7' Royal North Lancashire Regt. Dre agreed starting point him for 55' Brigade H.Q. 500 hrs allowed for water storage purposes. Notices "Nothing Normal" prepared for A.D.M.S. Carpenter engaged in meeting sanitary structure. One N.C.O and Divisional Bath Laundry. Infection Chacen chart prepared. Bath personnel from W. Brigade Manchester Regt. instructed in duties. Wash supplies in area noted and tested. Against of Company attacked men engaged in sanitary duties at AUTHIE. The following Units of Division inspected — A B C and D functions of 88th Brigade R.F.A., Transport and Officer of 9' Welch Regt. Transport of 9' Royal Welch Fusiliers Regt, 6th Wiltshire Regt and transport, 57' Brigade H.Q. 57' Brigade Machine Gun Corps, 57' Trench Mortar Battery, + 19' Divisional Train.	

Army Form C. 2118.

WAR DIARY
or
INTELLIGENCE SUMMARY

(Erase heading not required.)

Instructions regarding War Diaries and Intelligence Summaries are contained in F. S. Regs., Part II. and the Staff Manual respectively. Title Pages will be prepared in manuscript.

Place	Date	Hour	Summary of Events and Information	Remarks and references to Appendices
AUTHIE	14th Oct.		Batn personnel of 10th Royal Warwickshire Regt instructed in various Notices "walking wounded" attended to 59 Field Ambulance. The squad completed instruction of petrol tin in water storage purposes. Squad of Carpenters engaged in construction country appliances. Squad of temporary attached men under supervision of NCO of Section engaged in sanitary purposes at AUTHIE. Several manufacturing disinfectors by Justin Aronfrecta. The NCO and Personnel Laundry. One squad on trolls duties. Two temporarily attached men at Central Marine Dept. COIGNEUX. The following Men of Divisn inspected - Headqrs of A B C and D Batteries of 87th Brigade R.F.A., 9th Lncs & 6th R.E., 9th Cheshire Regt, 58th Machine Gun Corps, 87th Field Co R.E., Transport of 88th Brigade HQ, Transport of 87th Brigade HQ, Machine Gun Corps.	
AUTHIE	15 Oct.		M.O. visited 88th Brigade H.Q. Inspected water points at SAILLY-au-BOIS and supervised filling of petrol tins at SAILLY. Inspected	

WAR DIARY
or
INTELLIGENCE SUMMARY

(Erase heading not required.)

Army Form C. 2118.

Place	Date	Hour	Summary of Events and Information	Remarks and references to Appendices
			Held guards at COIGNEUX and ROSSIGNOL QUARRIES; interviewed M.O. 7 Lancashire Regt regarding diphtheria outbreak and arranged for re-swabbing. Proceeded to BERTRANCOURT to interview O.C. wash parties. One squad firing petrol tins with chloride of lime at SAILLY. One squad of personnel attached men, under supervision of NCO of Section, engaged in sanitary fatigues at AUTHIE. One ICC with Divisional Laundry. Struck of personnel attached men at SAILLY and COIGNEUX water supplies. Two men at manure dump COIGNEUX. Orderly manceuvring disinfected in Sodium Lorry Disinfector. Carpenter engaged in making sanitary appliances. Inspection and other sickness in division received. MRC	
AUTHIE	1st Oct		I.O. proceeded to MARIEUX and reported to ADMS 37th Division. Proceeded to	

WAR DIARY
or
INTELLIGENCE SUMMARY

Army Form C. 2118.

Place	Date	Hour	Summary of Events and Information	Remarks and references to Appendices
AUTHIE ROSSIGNOL	17th Oct		TERRA MESNIL and saw Sanitary Officer 31st Division, accompanied Sanitary Officer to AUTHIE and explained sanitary measures in present area. Proceeded to COIGNEUX and arranged to distribute contacts in 7/South Lancashire Regt. One squad engaged filling pitons cans with chloronated water at SAILLY water supply. Three of temporarily attached men at SAILLY and COIGNEUX water supplies. Two men at manure dumps COIGNEUX. One squad of temporarily attached men engaged in sanitary fatigues at AUTHIE under supervision of NCO of section. One NCO at Divisional Laundry, Poste Leng Disinfector disinfecting soiled underclothing. Inspected Bureaus and other sickness in Division visited.	
			C.O. proceeded with Sanitary Officer 31st Division to visit stations at SAILLY and COIGNEUX and arranged for taking over posts. Guards at their stations relieved and marched to new billets at ROSSIGNOL. C.O. handed over details and instructions regarding sanitation of area to Sanitary Officer 31st Division. Men of Section together with temporarily attached men and	

WAR DIARY
INTELLIGENCE SUMMARY

Details of Divisional Baths and Laundry marched to new billets at RUBEMPRE. Section stores and equipment removed in lorry to new billet. Guard at COIGNEUX means dump relieved. Two men as guard over petrol cans at SAILLY. Bath Station and supplies in new area worked and test prepared and forwarded to D.R.M.O. (copy attached). The following units moved:- 7" East Lancashire Regt, 7" North Lancashire Regt, 7" Kings Own Royal Lancaster Regt, 58 Brigade Machine Gun Corps and transport, 7" Loyal North Lancashire Regt, Transport, 58 Brigade HQ, 58 Brigade HQ, 57 Brigade MG 55 Brigade Machine Gun Corps, 58 Trench Mortar Battery, 10" Royal Warwickshire Regt, 10" Worcester Regt, 8 North Staffordshire Regt, 8" Gloucestershire Regt, 9 Welch Regt, 9 Royal Welsh Fusiliers Regt, 9" Cheshire Regt, 58 Brigade Machine Gun Corps, 8", 9" and 94" Field Cos R.E., A.B and D Batteries and HQ of 81" Brigade R.F.A., ABC and D Batteries HQ. 87 Brigade R.F.A., ABC and D Batteries 79 88 Brigade R.F.A., HQ and 1st, 2, 3 and 4 Columns, Divisional Ammunition Column.

Army Form C. 2118.

WAR DIARY
or
INTELLIGENCE SUMMARY
(Erase heading not required.)

Place	Date	Hour	Summary of Events and Information	Remarks and references to Appendices
RUBEMPRÉ	18th Oct.		O.C. visited AVELUY and examined main dump at CRUCIFIX CORNER and arranged for storage of petrol him at this point. Visited bath site at AVELUY and visited BOUZINCOURT to ascertain facilities for bathing. One squad of temporary attached men engaged in cleaning up technical stores and erecting sanitary appliances. One squad of temporary attached men engaged in sanitary fatigues at RUBEMPRÉ. 1196 petrol cans for storing water transferred from SAILLY-au-BOIS and dumped at supply dump.	m.a.
RUBEMPRÉ	19th Oct.		O.C. proceeded to WARLOY and arranged as to dump. On instructions from A.D.M.S. from Army Divisional proceeded to 137" Field Ambulance for temporary duty. Fatigue party of four temporary attached men accompanied Divisional Section lorry transported part of equipment and other to new level at WARLOY. Men of Section and temporary attached men paraded and men to march to new area when orders received.	

WAR DIARY
INTELLIGENCE SUMMARY
(Erase heading not required.)

Army Form C. 2118.

Place	Date	Hour	Summary of Events and Information	Remarks and references to Appendices
			Concluding move. Company attached men inspected as to sanitary condition and engaged in sanitary fatigues at RUBEMPRE under supervision of N.C.O. of R.A.M.C.	G.M.C.
RUBEMPRE	20th Oct		The following units of Division inspected as to sanitary condition and arrangements:— H.Q. 55th Infantry Brigade. 55th Brigade Machine Gun Corps. 7 Royal North Lancashire Regt. 7th East Lancashire Regt. 87th Field Co. R.E. 7th King's Own Royal Lancaster Regt. H.Q. 57th Infantry Brigade. 8th Gloucester Regt. 10th Worcestershire Regt. 10th Royal Warwickshire Regt. 8th North Staffordshire Regt. 82nd Field Co. R.E. Transport of 6th Wiltshire Regt. Transport of 55th Brigade Machine Gun Corps. 58th Infantry Brigade H.Q. Transport of 9th Welch Regt and A.B.C+D Cos + 5 Sub Males Brown Regt. A/part of Company attached men engaged in sanitary fatigue at RUBEMPRE under supervision of N.C.O of	

WAR DIARY
INTELLIGENCE SUMMARY

Army Form C. 2118.

Place	Date	Hour	Summary of Events and Information	Remarks and references to Appendices
			Section One N.C.O. at Divisional Laundry. Bath Supplies on arrival RUBEMPRE tested and output taken. Expedition Divisional Baths ordered arranged.	
RUBEMPRE to MARLOY	19/4/17		Section Lorry with stores and equipment proceeded from RUBEMPRE to MARLOY. Men of Section together with personnel attached men and details of Divisional Baths and Laundry marched to new billets at MARLOY. On arrival sanitary arrangements attended to and billets generally cleaned up. Bath Supplies in Headquarters Area tested. The following Units of Division inspected as to sanitary arrangements:- 57' Infantry Brigade H.Q. 9th Worcestershire Regt. 8th North Staffordshire Regt. 10th Manchester Regt. 10th Royal Manchester Regt. No.3 A.T.C. P2 Trench Mortar Battery, 5th Trench Mortar Battery, St Machine Gun Corps, 87th Field Co R.E., 7 East Lancashire Regt., 7 Royal Scots.	

WAR DIARY
INTELLIGENCE SUMMARY
(Erase heading not required.)

Army Form C. 2118.

Place	Date	Hour	Summary of Events and Information	Remarks and references to Appendices
			Lancashire Regt; 7" Kings Own Royal Lancaster Regt; 6"N.Lancs Regt transport and A and D Co. 58¹ Machine Gun transport; 9" W.Yks Regt transport and A, B, C and D Co. 58 Infantry Brigade HQ. A and C Co 9" Cheshire Regt. hrs.	
WARLOY	22ⁿᵈ Oct.		I.O. proceeded to BOVES and arranged as to washing and repairing of underclothing by civilians; arrangement made as to move. On instruction from RSMR arrangement made for inspecting and taking water outfits in the Divisional area. two N. COs sent forward to investigate. 1013 Infant hro (Stinlage) transferred from ASC Dumb to CRUCIFIX CORNER by lechris lorry and guard of this temporary attached men placed over him. Fatigue squads of temporary attached men engaged in ordinary fatigue at WARLOY under supervision of NCO of Section. T.U. men attended ADMS for fortnights examination.	hrs.

WAR DIARY
INTELLIGENCE SUMMARY

Army Form C. 2118.

Place	Date	Hour	Summary of Events and Information	Remarks and references to Appendices
WARLOY and W14.b.9.7 (Sheet 57D)	23rd Oct		Section lorry with pack of stores and equipment proceeded to camp at W14.b.9.7 (Sheet 57D). Men of Section together with Lieutenant attached men marched from WARLOY to new area. BHQ camp inspected as to sanitary and water arrangements. Fatigue squad of temporary attached men building incinerators at SHR. centre. Two men as guard on the water dumps at CRUCIFIX CORNER. Water supplies in forward area investigated, water supplies when on the duty accounted and commenced to C.C.S. when dealt occurred. Section lorry transported marquees to from Second Army Corps at CLAIRFAYE to 38 Field Ambulance. [signed]	
W14.b.9.7 (Sheet 57D)	24th Oct	6.0	O marched CRUCIFIX CORNER and inspected several dugouts in view to see whether they would be suitable for dugouts room and observed quarters with D.A.D.M.S. Two dugouts attached and selection suggested at interview with Town Major of AVELUY. Placed on patrol two containing chlorinated water inspected and further ground placed at water supply CRUCIFIX CORNER	

WAR DIARY
INTELLIGENCE SUMMARY
(Erase heading not required.)

Army Form C. 2118.

Place	Date	Hour	Summary of Events and Information	Remarks and references to Appendices
W 14 6-9-7 (Sheet 57 D)	23rd Oct		CO superintended erection of new latrines at DHQ Camp and arranged for storage of water. Making of portable water testing case demonstrated to MOs of Welch Regt. Water supplies inspected and tested. Squads of Company attached men engaged in sanitary fatigue under supervision of CO of Section. Sanitary inspections made 1 of Welch Regt and Transport, 9' Cheshire Regt and Transport and DHQ work. Section Lorry proceeded to SENLIS and VARENNES and transported two "59" Field Ambulances.	
		16.0	CO proceeded to AVELUY to select suitable site for bathi-house and also for Baths ovens and canteens at interview with Town Major of AVELUY when also the question of erecting Drying Rooms was discussed. Section Lorry proceeded to VARENNES and transported two 1/59' Field Ambulances. Squads of temporary attached men engaged on sanitary fatigues. Captain [?] temporary attached erecting latrines at DHQ camp. Guard at CRUCIFIX CORNER baths deeply and Dump. 6t Wiltshire Regt and Hampshire Yeth inspected as to sanitary arrangement. Water supplies tested and currently labelled. One of CO proceeded to BOUES work carried immediately for Section to [?] Guard at Section dump NAB LOY.	

WAR DIARY
or
INTELLIGENCE SUMMARY

(Erase heading not required.)

Army Form C. 2118.

Instructions regarding War Diaries and Intelligence Summaries are contained in F. S. Regs., Part II. and the Staff Manual respectively. Title Pages will be prepared in manuscript.

Place	Date	Hour	Summary of Events and Information	Remarks and references to Appendices
W.14.b.9-7 (Sheet 57D)	26th Oct		C.O. made arrangements with 2d ARMY for erection of baths at AVELUY; proceeded to WARLOY and arranged for removal of baths and stoves to new site at AVELUY. Proceeded to AVELUY and superintended erection of bath. Interviewed Town Major of AVELUY reference Drying Room at CRUCIFIX CORNER; arranged with Camp Commandant to take over works arrangements for 29th Div. Camp; engineer made reference cards of Workshops at 9th Royal W. Kent Regt. Approx 1 ten men including four carpenters engaged in erection of baths at AVELUY. Six squads of temporary attached men engaged in sanitary fatigue at 29th Div. Camp. Three of the temporarily attached men at CRUCIFIX CORNER Baths supply and Water Camp Water Supplies tested. 9th Cheshire Regt and 5th Brigade Transport inspected as to sanitary arrangements. Infectious Diseases and other accidents in Division reported. Return dealing with 2 men prosecuted to BEAUVAL and expected clean underclothing.	m.a.
W.14.b.9-7 (Sheet 57D)	27th Oct		9th Cheshire Regt and Transport, 9th Welch Regt and Transport inspected as to Sanitary arrangements. Water Supplies tested. Arrival of three men	

2449 Wt. W14957/M90 750,000 1/16 J.B.C. & A. Forms/C.2118/12.

WAR DIARY
or
INTELLIGENCE SUMMARY
(Erase heading not required.)

Army Form C. 2118.

Place	Date	Hour	Summary of Events and Information	Remarks and references to Appendices
			Ordinarily attached at CRUCIFIX CORNER Water Supply and Water Dumps. Squads of temporary attached men engaged in sanitary fatigues at 28th Camp. Our Carpenter erecting latrines. 3 Carpenters and 1 Sergeant & attached men engaged in erection of Drying Room and Spray Baths. One NCO proceeded to BOVES and sorted underclothing for distribution among civilian washerwomen. Section lorry proceeded to TYPE PRESS for surveying. Two men as dump at WARLOY. CO proceeded to AVELUY reference Baths and CRUCIFIX CORNER to inspect Drying Rooms, on arrival found dugouts occupied by Carrying Party of 56th Infantry Brigade, discovered that four dugouts had been allotted in error to the Divisions and interviewed Town Major and matter rectified. J.M.B.	
W.14.b.9.7 (Sheet 57D)	J.8.10.17		H.Q made arrangements for the erection of Dugouts as CRUCIFIX CORNER by 56th Brigade Carrying Party at noon today. Proceeded to AVELUY and arranged with O.T Baths for the carrying out of washing of soiled under-clothing from the Baths. Proceeded to DOULLENS to 17th Mobile Laboratory to obtain necessary re agents for fitting up of Special Divisional Bath Case, also	

WAR DIARY
or
INTELLIGENCE SUMMARY
(Erase heading not required.)

Army Form C. 2118.

Place	Date	Hour	Summary of Events and Information	Remarks and references to Appendices
			materials for the fitting up of 1 Drying Room. Prepared monthly sanitary report. Lectern lorry returned from Type Press. Lorry proceeded to MARLOY and Lectern surplus stores dumped at 19th Div. DADOS Store. On instruction from DHQ fatigue squad of four temporarily attached men proceeded to CRUCIFIX CORNER to unload lorry with permit him for water storage. Squad of four carpenters and attached men preparing dugouts as Drying Rooms. Stood of three men at CRUCIFIX CORNER Water Supply and Dumps. Stand at Lectern stores MARLOY. Inspection progress and other stores in Division visited. The squad of Water stores squad of temporary attached men made experiment of NCO & Lectern engaged in sanitary fatigues at DHQ Camp.	
W 14.4.97 (Sheet 5A)	29	10¢t	C.O. proceeded to AVELUY and superintended as to fitting out of Drying Rooms at CRUCIFIX CORNER. Squad of three carpenters and temporary attached men fitting up Drying Room. Squad of three temporary	

WAR DIARY
INTELLIGENCE SUMMARY
(Erase heading not required.)

Army Form C. 2118.

Place	Date	Hour	Summary of Events and Information	Remarks and references to Appendices
W 11. c 9.7 (Sheet 5)D	30th Oct		attached men at CRUCIFIX CORNER Water Supply. Two men as guard at Sechris Dump MARLOY. One man as guard at Divisional Bomb Store. Squads of temporary attached men engaged in sanitary fatigue at 194.8. temp water supply in [?] of section. Water supplies in area tested. Infection diseases and other sickness in Division recorded.	L.M.C.
			C.O. proceeded to AVELUY and inspected premises to be utilised as additional Divisional Rest and ascertain how much material was required for fitting up baths. Interviewed the Baths and informed him that water supply prospects was coming from WARLOY to AVELUY today. Proceeded to AMIENS and made sundry purchases in connection with Drying Room Section. Lorry proceeded to AMIENS and transport shin before to Drying Room. Saw L.C.O. of section. 3 carpenters and guard of temporary attached men engaged in preparing dugouts as Drying Room. Squad of men preparing oil drums as stoves for Drying Room. Water supplies in Divisional area tested and results tabulated. Squads of temporary attached men	

WAR DIARY
INTELLIGENCE SUMMARY
(Erase heading not required.)

Army Form C. 2118.

Place	Date	Hour	Summary of Events and Information	Remarks and references to Appendices
W14 6-9-7 (SW 57D)	31st Oct.		under supervision of NCO of techm engaged in sanitary fatigue at BHQ camp. One man as guard at Point Wire. Two men as guard at techm. Bomb. Three men as guard at CRUCIFIX CORNER latrine supply. Syphon Bracers and other latrines at Dunaven recruit. One carpenter and squad of attached men marking sanitary appliances. One NCO as Dunaven Kennion. [signature] The following Units employed as sanitary arrangement. HQ RA. RFA. Signal Co. Ironsby Working Party and BHQ Units. Latrine erected by attached men and carpenter near BHQ camp. One attached man attending incinerator. Squad of attached men under supervision of NCO of techm engaged in sanitary fatigue at BHQ camp. Three men as guard at CRUCIFIX CORNER latrine supply. Two men as guard at Dunaven Bomb Wire. Two men at techm dump MATLOV. techm lorry transported material for Dunaven Dugong Room. One NCO of techm attached squad and carpenter engaged in preparing dugouts as Drying Room. Squad of attached men preparing further side for baths. One NCO with	

WAR DIARY
-or-
INTELLIGENCE SUMMARY
(Erase heading not required.)

Army Form C. 2118.

Place	Date	Hour	Summary of Events and Information	Remarks and references to Appendices
			Personal Laundry. Water Supplies in area tested and critically inspected. Supplementary list of Water Supplies forwarded to all R.M.O. (copy attached) (C.O. made inspection of DHQ Camp and also camp of attached Laundry Working Party; proceeded to AVELUY and inspected Divisional Drying Rooms at CRUCIFIX CORNER and made arrangements for opening them on the 1st November; arranged with O/c Baths to supply Personnel, visited new Baths and Rest Room and arranged for necessary material for completion of new Room.	

G.N. Anderson, Capt. / S.M.O.

Supplementary List of Water Supplies
in 19th Divisional Area.

Map Reference (Sheet 57 D)	Description	Treatment
W 11 d 9.2.	CRUCIFIX Cnr. Water Station. 3. Stand Pipes	1 Scoop.
W 5 c 3.8.	AVELUY WOOD 5 Roadside Pipes	1 Scoop.
W 18 b 1.7.	OVILLERS POST. 2 Roadside tanks.	1 Scoop.
W 18 b 3.6.	do. Pipe fitted with 21 small Taps.	1 Scoop.
W 7 c central	Old Reserve Trench opposite DONNET ROAD. 4 Tanks fitted with 8 Taps.	1 Scoop.
X 1 b 7.7.	Tank near roadway. fitted with 4 Taps.	1 Scoop.
X 7 a central	Pipe near roadway, fitted with 2 small Taps	2 Scoops.
X 8 c 2.6.	8 Roadside Tanks S.W. of OVILLERS.	1 Scoop.
X 8 b 1.5.	Bennett St. OVILLERS. Tanks fitted with 6 Taps.	1 Scoop.
X 1 c 8.8.	WOOD POST. Tank fitted with 2 Taps.	1 Scoop.
R 33 c 6.4.	Tank fitted with 4 Taps & Hose for Water Carts	1 Scoop.
R 32 b 6.8.	Pipe fitted with 20 small Taps.	1 Scoop.

Note:- Owing to the difference in the strength of the Chloride of Lime supplied to Units, the above figures for Chlorination are only suggestive. Standards should be re-adjusted with the sample of Lime to be used.

G. N. Andrews. Capt. RAMC.
O.C. 19th Divn Sanitary Section.

31.10.1916.

List of Water Supplies in Rubempre and Neighbourhood.

No	Source of Supply and Locality.	Treatment
(1)	Rubempre. Piped Supply in Villers Bocage Rd.	1. Scoop
(2)	" Communal Well in Main Rd. S.E. of Village	1½ Scoop
(3)	LOUVENCOURT. Stand Pipe in main Rd. Next to Church. Army Hut.	1. Scoop
(4)	VAUCHELLES-les-AUTHIE. Nearest Water Station LOUVENCOURT.	1. Scoop
(5)	HARPONVILLE. Water Station at U5C8.8.	1. Scoop
(6)	" Communal Well Opposite Billet 62	1. Scoop
(7)	" Well No. 5 Near Canteen. (For Cooking Purposes)	2. Scoop
(8)	TOUTENCOURT. Water Station in Rue Haute du Mont Renard.	1. Scoop
(9)	" Communal Well in Rue Harponville.	1. Scoop
(10)	HÉRISSART. Piped Supply, in Church St.	1. Scoop
(11)	BÉHENCOURT. Running Stream (after Clarification)	1. Scoop
(12)	ST. GRATIEN. Water Station in main Rd. South of Village.	1. Scoop
(13)	MONTIGNY. Communal Pump in Church Square.	1. Scoop
(14)	" Running Stream. (After Clarification)	1. Scoop
(15)	BAIZIEUX. Water Station, at School, York St.	1. Scoop
(16)	CONTAY. Running Stream (after Clarification)	1. Scoop
(17)	MOLLIEN-au-BOIS. Water Station in Wick Rd.	1. Scoop
(18)	MIRVAUX. Communal Well, Opposite "Café de la Place".	1. Scoop
(19)	" Water Station. Near Church	1½ Scoop
(20)	PIERREGOT. Water Station in Shuttle Lane.	1½ Scoop
(21)	VILLERS-BOCAGE. Water Station at Gendarmerie.	1½ Scoop
(22)	" Communal Well in Argylle St.	2. Scoop
(23)	RAINNEVILLE. Water Station in Main Rd.	1. Scoop
(24)	FRANVILLERS. Piped Supply at Church.	2. Scoop
(25)	" Water Station between FRANVILLERS & HEILLY.	1. Scoop
(26)	HEILLY. Water Station in main Rd. Near Station Rd.	1. Scoop
(27)	VILLE-s-CORBIE. Water Station at X Roads ½ mile East of Village.	2. Scoop
(28)	" Pump in Jones. Yard. Queen St.	1. Scoop

29)	DERNANCOURT.	Running Stream (after Clarification)	1. Scoop.
30)	ALBERT	Water Station in Square.	1. Scoop.
31)	BOOZINCOURT.	Water Station in BOOZINCOURT – ALBERT RD.	1. Scoop.
32)	"	Communal Well in triangle.	2. Scoops.
33)	"	Piped Supply on bridge near Church.	2. Scoops.
33)	MARTINSART.	Water Station off Main Rd.	1. Scoop.
34)	MILLENCOURT.	Well at Church fitted with Horse Pump.	1. Scoop.
35)	AVELUY.	Well No. 3. at House next to Railway.	1. Scoop.
36)	LAVIEVILLE	Water Station in main Rd.	2. Scoops.
37)	"	Communal Well in main Rd.	1. Scoop.
38)	BRESLE.	WATER STATION.	2. Scoops.
39)	FRECHENCOURT.	Water Station near Chateau.	1. Scoop.
40)	HENENCOURT.	Water Station in Rd. next to Chateau.	1. Scoop.
41)	SENLIS.	Water Station in HENENCOURT RD.	1. Scoop.
42)	WARLOY BAILLON.	Water Station in Rue de la Croix.	1. Scoop.
43)	FRECHENCOURT.	Water Station in T Road at Railway.	1. Scoop.

NOTE :-

Owing to the difference in the strength of Chloride of Lime supplied to Units, and the variation in quality of small water supplies, from time to time, the above figures for chlorination are only suggestive. Standards should be re-adjusted with the sample of Lime to be used.

G. N. Anderson, Capt.
O.C. 19th Divisional Sanitary Section.

List of Main Water Supplies in 19th Divisional Area.

Water Stations.
(Map Sheet 57 D)

(1) AUTHIE I 10 c 5.5 Stand Pipe & Tank fed from Spring.   Treatment   1. Scoop

(2) COIGNEUX J 7 c 8.2. 4 Stand Pipes & Tanks.   Treatment   1. Scoop

(3) SAILLY-au-BOIS. J 16 c 8.3 4 Stand Pipes.   Treatment   1. Scoop

(4) I 17 c 84 2 Tanks and Standpipes   Treatment   1. Scoop

(5) I 23 c 8.8 Tanks near Y.M.C.A. Tent.   Treatment   1. Scoop

(6) HEBUTERN. Stand Pipes and Tanks.   Treatment   1. Scoop

(7) ROSSIGNOL FARM. WELL fitted with Windlass and Bucket.   Treatment   1. Scoop

Locality	Nearest Water Station	Emergency Supply
AUTHIE	No. 1 on List.	River AUTHIE
ST. LÉGER.	No. 2 " "	" "
COUIN.	No. 2 " "	" "
COIGNEUX.	No. 2 "	" "
ROSSIGNOL FARM.	No. 2 " "	" "
SAILLY-au-Bois.	No. 3 " "	
HEBUTERN.	No. 6 " "	

NOTE:—
M.O.s will take steps to prevent pollution of the River AUTHIE by men of their Unit, as it may be requisitioned for a water supply in case of emergency. Treatment, after passing through Clarifier of water cart 1. Scoop.

G. N. Anderson Capt.
O.C. 19th Divisional Sanitary Section

War Diary

No. 36 Sanitary Section
19th Divisional Sanitary Section

from 1st November to 30th Nov 1916

Vol 17

Army Form C. 2118.

WAR DIARY
or
INTELLIGENCE SUMMARY

(Erase heading not required.)

Instructions regarding War Diaries and Intelligence Summaries are contained in F. S. Regs., Part II. and the Staff Manual respectively. Title Pages will be prepared in manuscript.

Place	Date	Hour	Summary of Events and Information	Remarks and references to Appendices
W14 A.9.7 (Sheet 57 D) AVELUY	1st Novr		CO proceeded to AVELUY supervise Divisional Baths and Drying Room. CO inspected as to sanitary arrangements and accommodation the following units:- "A" "B" and "D" Batteries 85th Brigade RFA, A B C and D Batteries 87 Brigade RFA, A.B.C. and D. Batteries 88 Brigade R.F.A. and N.C.O. of Section attached carpenters and squad of temporary attached men engaged in adapting dugouts as Drying Rooms. One squad adapting NC dumps as stores for Drying Room. One carpenter and attached men making sanitary appliances. One squad of temporary attached men under supervision of N.C.O. of Section engaged in sanitary fatigues at 8th Camp, water supplies in Divisional area unchanged. Rested and suitably labelled. Two men preparing Water Notices. Three men as guard at Point One. Two men as guard at CRUCIFIX CORNER Water Supply. Two N.C.O.'s of Section with Divisional Sanitary Inspection Section and other sickness in Division received.	M.O.
IV14 A.9.7 (Sheet 57 D)	2nd Novr		CO proceeded to CRUCIFIX CORNER and inspected Drying Rooms and arranged for precautions to be taken against frostbite from stove. CO and squad of attached men posted for work in Drying Rooms. Two temporary attached men sent to	

WAR DIARY or **INTELLIGENCE SUMMARY**

Army Form C. 2118.

Place	Date	Hour	Summary of Events and Information	Remarks and references to Appendices
W14.b.9.7 (Sheet 57 D)	3" Nov.		Bull Dump. N.C.O. of section attached carpenters and signal of men engaged in anything urgent for Drying Room. The signal attaching stores. Squads of temporary attached men under supervision of N.C.O. of section engaged on sanitary fatigue at BHQ Camp. Three men as guard at CRUCIFIX CORNER Water Supply. Two men as section Camp and one man at Bomb Store. The men and carpenter making sanitary appliances. Water supplies in Divisional area investigated. Notes and exhibits labelled. Two men engaged in preparing notes. Infectious Diseases and their sickness in Divisional record. 56" and 57" Infantry Brigade Refilling Points inspected as to sanitary arrangements. N°1 and section Divisional Ammunition Column and R.A. HQ inspected as to sanitary arrangements. C.O. proceeded to Drying Rooms to view progress of work, also inspected designs for a further Drying Room; made arrangements for alteration in present Drying Room so as to accommodate more men and arranged for structures to be put up; arrangement made for further incising room to be erected in connection with new Drying Room.	

WAR DIARY
INTELLIGENCE SUMMARY
(Erase heading not required.)

Army Form C. 2118.

Place	Date	Hour	Summary of Events and Information	Remarks and references to Appendices

Arranged for bacteriological examination of wash cupps at CRUCIFIX CORNER. Interviewed OC Baths reference question as to laundry. The following Units inspected as to sanitary arrangements - No 2 and 4 Section of 19th Divisional Ammunition Column, No 1, 2, 3 and 4 Sections of 19th Divisional Train, Transports of 10th Royal Warwickshire Regt, 1st Gloucestershire Regt, 10th Worcestershire Regt and 8th North Staffordshire Regt. One M.G.O. Three carpenters and squad of attached men engaged in preparing dugouts as Drying Room. One squad working Drying Room. One squad adapting outdugouts for stoves. Three men as guard at CRUCIFIX CORNER baths supply. Two men at Section store and one man at Servt Stn. One man with Divisional Laundry. One carpenter and attached men preparing sanitary appliances. One man at bath supply LONE FARM. 1 squad of 1 temporary attached men engaged at sanitary fatigues at DHQ camp. Water supplies in Divisional area tested and outlets labelled. Two men preparing wash water. Cases of hyachism [?] Sources investigated and recorded. OC No 5 Mobile Hygiene Laboratory asked for chemical and bacteriological work on water at CRUCIFIX CORNER.

Army Form C. 2118.

WAR DIARY
or
INTELLIGENCE SUMMARY
(Erase heading not required.)

Place	Date	Hour	Summary of Events and Information	Remarks and references to Appendices
W14 b 9.7 (Sheet 57D)	4th Nov		M.O. made routine inspection of Drying Rooms at CRUCIFIX CORNER and superintended construction of new Drying Room; ascertained location of Divisional Units advanced in and around AVELUY; viewed camp of Country Working Party and interviewed M.O. The following Units inspected as to sanitary arrangements:— 58th Brigade Refilling Point, A.A. Refilling Point, Howitzers of A, B and D Batteries 80th Brigade R.F.A., 51st Brigade Machine Gun Corps, 7th Kings Own Royal Lancaster Regt., 7th Loyal North Lancashire Regt., 7th South Lancashire Regt. and 7th South Lancashire Regt. Squad of temporary attached men engaged on sanitary fatigues at SHQ (and with supervision of it completed. The carpenter and attached men constructing sanitary appliances. Men of section and attached carpenter engaged in adapting dugouts as Drying Rooms. Three men as guard at CRUCIFIX CORNER Water Supply. Two men at Latrine dump. One man at Bomb Pits, one man at LONE FARM Water Supply. Three attached men at Civil Burials. Water supplies tested and ordinary labelled. Two men preparing water another. Infectious Diseases received and investigated.	

2449 Wt. W14957/M90 750,000 1/16 J.B.C. & A. Forms/C.2118/12.

WAR DIARY or INTELLIGENCE SUMMARY

Army Form C. 2118.

Place	Date	Hour	Summary of Events and Information	Remarks and references to Appendices
W14.A.97 Sheet 57D	5th Nov.		C.O. Proceeded to CRUCIFIX CORNER reference Drying Room. Cases of Infection Diseases investigated. Men of Section and attached carpenter engaged modifying dugouts for Drying Rooms. One squad of attached men working Drying Room. Three men on guard at CRUCIFIX CORNER Water Supply. One man at LONE FARM Water Supply. Two men at Section Dump. One man at Pound Pine. One Squad engaged in making sanitary appliances. Squad of attached men under supervision of J.N.C.O. of Section engaged on sanitary fatigues on H.Q. Camp. Water Supplies in area investigated, tested and swiftly labelled. Two men preparing Water notices. The following Units inspected as to sanitary arrangements :- B Battery. 88th Brigade R.F.A. 58th Brigade Machine Gun Corps. 10th Worcestershire Regt, 8th North Staffordshire Regt. 31st Mobile Veterinary Section and Transport and camp of 34th Labour Sect. Royal Fusiliers Regt.	
W14.b.97 Sheet 57D	6th Nov.		C.O. investigated water supplies in forward area at X.7.a central, X.1.d.9.9, R.32.C.66 and R.32.A.6.6. Supplies at DONNET POST. X.7.a.7.3, X.8.c.3-5.	

WAR DIARY
INTELLIGENCE SUMMARY

Army Form C. 2118.

Place	Date	Hour	Summary of Events and Information	Remarks and references to Appendices
	7 Nov		BENNETT St OVILLERS, OVILLERS POST and Q.36.a.5-8 also investigated. Samples of water taken from Q.36.a.5-8, X&C.3-5 and R.32.b.6-8 and forwarded to C.O. 15 N°13 Motor Laboratory for bacteriological examination and report. Water passed at X&C.3-5 Supply. Men of section and attached carpenter engaged in preparing Drying Rooms. One squad of attached men working Drying Rooms. One squad making sanitary appliances. One squad of attached men under supervision of N.C.O. of Section engaged in sanitary fatigue at 1748 Camp. One N.C.O. with Divisional Laundry. Three men as guard at CRUCIFIX CORNER water Supply. Two Petrol Cans received at Water Supply for chlorinating and filling with chlorinated water. Two men at Section Dump. One man at Bennet Mill. One man at LONE FARM water supply. The following Units inspected as to sanitary arrangements:- A and D Batteries 5th Brigade R.F.A., "A" "B" "C" and "D" Batteries 87 Brigade R.F.A. N°s 2, 3, 4 and No. No. 1 Divisional Train. OVILLERS inspected as to sanitary condition.	6.6. inspected transport 5th Brigade Units. inspected Drying "Rooms at CRUCIFIX

W14697
Sheet 57D

WAR DIARY
INTELLIGENCE SUMMARY

Army Form C. 2118.

(Erase heading not required.)

Place	Date	Hour	Summary of Events and Information	Remarks and references to Appendices
			CORNER N.6.8 and men of section together with attached carpenter adapting dugout as Drying Room. The squad of attached men working Drying Room. Bn. H.Q. with Divisional Laundry. Headquarter Work inspected as to sanitary condition. Squad of temporary attached men under supervision of N.C.O. of section engaged in sanitary fatigues at 1/4th Bn camp. Water supplies in area investigated. Tested and carefully labelled too fit or came chlorinated and 150 filled with chloronated water. One man preparing water notices. Three men at CROCIFIX CORNER Water supply. One man at LONE FARM water supply. Two men at latrine trunk and one man at Sandy Stone pages of infection diseases investigated and needed. [signature]	
W.14-1.97 (Rev. 5)?	8 May		I.S. inspected camps of 9th Worcestershire Regt and 10th Worcestershire Regt at OWLLERS POST and investigated cases of infection disease at these camps. Accompanied Staff Capt. 58 Brigade to Drawing Room and made arrangements for drying clothes of troops, arranged scheme for water guards and chlorination of water supplies in Divain. Report on examination of water received from O.C. [signature] Forms/C.2118/12. Laboratory. Squad of temporary attached men	

WAR DIARY
or
INTELLIGENCE SUMMARY

Army Form C. 2118.

(Erase heading not required.)

Instructions regarding War Diaries and Intelligence Summaries are contained in F. S. Regs., Part II. and the Staff Manual respectively. Title Pages will be prepared in manuscript.

Place	Date	Hour	Summary of Events and Information	Remarks and references to Appendices
W.14.6.9.7. (Sheet 57D)	9 Nov.		under supervision of 1 NCO of section engaged in sanitary fatigues at C.9.4.40. Camp. Water supplies in area tested and investigated. 1.30 Elliot Huts tried with chlorinated water at CRUCIFIX CORNER. One man preparing water notices. Three men at CRUCIFIX CORNER water supply. Two men at section dump. One man at Point Pire. One man at LONE FARM water supply and one man at X.F.C.35 water supply. One squad of attached men working Drying Room. Men of section and attached carpenter preparing Drying Rooms. The following Units inspected as to sanitary arrangement and cleanliness:— H.Q. R.A. 3rd Mobile Veterinary Section, 172nd Battery R.G.A. and Transport & 57 Brigade Machine. M.O. accompanied A.D.M.S. of Division in sanitary inspection of Trucks occupied by 6th Wiltshire Regt. Visit for Bathe Latrine chosen at DIVIERS and inspection made of several latrines made by Artillery Units. Stock of water sterilising tablets obtained from HARLEY. Two N.C.Os with Divisional Laundry. Headquarter Units inspected and squad of temporary attached men under supervision of N.C.O. of section engaged in sanitary fatigues at C.9.4.40. Two men preparing sanitary appliances. One	

2449 Wt. W14957/M50 750,000 1/16 J.B.C.& A. Form/C.2118/12.

WAR DIARY or INTELLIGENCE SUMMARY

Army Form C. 2118.

Place	Date	Hour	Summary of Events and Information	Remarks and references to Appendices
W14 b-9-7 (Sheet 57D)	10th Nov		Squad of attached men working Drying Rooms. One man as guard at LONE FARM Water Supply and one man at Water Supply at X.8.C. 3.5. Water Supplies tested and correctly labelled. One man preparing Water stores. Two men at Section dumps and one man at Point Store. The following Units inspected as to sanitary arrangements and conditions — Headquarters Transport and A.B.C and D'Ecs. / 5th South Wales Border Regt. Divisional Point Store. H.Q. A. B. C and D. Batteries of 88th Brigade R.F.A. 56th Brigade Refilling Point. 57th and 58th Refilling Points. H.Q. Refilling Point. Sanitary arrangements at OVILLERS further inspected. Three inter at CRUCIFIX CORNER Water Supply.	
			C.O. proceeded to OVILLERS in order to inspect dugouts occupied by Division and ascertain whether they were fit for occupation by troops; made arrangements for erection of Latrines at OVILLERS. Inspected water system at OVILLERS. Inspected Drying Rooms in CRUCIFIX CORNER, Inbournout of Baths Concerning bathing and washing facilities in the area. Inspected camps occupied by Nos 2, 3 and 4 Sections Divisional Ammunition Column and Divisional Point Stone. Renewed Report Stations on bathing of troops and washing clothes on the Divisional area. One squad of attached men working Divisional Drying Rooms. Two NCOs with Divisional	

WAR DIARY or INTELLIGENCE SUMMARY

Army Form C. 2118.

Place	Date	Hour	Summary of Events and Information	Remarks and references to Appendices
W12 b 9.7 (Sheet 57 D)	11th June		Sunday. One squad of Temporary attached men under supervision of 1 C.S. of Section engaged in sanitary fatigue at DHQ camp. One squad making sanitary appliances. One man at LONE FARM Water Supply and one man at X 8 c 3.5 Supply. Two men at Section Dump and one man at Point One. Three men at CRUCIFIX CORNER Water Supply. One man as guard at X 3 c 1.9 and X 8 b 1.5. The following Units inspected as to sanitary arrangements. Cavalry Working Party, 6" Wiltshire Regt. H.Q. 58th Infantry Brigade. Horselines of A, B, C and D Batteries 80th Brigade R.F.A., 7th Loyal North Lancashire Regt, 7th Kings Own Royal Lancaster Regt, 34th Machine Gun Corps. Water Supplies Maps and privately labelled. One man preparing Water Notices. G.R.A. E.O. inspected Refilling Points of H.Q. Short 56th, 57th and 58th Brigades. Arranges for digging of soakage pits at DHQ camp and cleaning at of attached Cavalry working Parties camps another office work. Squad of attached men working Personnel Drying Rooms. One squad engaged erecting further latrine air	

WAR DIARY
or
INTELLIGENCE SUMMARY
(Erase heading not required.)

Army Form C. 2118.

Place	Date	Hour	Summary of Events and Information	Remarks and references to Appendices
OVILLERS			The N.C.O. and two men posted as guard at Ration Supply THIEPVAL ROAD. The man at LONE FARM Ration Supply, and the manual supply at X 8 c 3.5. The man as guard at Ration Supplies at X 3 c 1.9 and X 8 6.1.5. Three men at CRUCIFIX CORNER Ration Supply. The man at Bomb Store and two men at Section Dump. One squad of attached men under supervision of N.C.O. 1 Section, engaged in sanitary fatigues at OPP Camps. Water supplies in area investigated, tested and carefully labelled. The men preparing baths & huts. Latrine screens investigated and renewed. The following Units inspected as to sanitary arrangement and cleanliness:- 3rd Battn South Royal Fusilier Regt. 108th Heavy Battery R.G.A. N° 23 +and 4th Co Divisional Train. G.N.A.	
W14 6.9.7 (Sheet 57D)	12th Nov		C.O. proceeded to AVELUY and inspected contacts of Pte BARNES 6th Wiltshire Regt suspected Cerebro Spinal- Meningitis and arranged for disinfection of quarters and isolation of contacts. Squad working Divisional Drying Rooms. One squad of temporary attached men under supervision of NCO. 1 Section engaged as carpenters engaged in making sanitary	

WAR DIARY or INTELLIGENCE SUMMARY

Army Form C. 2118.

Place	Date	Hour	Summary of Events and Information	Remarks and references to Appendices
			appliances. Water supplies in area investigated and tested. Weekly Report on result of inspection of water carts forwarded to ADMS. One man preparing water notices. Two men at Lechure dump and one man at Front-line. One NCO and two men at THIEPVAL ROAD water supply. One man at LONE FARM water supply and one man at supply at X 8 c 3-5. One man at supplies X 3 C 1-8 and X 8 6 1-5. Three men at CRUCIFIX CORNER water supply. Inspection of various incinerators and disinfection carried out. The following Units inspected as to sanitary arrangements - Polish Chiffrataire Regt, 3rd Mobile Veterinary Section, 122nd Heavy Battery R.G.A. and No 2 Section Divisional Ammunition Column. Two dugouts at OVILLERS placed out of bounds owing to insanitary condition. The N.CO with Divisional Laundry F.B and D Battens (Howitzers) (th Brigade RFA inspected. G.R.A.	
W14.b.9.7 (Aberyd)	13th Nov.	6.0	engaged in office routine work. On instruction from ADMS eight men proceeded to AVELUY POST to assist with wounded and eight men to BOUZINCOURT for similar duty.	

WAR DIARY
or
INTELLIGENCE SUMMARY

Army Form C. 2118.

Place	Date	Hour	Summary of Events and Information	Remarks and references to Appendices
	14th March		A squad of attached men working Divisional Drying Rooms. Water supplies in Divisional area investigated and noted. One man preparing water notices. Guard of one NCO and three men at CRUCIFIX CORNER Water Supply. Guard of one NCO and two men at THIEPVAL ROAD Supply. One NCO and two men as guard at OVILLERS Water Supplies. One NCO and two men as guard at X 7 a central and X 1 at 9·9 Supplies. The men at LONE FARM Water Supply and six men at Bomb Store. Squad of attached men carpenters at X.6.0 of Schwm engaged in sanitary fatigue in R.H.Q. Camp. Attached carpenters re-erecting huts for Camp Commandant. Latrines chosen received and investigated. The following units inspected as to sanitary arrangements — 56th 57th and 58th Brigades and H.Q. Dump. A.B.C and D Batteries and H.Q 87 Brigade R.F.A.	
			[signed]	
			6 O.R. admitted to 57th Field Ambulance suffering from influenza. One squad of attached men working Divisional Drying Room. Water supplies in Divisional area	

WAR DIARY or INTELLIGENCE SUMMARY

Army Form C. 2118.

Place	Date	Hour	Summary of Events and Information	Remarks and references to Appendices
			investigated and noted. Guard of one N.C.O and four men at CRUCIFIX CORNER Water Supply. One man at LONE FARM Supply relieved and returned to section for duty. Guard of one N.C.O. and two men at THIEPVAL ROAD Supply. One N.C.O and four men as guard at OVILLERS Water Supplies. One N.C.O and two men as guard at X7a central and X1d 9.9 Supplies. One man preparing Water Meters. Infectious Diseases etc reviewed. One Squad of attached men sworn supervision of N.C.O of Section engaged on sanitary fatigues at DHQ Camp. Attached Carpenters erecting huts for Camp Commandant. One Squad engaged erecting Police Hutment at OVILLERS. Sections of A.R. + A.B.C + D Batteries 81st Brigade R.F.A. inspected. Refilling Points of 56', 57' and 58' Brigades near 4th Army inspected and found in satisfactory condition after move.	
W14 c-9-7 (Sheet 57D)	15th Mar		AUTHUILLE visited afternoon sanitary accumulations and fouling of River ANCRE. No 1, 2, 3 and 4 Sections Personnel Ammunition Columns inspected as to sanitary arrangements. One Squad of temporary attached men worked	C.I.F.

WAR DIARY or INTELLIGENCE SUMMARY

Army Form C. 2118.

Place	Date	Hour	Summary of Events and Information	Remarks and references to Appendices
			Afternoon. 1 N.C.O. 4 section engaged on sanitary fatigues at Bttn. Hdqrs. Water supplies in area investigated and tested. One man preparing bath notices. Eight men with 59 Field Ambulance. Two carpenters making sanitary appliances. Guard of one NCO and four men at CRUCIFIX CORNER bath supply. Guard of one N.C.O. and two men at THIEPVAL ROAD bath supply. One NCO and four men on guard at OVILLERS bath supplies. One NCO and two men on guard at X7a central and X1d 9.9 supplies. Two men at Section Dump, and one man at Bomb Store. One guard working Divisional Drying Rooms.	
W14 b 9.7 (Sheet 57 D)		10 a.m.	The following trunk of Division inspected as to sanitary arrangements. A 2, 3, 4 and HQ Companies Divisional Train. A.B. and D Batteries 82nd Brigade R.F.A. Bath supplies at ST PIERRE DIVION and district inspected and reported upon. One man preparing bath notices. Guard of one NCO and four men at	C.C.J.

WAR DIARY
or
INTELLIGENCE SUMMARY

(Erase heading not required.)

Army Form C. 2118.

Place	Date	Hour	Summary of Events and Information	Remarks and references to Appendices
			CRUCIFIX CORNER Halt Supply. Guard of one N.C.O and two men at THIEPVAL ROAD Halt Supply. One N.C.O and four men as guard at OVILLERS Halt Supply. One N.C.O and two men as guard at X7a. Central and X1 & X9 Supplies. One signal orderly missing Burying Room. One guard of attached men under experiment of 100 of section engaged in sanitary fatigues at R.H.Q. Kennels. Two men at Section Dumps and one man at Scout Place. One signaller engaged making sanitary appliances. Capt C.C. Anderton. R.A.M.C. OC 19th Divisional Baths and Laundry took over duties as OC of section during absence of Capt Anderson, RAMC (Inh). Eight men working with 59' Field Ambulance.	
W14.6.9.7. (Sheet 57D)	17th Nov		Halt Supplies in and around ST PIERRE DIVION further investigated and reports forwarded to ADMS and 19th Division Q. One N.C.O and four men as guard at Halt Supply CRUCIFIX CORNER. Guard of one N.C.O and two men at THIEPVAL ROAD Halt Supply. One N.C.O and four men as guard at OVILLERS Halt Supplies. One	R.C.D

WAR DIARY or INTELLIGENCE SUMMARY

Army Form C. 2118.

Place	Date	Hour	Summary of Events and Information	Remarks and references to Appendices
			2nd CO. and two men as guard at Supplies at X 7 a central and X 1 d 9 9. Two men at Rations dump and one man at Bomb Sto. One squad of henchmen attached men engaged in sanitary fatigue at B.H.Q. Camp. One squad making sanitary appliances. One squad working Drying Rooms, Lorry (transport) received from SOUZINCOURT to CABSTAND (59th Field Ambulance). Eight men assisting with 59th Field Ambulance. The following Units inspected as to sanitary conditions - 37th Mobile Veterinary Section. H.Q. A, B, C and D Batteries 87th Brigade R.F.A. C.C.T	
N14 & 9.7 (Sheet 57?)	18 Nov		Eight men assisting with 59th Field Ambulance and eight men at DONNET POST. Eight men with 58th Field Ambulance. A N.C.O with 58th Brigade Headquarters for water duty. One N.C.O with 57th Brigade Headquarters for water duty. One squad working Drying Rooms. One squad of attached men under supervision of N.C.O of Section, engaged on sanitary fatigue. 2nd H.C.O and four men as guard as	

WAR DIARY or INTELLIGENCE SUMMARY

Army Form C. 2118.

Place	Date	Hour	Summary of Events and Information	Remarks and references to Appendices
W14.c.9.7 (Sheet 57D)			CRUCIFIX CORNER Water Supply. One NCO and two men as guards at THIEPVAL ROAD Supply. One NCO and four men as guard at OVILLERS Supplies. One NCO and two men as guard at Supplies X7a central and X1a 9.9. Two men at Authuille dump and one man at Bomb Store. Infantry Prisoners to recount. C.C.T.	
W14.c.9.7 (Sheet 57D)		10'/10 A	Eight men with 58th Field Ambulance. Sixteen men with 59th Field Ambulance. One N.C.O. with 57 Brigade Headquarters for water duty. One N.C.O. and four men as guard at CRUCIFIX CORNER Water Supply. One N.C.O. and two men as guard at THIEPVAL ROAD Supply. One N.C.O. and four men as guard at Supplies X7a central and X1a 9.7. Two men at Authuille Mine and one man at Bomb Store. Infantry Prisoners attached. One squad of attached men working Drying Room. One squad of attached men cleaning up camp. C.C.T.	
W14.c.9.7 (Sheet 57D)		10 A.M.	Eight men with 58th Field Ambulance. Sixteen men with 59th Field Ambulance.	

WAR DIARY or INTELLIGENCE SUMMARY

Army Form C. 2118.

Place	Date	Hour	Summary of Events and Information	Remarks and references to Appendices
			One NCO and four men on guard at CRUCIFIX CORNER Water Supply. One NCO and two men on guard at THIEPVAL ROAD Water Supply. One NCO and four men on guard at OVILLERS Water Supply. One NCO and two men on guard at Ovillers X7a central and X1 d 9.9. Two men on guard at Decline Wire and one man at Bomb Store. One squad engaged under supervision of NCO of Section on sanitary fatigues at D.H.Q. Camp. Specimen Sheets recorded etc. One squad working Drying Rooms. Water supplies in area visited and tested.	
			C.I.T.	
W 14 1-9-7 (Sheet 57 D)	12th Nov		Relieve men with 59th Field Ambulance. One NCO and four men on guard at CRUCIFIX CORNER Water Supply. One NCO and two men on guard at THIEPVAL ROAD Water Supply. One NCO and four men on guard at OVILLERS Water Supply. One NCO and two men on guard at Ovillers X7a central and X1 d 9.9. Two men on guard at Decline Wire and one man at Bomb Store. One squad engaged under the supervision of NCO of Section on sanitary fatigues at D.H.Q. Camp. Specimen Sheets recorded. One squad working Drying Rooms. Water supplies in area visited and tested. N.O. returned from Hospital and assumed command of Section. Sanitary arrangements — 5th Machine Gun Corps	

WAR DIARY
INTELLIGENCE SUMMARY

Army Form C. 2118.

Place	Date	Hour	Summary of Events and Information	Remarks and references to Appendices
M14697 (M.W.57) 2)	22/VIII		B/North Wales Border Regt. 7 King's Own Royal Lancaster Regt. 48 Rds. 19 Offrs. Bomb Store. No. 1, 2, 3 and 4 Sections Divisional Ammunition Column. [signature]	
			C.O. made arrangements as to move to new area, prepare and submitted to DMS monthly report on sanitation, rats and epidemic disease, general office routine. One squad working Divisional Drying Room. One squad of attached men under supervision of NCO of Section engaged on sanitary fatigues at DHQ camps. Eight men with Sgt. Field Ambulance. Water supplies noted and tested. One NCO and four men as guard at CRUCIFIX CORNER Water Supply. One NCO and two men as guard at THIEPVAL ROAD Water Supply. One NCO and four men at OVILLERS Water Supplies. One NCO and two men as guard at Divilers X7a central, and X1 a 9.9. Two men at Section Store and one man at Bomb Store. The following units inspected:- Anselmes 7, D Battery, A & B, C & D Batteries 87 Brigade RFA. Anselmes 7, A & D, A & B, C & D Batteries 88 Brigade RFA, Anselmes J.A., B & D Battery M" Brigade RFA, A&C Section 87 Brigade RFA, Anselmes J.A. Anselmes 5th, 7th, 6th & 7th Sections 87 Brigade RFA Divisional Train. [signature]	

WAR DIARY or INTELLIGENCE SUMMARY

Army Form C. 2118.

Place	Date	Hour	Summary of Events and Information	Remarks and references to Appendices
CONTAY	23rd Nov		C.O. interviewed Sanitary Officer McGovern and handed him particulars as to area. C.O. proceeded to new billets at CONTAY. Men of Section arrived attached men marched to new billets at CONTAY. Regtl. Lorry conveyed equipment and others to CONTAY. All tools and other grenades returned and men again went those at MIRLOT removed to CONTAY. Water supplies at CONTAY moved and fixed. R.M.O. Camp cleaned out by attached fatigue squad. G.M.A.	
DOULLENS	24th Nov		C.O. proceeded to new billets at DOULLENS. Men of Section together with attached men marched from CONTAY to DOULLENS. Regtl. Lorry transported equipment and others. C.O. visited Rest Area and BERNAVILLE. G.M.A.	
BERNAVILLE	25th Nov		C.O. proceeded to BERNAVILLE. Men of Section together with attached men marched from DOULLENS to new billets at BERNAVILLE. Regtl. Lorry transported equipment and others. G.M.A.	

WAR DIARY
or
INTELLIGENCE SUMMARY

Army Form C. 2118.

Place	Date	Hour	Summary of Events and Information	Remarks and references to Appendices
BERNAVILLE	26th Nov		6.0 in company with Town Major inspected sanitary arrangements at BERNAVILLE and suggested improvements; arranged with Q. Sgt for having sanitary squad for H.Q. town. Made supplies in Divisional area investigated and tested. List of train supplies furnished to all R.M.Os (copy attached). Squad engaged in putting filter of system in sanitary condition. Squad engaged in town sanitation under supervision of NCO of system. One NCO with Divisional Baths Laundry.	
BERNAVILLE	27th Nov		6.0 proceeded to BEAUVAL and GEZAINCOURT; interviewed Staff Capt 57 Infantry Brigade and arranged for him to supply fatigue party for cleaning up village and arrange for sanitary squad for village to be supplied by the Divn, interviewed Town Major regarding sanitation, inspected billets of 8th Worcester Regt in company with Major and Medical Officer, inspected public latrines and incineration in village with Town Major, arranged to take over sanitation of GEZAINCOURT. Two inspectors with 58th Brigade. Two inspectors with 57 Brigade. Two inspectors with 58th Brigade.	

WAR DIARY / INTELLIGENCE SUMMARY

Army Form C. 2118.

Place	Date	Hour	Summary of Events and Information	Remarks and references to Appendices
			Ration supplies in area investigated and taken. One NCO with Divisional Laundry squad & attached men under supervision of NCO of section engaged in sanitary fatigue at BERNAVILLE. R.S. wagon supplies for collection of refuse from billets. 40th Tank inspected.	
BERNAVILLE	28/1/17		R.M. rode to GEZAINCOURT and inspected in company with G.O.C. 37 Infantry Brigade billets occupied by 10th Worcester Regt. Billets occupied by 8th Gloucester Regt also inspected. One squad of attached men engaged in sanitary fatigue at BERNAVILLE under supervision of NCOs of section. R.S. wagon supplies for collection of refuse from billets. Ration supplies in area inspected and found satisfactory. Supplementary list of ratio supplies prepared and forwarded as att. R.M.O. (copy attached.) Two inspections with 58th Brigade. Two inspections with 57th Brigade. Two inspections with 58th Brigade. 3rd Brigade. 58th Somerset Light Infantry, Border and 7th East Lancashire Regt inspected. One NCO of section and one attached man engaged in sanitary work at GEZAINCOURT. 7th Cheshire Regt inspected.	

WAR DIARY
INTELLIGENCE SUMMARY

Army Form C. 2118.

Place	Date	Hour	Summary of Events and Information	Remarks and references to Appendices
BERNAVILLE	29 June		C.O. visited FIENVILLERS. C.O. in company with A.D.M.S. inspected billets of 7th South Lancashire Regt. and 7th Kings Own Royal Lancaster Regt. at CANDAS; investigated case of Rubella at 7th Kings Own Royal Lancaster Regt. C.O. in company with C.O. R.A.M.C. proceeded to BEZAINCOURT and inspected billets of 8th Worcestershire Regt. and 10th Worcestershire Regt. Two inspections with 57th Brigade. Two inspections with 58th Brigade. The following units inspected - A, B, C and D Cos. 6th Wilts Regt.; A, B, C and D Cos. and transport of 7th South Lancashire Regt. and H.Q. to Divisional Train. The M.O. and C.O. men on sanitary duties at GEZAINCOURT. Squad of temporarily attached men under supervision of M.O. of Section engaged in sanitary fatigues at BERNAVILLE. U.S. Wagon equipped for removal of refuse etc. The M.O. with Divisional Sanitary Section. Refection Screen resented etc. Water carts examined and tested for free chlorine. [signature]	
BERNAVILLE	30 June		Two inspections with 57th Brigade. Two inspections with 58th Brigade. The M.O. of Section and one attached men as sanitary squad at BEZAINCOURT. Squad of temporarily attached men under supervision of M.O.	

WAR DIARY
INTELLIGENCE SUMMARY
(Erase heading not required.)

Army Form C. 2118.

Place	Date	Hour	Summary of Events and Information	Remarks and references to Appendices
			1/ Action engaged in sanitary fatigues at BERNAVILLE. A.S. Wagon supplied for removal of refuse etc. to incinerators at BERNAVILLE. Units' water carts inspected for the chlorine. Latrines Bivouacs investigated and noted. The following Units inspected as to sanitary arrangements:- H.Q, A, B, C and D, 11th and transport of 7th King's Own Royal Lancaster Regt. A, B, C and D, 1/5 Kings and transport of 9th Royal West Fusilier Regt. Also No.1 with Divisional Laundry. E.0 inspected sanitation of BERNAVILLE and also made arrangement for the incineration of all refuse and inspected incineration of area of the town; interviewed Town Mayor regarding sanitation.	
				M.M. Anderson Capt

List of Main Water Supplies in the 19th Divisional Area.

Place	Description	Treatment
AUTHEUX.	Communal Well in front of Café de la Place.	1 scoop.
BEAUVAL.	Hydrants and Communal Wells.	1 scoop.
BERNAVILLE.	Communal Wells.	1 scoop.
BERNEUIL.	do.	1 scoop.
CANDAS.	do.	1 scoop.
DOULLENS.	Hydrants.	1 scoop.
EPECAMPS.	Communal Well near Church.	1 scoop.
FIENVILLERS.	Communal Wells.	1 scoop.
FROHEN LE GRAND.	Farmhouse pump 200 yds N. of Bridge.	1 scoop.
do.	Spring near Shrine on DOULLENS Rd. 200 yds E. of Church	1 scoop.
GORGES.	Communal Wells.	1 scoop.
HARDINVAL.	do.	1 scoop.
HEUZECOURT.	do.	1 scoop.
LE MAILLARD.	Pump at Billet No. 21.	1 scoop.
OCCOCHES.	Roadside pump between Church and DOULLENS Rd.	1 scoop.
OUTREBOIS.	River AUTHIE. (after Clarification).	1 scoop.
VACQUERIE.	Communal Wells.	1 scoop.

NOTE :-

Owing to the difference in the strength of the Chloride of Lime supplied to Units, and the variation in quality of small supplies, the above figures for chlorination are only suggestive, and should be re-adjusted with the sample of Lime to be used.

J. M. Anderson, Capt. R.A.M.C.
O.C. 19th Divisional Sanitary Section

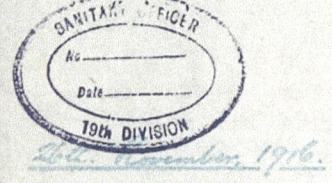

26th November 1916.

Supplementary List of Main Water Supplies in 19th Divisional Area.

PLACE	DESCRIPTION	TREATMENT
BEAUMETZ	Communal Wells	1 scoop
BERTEAUCOURT	Roadside Pumps	1 scoop
	Communal Well on L. of BERTEAUCOURT- HALLOY road	1 scoop
BONNEVILLE	Pump at Billet No 41	1 scoop
NAPLES	Spring E. of town, after clarification	1 scoop
DMART	Two pipes fitted with hand pumps, fed from spring	1 scoop
MESMONT	Well next to school	1 scoop
EPPES	Stream nr church, after clarification	1 scoop
EZAINCOURT	Pump at Billet No 49	1 scoop
RIMONT	Communal well	1 scoop
ANCHES	Communal well nr. church	1 scoop
	do. 200 yds. S. of church	1 scoop
LONGUEVILLETTE	Communal well	1 scoop
MONTRELET	Well at farm next CAFE DUFRENOY at T roads	1 scoop
	Stream S. of village, after clarification	1 scoop
PROUVILLE	Well in place at BEAUMETZ end of village	1 scoop
ST. ACHEUL	Communal well nr church	1 scoop
ST. LEGER - ST. OUEN RD	pump on left of road, nr. railway	1 scoop
ST. OUEN	Pump nr railway N.E of town	1 scoop
	Roadside pump N.W. of town	1 scoop
VALHEUREUX	350 gall. tank filled twice daily by water column	1 scoop

NOTE:- Owing to the difference in strength of the chloride of lime supplied to Units, & the variation in quality of small supplies, the above figures for chlorination are only suggestive & should be readjusted with the sample of lime to be used.

G. N. Andrews, Capt. R.A.M.C.
O.C., 19th Divisional Sanitary Section.

28th November, 1916.

140/1903

1st Div.

36th Sanitary Section

COMMITTEE FOR THE
MEDICAL HISTORY OF THE WAR
Date 31 JAN. 1917

Dec 19th

Army Form C. 2118.

WAR DIARY
or
INTELLIGENCE SUMMARY.

(Erase heading not required.)

War Diary
of
36th Sanitary Section
R.A.M.C.
From 1st December to 31st December 1916.

Vol 18

WAR DIARY
INTELLIGENCE SUMMARY

Army Form C. 2118.

Place	Date	Hour	Summary of Events and Information	Remarks and references to Appendices
BERNAVILLE	1st December		60 proceeded to CANDAS and saw Town Mayor re Clerk re French Interpreter, also re water supply of village of CANDAS. Visited GEZAINCOURT and interviewed Staff Capt 57th Infantry Brigade and Town Mayor and motored the latter Clerk as to the necessity for arranging for proper bushels for Public Latrines in GEZAINCOURT. Visited Field Cashier at DOULLENS; made enquiries regarding Laundry at DOULLENS. Proceeded to MONPLAISIR, 58th Infantry Brigade HQ, proceeded to AUTHEUX and interviewed MO of Cheshire Regt and inspected some of the lines and latrines in company with MO, gave Brigade sanitary reports necessary instructions; visited BOISBERGUES and informed MO of Wiltshire Regt and inspected some lines and latrines, proceeded to LE MEILLARD to an MOT of Wilts Regt. Two inspections with 57th Brigade. Two inspections with 58th Brigade. One NCO and 6 attached men engaged in sanitary duties at GEZAINCOURT. Squad of attached men under supervision of NCO of Cheshire engaged in sanitary fatigue at BERNAVILLE. NCO began supplies for removal of refuse. Squad of carpenters engaged in erecting and constructing Latrine Seats. Squad of painters engaged in making water carts of known hammer to fill Chlorine. The CO visited Divisional Laundry. The following units inspected:- 1st North Staffordshire Regt, 57th Machine Gun Corps, 7th Kings, 8th North Lancashire Regt, transport and of Wilts Regt and transports.	[signature]

WAR DIARY
or
INTELLIGENCE SUMMARY.

Army Form C. 2118.

(Erase heading not required.)

Instructions regarding War Diaries and Intelligence Summaries are contained in F.S. Regs., Part II. and the Staff Manual respectively. Title pages will be prepared in manuscript.

Place	Date	Hour	Summary of Events and Information	Remarks and references to Appendices
BERNAVILLE	2nd Dec		A.D.M.S. company with Town Major BERNAVILLE visited DOMESNYONT and inspected huts of 56th Brigade Machine Gun Units proceeded to GRIMONT and interviewed O.C. 58th Brigade. Machine Gun Units advance main cart. Two inspections with 58th Brigade. Two inspections with 57th Brigade. Two inspections with 58th Brigade. The following Units inspected as to sanitary arrangements - 58th Trench Mortar Bn, Transport, Machine Gun Section, Depot and D.M. Stores of 9th Cheshire Regt. 58th Brigade H.Q. 5th Machine Gun Coys and Transport and 10th Lancashire Regt. One squad of attached men engaged in sanitary fatigues at BERNAVILLE. 15 men supplied for removal of rubbish. Squad of attached carpenters renovating and erecting latrines. Water notices prepared. Train carts of Division inspected and tested for fleas and chlorine. One W.O. sent to attached men engaged in sanitary duties at GEZAINCOURT. Luncheon preceded and other matters received. Pri 175 ml Divisional Laundry. MMR.	
BERNAVILLE	3rd Dec		A.D.M.S. company with M.O. of 7th East Lancashire Regt inspected huts and sanitation of FIENVILLERS. Two inspection with 58th Brigade, two with 57th Brigade and two with 58th Brigade. The following Units inspected as to sanitary environs - 9th Cheshire Regt, Refilling Point No 2 & Divisional Train, 58th Brigade Transport.	

WAR DIARY
OR
INTELLIGENCE SUMMARY.
(Erase heading not required.)

Army Form C. 2118.

Place	Date	Hour	Summary of Events and Information	Remarks and references to Appendices
			10th Worcestershire Regt and 10th Warwickshire Regt. One M.O. and 6 attached men engaged on sanitary duties at GEZAINCOURT. Water tables prepared, latrines & urinals inspected and holes dug for fire cleansing. One Officer & 7 attached men engaged on sanitary fatigues at BERNAVILLE main supervision. 1 NCO & 1 section H.S. wagon supplied for removing rubbish. Squads of carpenters engaged in constructing and erecting latrines. One NCO with Divisional Laundry T.U. men attached for examination by A.D.M.S. Inspection Section and other sections needed. Two NCOs and men attached men at Reinforcement camp.	
BERNAVILLE	4th Dec		M.O. inspected 81st Field Bn R.E. at GORGES and 7 Loyal North Lancashire Regt BERNEUIL. Interviewed Town Mayor BERNEUIL. Two inspection with 58th Brigade, two with 57th Brigade and two with 58th Brigade. The following units inspected on its sanitary arrangement – 8th Worcestershire Regt, 6th Wiltshire Regt and Machine Gunners and 8th Field to R.E. and Transport. Water filters prepared, water supplies in area tested. One M.O. and six attached men employed on sanitary duties at GEZAINCOURT. Carpenters erecting and constructing latrines. One squad of attached men main supervision. 1 NCO 1 section engaged in constructing water tables and fire cleansing. BERNAVILLE H.S. wagon supplied for removal of refuse.	

Army Form C. 2118.

WAR DIARY
or
INTELLIGENCE SUMMARY.
(Erase heading not required.)

Instructions regarding War Diaries and Intelligence Summaries are contained in F. S. Regs., Part II. and the Staff Manual respectively. Title pages will be prepared in manuscript.

Place	Date	Hour	Summary of Events and Information	Remarks and references to Appendices
BERNAVILLE	5th Oct		The M.O. visit Divisional Laundry. Lieut McMahon Brennan review case investigated party of attached men returned from Reinforcement Camp. DMS	
			S.O. proceeded to HARDINVAL and HEM and inspected 182,161 A.S.C.; proceeded to LONGUEVILLETTE and inspected S/North Staffordshire Regt; proceeded to GEZAINCOURT and ordonnance Town Major. Took reference sanitation of village. Saw Brigade Sanitary Inspector and gave him instructions; proceeded to CANDAS saw acting Town Major and gave information regarding relation of Permanent Latrines in village; interviewed M.O. 7 Kings Own Royal Lancaster Regt and M.O. 7 South Lancashire Regt regarding ordonnance and erection of latrines. Two inspections with 58th Brigade, this unit 57 Brigade and two unit 58th Brigade. The forenoon units inspected as to sanitary arrangement and conditions – 9 Royal Welsh Fusilier Regt, 7 East Lancashire Regt, 57 Brigade HQ, 57 Trench Mortar Battery. The N.C.O. and one men engaged in sanitary duties at GEZAINCOURT. One squad of attached men under supervision of NCOs of Section engaged in sanitary fatigues at BERNAVILLE.	

WAR DIARY
— or —
INTELLIGENCE SUMMARY.
(Erase heading not required.)

Army Form C. 2118.

Instructions regarding War Diaries and Intelligence Summaries are contained in F. S. Regs., Part II. and the Staff Manual respectively. Title pages will be prepared in manuscript.

Place	Date	Hour	Summary of Events and Information	Remarks and references to Appendices
			US wagon supplied for removal of refuse etc. Water bottles prepared duplicates in area boiled and labelled. Water cart holes for free chlorine. In N.C.O. with Divisional laundry. Inspection carried on with 57th Brigade and two with 58th Brigade. The following work: carpentry, concreting and erecting latrines.	
BERNAVILLE	6 Dec		A.D. visited FIENVILLERS AUTHEUX and BOIS BERGUES in view to ascertain facilities for watering horses in these places, inspected 58th Brigade baths at BOIS BERGUES and gave instructions for completion of offtake. Two sanitary inspectors with 58th Brigade, two with 57th Brigade and two with 58th Brigade. The following units inspected: 7 South Lancashire Regt. No 3 Co. A.S.C, 9 Welsh Regt. and 58 Brigade Machine Gun Corps. One N.C.O. and six attached men engaged on sanitary duties at SEZAINCOURT. The usual of attached men under supervision of N.C.O. Section engaged on sanitary fatigues at BERNAVILLE. Latrine and incinerator constructed. US wagon supplied for removal of refuse. Water bottles prepared water supplies labelled. Units water cart inspected and tested for free chlorine. Inspection carried out this evening needed. One A.C.O. with Divisional laundry. Lorry proceeded to workshops for repairs.	

WAR DIARY
of
INTELLIGENCE SUMMARY.
(Erase heading not required.)

Army Form C. 2118.

Place	Date	Hour	Summary of Events and Information	Remarks and references to Appendices
BERNAVILLE	7th Dec		C.O. proceeded to AEUBECOURT and inspected in company with M.O. billets and sanitation of 9th Welch Regt, inspected truck and sanitation of 58th Brigade Machine Gun Corps at GRIMONT accompanied by D.C., proceeded to GEZAINCOURT and interviewed Town Major regarding supply of bricks for further latrines and saw Brigade Inspector regarding sanitation in the battalion, also inspected baths in course of erection at GEZAINCOURT, proceeded to CANDAS and investigated case of suspected enteric fever. Memorphis. Two sanitary inspectors with 57th Brigade, two with 57th Brigade and two with 58th Brigade. The following Units inspected — 8th Gloucestershire Regt, 8th North Staffordshire Regt, 57th Brigade Machine Gun Corps and transport, 8th Wiltshire Regt Reserve on Machine Gun School, 57th Brigade Machine Gun Corps and transport, No 2 Co A.S.C. and 58th Trench Mortar Battery. The N.C.O. and 6 attached men engaged in sanitary duties at GEZAINCOURT. Squad of attached men engaged in sanitary fatigues at BERNAVILLE under direction of N.C.O. of Section. W.S. wagon supplies for removal of refuse etc. from camps and latrines constructed. Wash house prepared. Supplies issued. Water carts inspected and tested for free chlorine. The N.C.O. attached to Divisional Artillery. Two inspected	

WAR DIARY
INTELLIGENCE SUMMARY

Army Form C. 2118.

Place	Date	Hour	Summary of Events and Information	Remarks and references to Appendices
BERNAVILLE	8 Dec		C.O. proceeded to DOMESMONT and VACQUERIE with him Major J. BERNAVILLE and called orders for further latrines in these places; inspected latrines of 5th South Antrim Borders Regt at VACQUERIE and machine Gun Corps at DOMESMONT; afterwards proceeded to CRMS on proposed scheme of pultic latrines in billets two inspection with 58th Brigade, two with 57th Brigade and two with 58th Brigade. The following units inspected as to sanitary arrangements – 7th King's Own Royal Lancaster Regt. and Sanopush, 9th Cheshires, 88th Brigade R.F.A. and 10th Hussars Regt. Are N.C.O. and squad of one attached men engaged in sanitary duties at GEZAINCOURT. Squad of attached men under supervision of 100th Sectn. engaged in sanitary fatigues at BERNAVILLE. D.S. wagon applied for removal of refuse etc. Carpenter making sanitary appliances. Incinerator (public) in course of erection. Pratt stoves inspected and supplies battled. Triptur tested and flipints medicants inspected and tested for the chlorine. The 100th Divisional Laundry, Infection Diseases investigated and reviewed. MLO	
BERNAVILLE	9 Dec		C.O. proceeded to OUTREBOIS and inspected billets and occupation of 81st Brigade R.F.A. accompanied by M.O. also talks at OUTREBOIS. Two inspections with 58th Brigade two	

WAR DIARY
or
INTELLIGENCE SUMMARY.

Army Form C. 2118.

(Erase heading not required.)

Instructions regarding War Diaries and Intelligence Summaries are contained in F. S. Regs., Part II. and the Staff Manual respectively. Title pages will be prepared in manuscript.

Place	Date	Hour	Summary of Events and Information	Remarks and references to Appendices
			with 57 Brigade and two with 58 Brigade. One HQ and one attached men engaged on sanitary duties at BEZAINCOURT. Squad of attached men under supervision of R.C.O. of section engaged on sanitary fatigue at BERNAVILLE. Gas masks supplied for carting of refuse etc. Incinerators in course of erection. Carpentier performing sanitary appliances. Main stores prepared incl. supplies. Watered. Main carts used for the collection the 400 unit Divisional Laundry. Divisional Bioscope received etc. The following units inspected as to sanitary arrangements - 9' Royal Welsh Fusiliers Regt. 6th Wiltshire Regt transport and depot, HQ and A Battery 88th Brigade R.F.A. 7 Loyal North Lancashire Regt. Two sanitary inspectors with Divisional Artillery. [signature]	
BERNAVILLE	10 Decr		C.O. preparing notes for lecture on sanitation, routine office work. Two sanitary inspectors with 58 Brigade, two with 57 Brigade. The following units inspected as to sanitary arrangements - 14th C. Divisional Train No 2 Co Divisional Train. HQ 58 Infantry Brigade. HQ 58 Infantry.	

WAR DIARY
or
INTELLIGENCE SUMMARY.

Army Form C. 2118.

Place	Date	Hour	Summary of Events and Information	Remarks and references to Appendices
			Brigade HQ Reporting Point. Officers of 7 Cheshire Regt met MO Royal Artillery, 57 Infantry Brigade HQ. One NCO and one attached men engaged in sanitary duties at GEZAINCOURT. Spare of attached men under supervision of NCO of 7 Ches. engaged in sanitary fatigues at	
BERNAVILLE			HQ wagon supplies for removal of refuse etc. Two inspections with Divisional Artillery. Carpenters engaged in making sanitary appliances. Incinerator in course of erection. Trash stores received and supplies issued. Motor cart taken for full chlorine. Inspections Discriminated. The NCO with Divisional Cavalry. [signed]	
BERNAVILLE	11 Dec		CO proceeded to CANDAS and interviewed MO's of South Lancashire Regt and 7 Kings Own Royal Lancaster Regt regarding Infection cases and construction of Incinerator and latrines; proceeded to GEZAINCOURT and inspected billets of 10th Royal Manchester Regt in company with MO; proceeded to DOCHIES and OUTRE BOIS: proceeded to AUTHEUX in order to obtain information regarding infectious cases. Acting on [illegible] [signed] Secondary inspection with 58th Brigade this week.	

WAR DIARY
or
INTELLIGENCE SUMMARY.
(Erase heading not required.)

Army Form C. 2118.

Place	Date	Hour	Summary of Events and Information	Remarks and references to Appendices
			57th Brigade, two with 58th Brigade and Divisional Artillery. The M.O. and one attached man assigned on sanitary duties at JEANCOURT. Agreed attached men, under supervision of M.O. of section, engaged in sanitary fatigue at BERNAVILLE. O.C. wagon supplied for removal of refuse. Inspection of Inoculation Protocol with one attached inspector making sanitary appliances. Inspection of Trench Standards with 61st Brigade R.F.A. Water supplies labelled and rest rooms inspected and tested for his columns. The following units inspected as to sanitary arrangement and construction:- No 5 Command Supply Column Workshop, 8th Worcestershires Regt, 8th Field Co. R.E., 58th Trench Mortar Battery, M.R. Dann B Battery 8th Brigade, R.F.A. Y and Z Batteries 7 Trench Mortars 58th Trench Mortar Battery 9th Middx Regt. and 58th Machine Gun Co.	
BERNAVILLE 11th Dec.			M.O. proceeded to 59th Field Ambulance, lectures on sanitation prepared. Inspection of Trench Mortar Standards with 88th Brigade R.F.A. Two sanitary inspections with 57th Brigade, two with 57th Brigade, two with 58th Brigade and two with Divisional Artillery. The M.O. and one attached man engaged	

WAR DIARY or INTELLIGENCE SUMMARY.

Army Form C. 2118.

(Erase heading not required.)

Place	Date	Hour	Summary of Events and Information	Remarks and references to Appendices
BERNAVILLE	1st Dec		On sanitary duties at GEZAINCOURT. Squad of attached men under supervision of N.C.O. of detm. engaged in sanitary fatigues at BERNAVILLE. US men employed in removal of refuse etc. Construction of manueash proceeded with and attached carpenter making sanitary appliances. Bath service started and used vats carts used for the columns. The following Units inspected - L.No3 Co ASC, 9th Field Amb R.E. 7th Lancashire Regt. 9 Cheshire Regt, 58 Brigade HQ, Refilling Point, RFA, and BHQ Units. EMA	
			M.O. investigated outbreak of Diarrhoea at 5th South Wales Border Reg at EPECAMPS. Visited Machine Gun sectn and Salvage bn billets at DOMESMONT. attended conference at DDM.S. Office I Corps. DOULLENS. Two sanitary inspection with 58 Brigade. two with 57 Brigade. two with 58 Brigade and two with Divisional Artillery. One NCO and squad of disc attached men engaged in sanitary duties at GEZAINCOURT. One squad of attached men engaged in sanitary fatigue at BERNAVILLE	

WAR DIARY or INTELLIGENCE SUMMARY.

Army Form C. 2118.

(Erase heading not required.)

Instructions regarding War Diaries and Intelligence Summaries are contained in F.S. Regs., Part II. and the Staff Manual respectively. Title pages will be prepared in manuscript.

Place	Date	Hour	Summary of Events and Information	Remarks and references to Appendices
			Made extension of N.C.O. of Section. U.S. surgeon supplied for conveyance of office carpenter constructing sanitary appliances. Inspection Disease investigated and needed the I.C.O. with Divisional Laundry. The following units inspected as to sanitary arrangements and anti-vermin:- 9 South Lancashire Regt, N°2 Coy A.S.C. (1st Worcestershire Regt 37 Brigade, Machine Gun Corps 57 Trench Mortar Battery, T.R. N°12a/m 3 Section Divisional Ammunition Column, W Satty, Trench Mortar 58 Trench Mortar Battery, 9 Corps Trench Mortar Regt 9 Welch Regt and 5 South Wales Border Regt. JMd	
BEAUVILLE	14th Dec		L.O. prepared orders for ADMS reference outbreak of Diarrhoea at 5 South Wales Border Regt; gave lecture to sanitary personnel of 58th Infantry Brigade attached K Section for two days course of instruction; attended conference of MO at VACQUERIE. Two sanitary inspectors with 58 Brigade, one with 57 Brigade. Two with 58 Brigade and two with Divisional Artillery. One N.C.O and O.R. attached men engaged in sanitary duties at GEZAINCOURT.	

WAR DIARY
or
INTELLIGENCE SUMMARY.

(Erase heading not required.)

Army Form C. 2118.

Place	Date	Hour	Summary of Events and Information	Remarks and references to Appendices
			Agnes of Employment attached men engaged on sanitary fatigue at BERNAVILLE under supervision of JCO of section. U.S. Major supplied for removal of refuse etc. Attached carpenter constructing sanitary appliances. Make supplies in use latrines and water carts of Work House for fire shelters. Infection shown investigates and remedied. The following units of Division inspected as to sanitary conditions - 6" Wiltshire Regt; 2nd Royal St. Brigade Machine Gun Corps and Transport; Salvage Co; S Trench Mortar Battery, 87th Brigade; HQ 87 Brigade R.F.A. A section of Divisional Ammunition Column and S. Staff Staffordshire Regt. MCD	
BERNAVILLE	15 Dec		C.O. provided KNOWLLERS and provided two men for sanitary duties in Town. Visited B.8 and SH.II Corps; provided 16 TERRAMESNIL and inspected combine with Town Major; visited BEAUVAL and interviewed Town Major and visited 58 Field Ambulance; provided to GEZAINCOURT and interviewed Town Major. The following units inspected - 7 Kings Own Royal Lancaster Regt and Transport; 94 Field Co R.E. No 1 Section Divisional Ammunition Autumn, C Battery 148 87 Brigade R.F.A. Attached men engaged in sanitary duties at	

Army Form C. 2118.

WAR DIARY
or
INTELLIGENCE SUMMARY.
(Erase heading not required.)

Instructions regarding War Diaries and Intelligence Summaries are contained in F. S. Regs., Part II. and the Staff Manual respectively. Title pages will be prepared in manuscript.

Place	Date	Hour	Summary of Events and Information	Remarks and references to Appendices
			GEZAINCOURT. Bn. squad of attached men engaged in sanitary fatigues at BERNAVILLE under supervision of MO. 1 action. OLS wagon supplies for removal of refuse etc. Two sanitary inspection with 57th Infantry Brigade, one with 57 Brigade, two with 58 Brigade, two with Divisional Artillery and two vitrines at DOULLENS. Attacked carpenters engaged in making sanitary appliances. Water writer repair and supplies batteries. Water carts inspected and used for tea chlorine. Lieutenant Johnson discovered sanitary personnel of 58th Infantry Brigade instructed. Ma	
BERNAVILLE	10 Dec	6.0	Proceeded to GEZAINCOURT and conferred with Town Mayor and MO 1 Work concerned as to erection of flybarot two latrines; interviewed Town Mayor of GARTON and arranged correction of village with him, interviewed Town Mayor of MARIEUX. The following units inspected - B. Coys field Amb. Bgn Sections Heavy Trench Mortar Battery, 80th Brigade R.F.A. X+Y, Wilshire Regt. Two sanitary inspection with 58th Infantry Brigade, two with 57 Brigade, two with 58 Brigade, two with Divisional Artillery and	

WAR DIARY or INTELLIGENCE SUMMARY.

Army Form C. 2118.

(Erase heading not required.)

Instructions regarding War Diaries and Intelligence Summaries are contained in F. S. Regs., Part II. and the Staff Manual respectively. Title pages will be prepared in manuscript.

Place	Date	Hour	Summary of Events and Information	Remarks and references to Appendices
			GEZAINCOURT. One squad of attached men engaged on sanitary fatigues at BERNAVILLE under supervision of A.D. of Section. O.S. major supplied for removal of refuse etc. Two sanitary inspectors with 58th Infantry Brigade, one with 57th Brigade, two with 58th Brigade, two with Divisional Artillery and two stationed at DOULLENS. Detached Corporation engaged in making sanitary appliances, lath screens, hygiene and supplies received. Both carts inspected and taken for fine cleaning. Inspection disinfector received. Sanitary personnel of 58th Infantry Brigade inspected. Mills	
BERNAVILLE	11 Sept		S.O. proceeded to GEZAINCOURT and conferred with Town Mayor and A.D. of Works. Examined no. & erection of Hyprowl box latrines, interviewed Town Mayor of CANDON and discussed orientation of village with him, returned via Mayor of MARIEUX. The following units inspected – 9 Royal Field Arc. Reg. Transport and orders, 58 Trench Mortar Battery, 58 Brigade RFA. X & Y Batteries, Heavy Trench Mortars, 1 Forge North Lancashire Rgt. 1 Machine Reg. Two sanitary inspectors with 58 Infantry Brigade, one with 57 Brigade, two with 58 Brigade, two with Divisional Artillery on	

WAR DIARY or INTELLIGENCE SUMMARY

Army Form C. 2118.

(Erase heading not required.)

Instructions regarding War Diaries and Intelligence Summaries are contained in F. S. Regs. Part II. and the Staff Manual respectively. Title pages will be prepared in manuscript.

Place	Date	Hour	Summary of Events and Information	Remarks and references to Appendices
EZAINCOURT			His of part of attached new engaged on sanitary fatigues at EZANVILLE under supervision of M.O. of Section. A.S. wagon supplied for removal of refuse &c. Two sanitary inspection with 58th Infantry Brigade one with 57 Brigade two with 51st Brigade two with Divisional Artillery and two divisions at DOULLENS. Attacked carpenter engaged in making sanitary appliances. Water troughs prepared and supplies between from carts in used and taken for use chlorine. Inspection Division received Sanitary inspection 1/58 Infantry Brigade instituted.	
[MARIEUX?]			Attended to EZAINCOURT and conferred with Town Mayor and M.O. of Units. Proceeded to K section of Hydrogen and Latrines; interviewed Town Mayor of BARTON and discussed sanitation of village with him. Interviewed Town Mayor of MARIEUX. The following units inspected - Royal Field Amb Regt transport and others. S.S. Signal Water Battery, 88th Brigade R.F.A, X & Y Batteries Heavy Trench Mortar, of Royal North Lancashire Regt of 9/ Cheshire Regt. Two sanitary inspection with 58th Infantry Brigade, two with 57 Brigade two with 58 Brigade two with Divisional Artillery and	

WAR DIARY or INTELLIGENCE SUMMARY.

Army Form C. 2118.

Place	Date	Hour	Summary of Events and Information	Remarks and references to Appendices
			Two Officers at DOULLENS. One NCO and one attached men engaged on sanitary duties at BERNAVILLE. One officer and one attached men under supervision of MO of Section engaged on sanitary fatigue at BERNAVILLE. Attached carpenter constructing sanitary appliances. NCO's engaged inspecting for removal of refuse etc. One officer visited public latrine, inspection of latrines and unveiled urea arrangement. Water carts tested for free chlorine and supplies taken. MA	
BERNAVILLE	17 Dec		The following units inspected as to sanitary arrangements - 58th Brigade M.G., 58th Brigade Stokes Mortar Batt, No 2 & 5 Refilling Points, 91st Field Co R.E., No 3 Co A.S.C. Two officers with 58th Infantry Brigade two with 57th Brigade, one with 59th Brigade. Two with Divisional Artillery and two Officers at DOULLENS. One NCO and one attached men engaged on sanitary duties at BEZAINCOURT. Officer & attached men under supervision of NCO of Section engaged on sanitary fatigues at	

WAR DIARY
or
INTELLIGENCE SUMMARY.

Army Form C. 2118.

Place	Date	Hour	Summary of Events and Information	Remarks and references to Appendices
BERNAVILLE			O.C. began supplies for removal of refuse &c. Carpenter constructing sanitary appliances. Water supplies tested and water carts inspected and tested for free chlorine. Inspections shewed as required. C.O. attended conference at Office of M.G.A. 1st ARMY, I Corps DOULLENS, inspected sanitation of 143 B. Divisional Train, 1st Indian Divisional Ammunition Column, H.Q. 143 Indian Divisional Ammunition between HARDINVAL and Headquarters of 58 Brigade at MON PLAISIR.	
BERNAVILLE	18th Dec.		C.O. inspected huts and latrines of 59 Field Ambulance and 9th Royal Welch Fusiliers Regt. at LE MEILLARD and 9th Welch Regt at HEUZECOURT. Marched thro' bivouac at GRIMONT. Passed BEAUVAL and interviewed Town Major re future sanitation of town and inspected further latrines and incinerator. Two sanitary inspectors with 58th Brigade one with 57 Brigade, two with 56th Brigade, two with Divisional Artillery and two stationed at DOULLENS. The following huts inspected 1st Wiltshire Regt and Transport, 57 Trench Mortar Battery, 10 Royal Warwickshire Regt. and Transport, 8th Field Co. R.E., 58 Trench Mortar Battery	

WAR DIARY
or
INTELLIGENCE SUMMARY.
(Erase heading not required.)

Army Form C. 2118.

Place	Date	Hour	Summary of Events and Information	Remarks and references to Appendices
			5th Ammunition Sub-Park, 85th Brigade R.F.A. X Battery Heavy Ft and Mortar Bie S.A.C. and squad of 200 attached men engaged in sanitary duties at 9 EZAINCOURT. Squads of attached men worked expansion of H.Q. of Lechin engaged on sanitary fatigue at BERNAVILLE. R.S. major applied for removal of report. Carpenter constructing new cooking latrine at SEPMERIES. Main Section prepared bath erection inspected Water Carts inspected and tested for time Chlorine Infection Broken in reverse. As H.Q. with Divisional Laundry.	
			Mla.	
BERNAVILLE	19 Nov	16.0	Visited DOBGIES, BERNEUIL and EPECAMPS and inspected sanitation of 1 pt Section to R.E. Two inspections with 50th Brigade. One with 57 Brigade. Two with 59th Brigade. Two with Divisional Artillery and two stationed at DOULLENS. The following units inspected as to sanitation – 9 Wilts Regt, 50 Brigade Machine Gun Corps, 7 South Lancashire Regt, 7 Kings Own Royal Lancaster Regt. 17th Brigade H.Q. 50th Machine Gun Corps. 5 Ammunition Sub Park, Salvage Co. A.S. Nos 1, 2, 3 and 4 Sections Divisional Ammunition Column, two 10th Worcestershire Regt and 5 South Wales Border Regt. Brie N.60 and 0100	

WAR DIARY
INTELLIGENCE SUMMARY.

Army Form C. 2118.

Place	Date	Hour	Summary of Events and Information	Remarks and references to Appendices
			attached men engaged in sanitary duties at GEZAINCOURT. Agricao of Employers attached men engaged in sanitary fatigues on BERNAVILLE undertaken 9-10A. of Section. U.S. wagon supplied for removal of refuse etc. Carpenters constructing sanitary appliances. Moto Notors prepared and supplies Section Moto cars inspected and tested for fir Schemes. Inspection and oil schemes received. bus ACC with Divisional Laundry. Mpa.	
BERNAVILLE	20 Oct		C.O. visited AMPLIER and AUTHIEULE and interviewed respective Town Majors regarding sanitation. C.O. attended conference at Offices of 57th & 58th Infantry Brigades DOULLENS. The sanitary inspector with 56th Infantry Brigade. Sow with 57 Brigade Sow with 58 Brigade Two not Divisional Artillery and her Stationed at DOULLENS. Bus F.A.C. and ane attached men engaged in sanitary duties at GEZAINCOURT. Agricao of attached men under supervision of NCOs of Section engaged in sanitary fatigues at BERNAVILLE. U.S. wagon supplied for removal of refuse etc. Carpenters engaged in constructing sanitary appliances. Motor Lorries prepared and supplies Section. Inspection of Units inspected and test for fir Scheme. Inspection reports received as to sanitary conditions — 5 South Wales Borderer Regt.	

A 5834 Wt. W4973/M657 750,000 8/16 D D & L Ltd. Form C.2118/13.

Army Form C. 2118.

WAR DIARY
or
INTELLIGENCE SUMMARY.
(Erase heading not required.)

Instructions regarding War Diaries and Intelligence Summaries are contained in F.S. Regs., Part II. and the Staff Manual respectively. Title pages will be prepared in manuscript.

Place	Date	Hour	Summary of Events and Information	Remarks and references to Appendices
			7 North Lancashire Regt. No 1 & 19 Divisional Train; 8th Worcestershire Regt. 57 Brigade Machine Gun Company; transport of Royal M.T.K. Section Regt. 58 Trench Mortar Battery 9th Welsh Regt. No 1 & 2. 19 Divisional Train; 'Y' and 'Z' Trench Mortar Sections and 19 Divisional Artillery Headquarters. JMcN.	
BERNAVILLE	7th Dec		C.O. investigated infectious areas for cases of dysentery and diarrhœa carriers. Visit Bureaux K.A.D.M.S. 19 Division; various D. Branch in connection with Divisional Laundry and sanitation report; sanitation of BERNAVILLE area not altogether satisfactory and letters and reports examined. Two sanitary inspections made 56th Infantry Brigade; one visit 57 Brigade; two visits 58 Brigade two visits Divisional Artillery and two detained at DOULLENS. D.x. A.D. and O.C. attached men engaged in sanitary duties at GEZAINCOURT. General of temporary attached men engaged in sanitary fatigue at BERNAVILLE with approvement of K.A.B.A. Section. U.S. wagon supplied for removal of refuse the train motor supplied and supplies detailed. Rainwater	

WAR DIARY
INTELLIGENCE SUMMARY.

Army Form C. 2118.

Place	Date	Hour	Summary of Events and Information	Remarks and references to Appendices
			of Mules inspected and held for use Chlorine Asphyxiated Carpentier ammunition sanitary appliances. The following Units inspected - 3/North Wales Border Regt, 1/West Lancashire Regt, 58th Brigade HQ, 8th North Staffordshire Regt, 57 Brigade HQ, YMCA Hut, GEZAINCOURT, 9 Sherw Regt, Transport and billets and B, C and D Batteries 58th Brigade RFA, also HQ and	
BERNAVILLE	22nd Oct		I.O. investigated case of Measles at AUTHIEULE; inspected the QUESNOY-PAROY and inspected sanitation and camp of A Battery 81st Brigade RFA and baths and sanitation of OUTREBOIS, proceeded to FROHEN LE PETIT and inspected HQ of 58th Brigade RFA and 2nd Battery, proceeded to SCOCHES and inspected sanitation and billets of A Battery 81st Brigade RFA and interviewed Town Major. Inspected GEZAINCOURT and inspected tanks and interviewed Town Major, interviewed Town Major of CANDAS and FIENVILLERS regarding sanitation. The sanitary inspector with 58th Brigade one with 57 Brigade, one with 58 Brigade, he with 19 Divisional Artillery and two stationed at DOULLENS. The M.O. and also attached men	

WAR DIARY
INTELLIGENCE SUMMARY.
(Erase heading not required)

Army Form C. 2118.

Place	Date	Hour	Summary of Events and Information	Remarks and references to Appendices
			Engaged in sanitary duties at GEZAINCOURT. Squads of attached men engaged in sanitary fatigue at BERNAVILLE under supervision of NCO of Section. A.S. wagon supplied for removal of refuse etc. Carpenter engaged in constructing sanitary appliances. Water Potion prepared and supplies issued. Water carts inspected and tested for the Columns. Inspection duncan etc. needed. The following units inspected - 83rd Brigade R.F.A. 10 Royal Warwickshire Regt & Wiltshire Regt and transport. Inspected 8 R.E. 5 Divisional Amm Park. and 94 Section 94 Field Co.	
BERNAVILLE	23 Dec		D.O. inspected billets and sanitation of 19 Divisional Train (transport) at BERNAVILLE also H.Q. Royal Engineers. Engaged in many sanitary report for A.D.M.S 19 Division. Proceeded to DOULLENS and accompanied M.O. on tour of sanitary inspection. Two inspections with 56th Brigade, one with 57 Brigade, two with 58th Brigade. Two with 19 Divisional Artillery and two others at DOULLENS. One M.O. unit	

WAR DIARY
INTELLIGENCE SUMMARY.

(Erase heading not required.)

Army Form C. 2118.

Place	Date	Hour	Summary of Events and Information	Remarks and references to Appendices
			One attached man engaged on sanitary duties at BEZAINCOURT. Officers of attached men under supervision of M.O. of Section engaged on sanitary fatigues at BERNAVILLE. E.S. wagon supplied for removal of refuse etc. Bakehouse constructed & latrines. Water trucks prepared and troops placed "Out of Bounds". Water carts inspected and passed for the Division. Inspection duties recorded &c. The following units inspected as to sanitary conditions:— 9 Welch Regt, 9 Royal Welch Fusilier Regt, 7 Royal North Lancashire Regt, Pilgrim Corps 112 & 119 Divisional Train, Post Office 57 and 58 Brigade, 113 & Divisional Train, 94 Field & C.S. HQ and B Battery, 81 Brigade R.F.A., A Battery 28 Brigade R.F.A. and X and Y Batteries, and Mortars. G.M.A.	
BERNAVILLE	11 Dec		M.O. accompanied by A.A.D.M.S. 19 Division visited AMPLIER and inspected Z Supply Baths. Proceeded to SARTON and interviewed Town Major. Two sanitary inspectors with 57 Brigade, one with 57 Brigade two with 58 Brigade, two with 19 Divisional Artillery, two stationed at DOULLENS. One M.O. and two also attached men engaged on sanitary duties at BEZAINCOURT. Officers of temporarily attached men under supervision of M.O. of Section	

Army Form C. 2118.

WAR DIARY
or
INTELLIGENCE SUMMARY.
(Erase heading not required.)

Instructions regarding War Diaries and Intelligence Summaries are contained in F.S. Regs. Part II. and the Staff Manual respectively. Title pages will be prepared in manuscript.

Place	Date	Hour	Summary of Events and Information	Remarks and references to Appendices
			Engaged on Sanitary duties at BERNAVILLE. U.S. wagon detailed for removal of refuse &c. Attached carpenters constructing sanitary appliances. Inspection and defences nearly ct. The following were inspected as Regimental environs :- "A" Barnard Farm. Garage &c. 1/9 D.W.R. 5t Arnd Mortar Battery. "C" Machine Gun Coy & Worcestershire Regt. 57 Brand Mortar Battery. Horse lines prepared and supplies detailed. Water carts inspected and tested for free chlorine. GM.	
BERNAVILLE	25th Decr		C.O. visited 7th South Lancashire Regt at VANDAS and made enquiries into cases of Dysentery on this unit. One officer & attached men under the supervision of N.C.O. of Sedan engaged on sanitary duties at BERNAVILLE. Squad of men attached men engaged on sanitary duties at GEZAINCOURT. U.S. wagon supplies for removal of refuse &c from BERNAVILLE. GM.	
BERNAVILLE	26th Decr		C.O. visited MT RENAULT FARM and inspected this unit with a view to extension of Pleury Baths. Inspected billets of one company of 2/9 Royal W.Yorks in BEAUVAL. Two sanitary inspection with 55 Brigade	

MIELLARD and ONTARCOURT M.O.

Army Form C. 2118.

WAR DIARY
INTELLIGENCE SUMMARY.
(Erase heading not required.)

Place	Date	Hour	Summary of Events and Information	Remarks and references to Appendices
			One with 57th Brigade, two with 58th Brigade, two with 19th Divisional Artillery and two stationed at DOULLENS. One M.O. and one attached man engaged in sanitary duties at BERNAVEOURT. Surgeons & attached men render expenses of W.O.& of tedium engaged in sanitary duties at BERNAVILLE. N.C.O.s began carpentry for removal of refuse etc. Water service prepared. Water carts inspected & tested for free chlorine. Attached carpenter continuing latrine Disinfector Unit & also overhauls needed of Worcestershire Regt and 10th Warwickshire Regt inspected as to sanitary arrangements. L.M.A.	
BERNAVILLE	27 Nov		Two sanitary inspectors with 56th Brigade, one with 57th Brigade, two with 58th Brigade two with 19th Divisional Artillery, and two stationed at DOULLENS. The following Units inspected as to sanitary arrangements - 1R., 191, 2.3 and 4 Sections 19 Divisional Ammunition Column. Artillery Refilling Point. 6th Worcestershire Regt and transport. 57th Machine Gun Co. 58th Machine Gun Co and transport. 19 Divisional Salvage Co and 7 Kings Own Royal Lancasters. Water carts inspected	

WAR DIARY
or
INTELLIGENCE SUMMARY.
(Erase heading not required.)

Army Form C. 2118.

Instructions regarding War Diaries and Intelligence Summaries are contained in F. S. Regs., Part II. and the Staff Manual respectively. Title pages will be prepared in manuscript.

Place	Date	Hour	Summary of Events and Information	Remarks and references to Appendices
			and looks for his return. But A.D.M.S. was attacked motor engaged on sanitary duties at GEZAINCOURT. Squads of attached men engaged on sanitary duties under supervision of N.C.O.'s Recton at BERNAVILLE. 62 men supplied for removal of refuse. Wooden carpenters constructing latrines etc. Brown spent December proceeded to V Corps Post Station BEAUVAL. Inspections and other actions carried. 6.0 prepared monthly report on sanitation and deserves before at 19 Divisional School of Instruction in Sanitation. Lectures Room went to workshops to complete scheme. E.M.a.	
BERNAVILLE	28 Dec.		6.0 visited BEZAINCOURT and inspected Baths and interviewed Town Major reported at office of D.A.M.S. V Corps: 6.0 proceeded on leave to England. Lieut E.C. PINEATOR 58th Field Ambulance, acting during absence. Two sanitary inspection with 58th Brigade, one with 57th Brigade, two with 58th Brigade, two with 19 Divisional Artillery and two claimed at DOULLENS. The following units inspected as to sanitary condition. 10th Warwickshire Regt. 57 French Mortar Battery	

WAR DIARY
or
INTELLIGENCE SUMMARY.
(Erase heading not required.)

Army Form C. 2118.

Place	Date	Hour	Summary of Events and Information	Remarks and references to Appendices
			9th Divisional Train A, B, C and D Coys and M.T. 187th Bgde R.F.A. W and Z Batteries. 6th Wiltshire Regt. Transport and depot 58th Brigade M.R. and transport and 7th South Lancashire Regt. The M.O. and men attached men engaged in sanitary duties at BERNAVILLE. Squads of attached men engaged in sanitary duties at BERNAVILLE made openings of M.R.'s latrines. All urgin supplied to remove if refuse etc. All been carried in anointing and bathing latrines at BERNAVILLE. Kitchens and other schemes inspected. Bath place prepared and supplied to R.M.O. Bath took inspected and later to fire stations. C.O.	
BERNAVILLE	29 Dec		16 C inspected Baths at BOISBERGUES, BOTRE-BOIS, GEZAINCOURT and CANDAS, inspected 57 Bgde R.A. ages public incinerator at GEZAINCOURT, main outlets at DOULLENS Trench and rubbish infant (rubbish) latrines at GEZAINCOURT. I hope, inspected stores at CANDAS occupied by 116th and 117th Reserve Park. M.T. A.S.C. Two sanitary inspectors with 58th Brigade, one inspector with 57th Brigade, two with 58th Brigade, two with 19th Divisional Artillery and two stationed at DOULLENS. The following Units inspected. 83rd Brigade R.F.A. C33 6" 19th Divisional Train 9 H. Field & R.E.	

WAR DIARY
or
INTELLIGENCE SUMMARY.
(Erase heading not required)

Army Form C. 2118.

Place	Date	Hour	Summary of Events and Information	Remarks and references to Appendices
			57 Brigade HQ. 58 Trench Mortar Battery, 51st Brigade Machine Gun Co. 7 East Lancashire Regiment & Welsh Regt. One NCO and one attached man of & pioneer sanitary duties at GEZAINCOURT. Squads of attached men under supervision of MO of Section engaged on sanitary duties at BERNAVILLE. O.C. main supplies to improvement of refuse. Attended to sanitary construction, latrines, kitchens and other services required. Main stoves inspected and supplies to R.M.O. Main cookhouses were there for rations.	C.C.T.
BERNAVILLE	30/8/16		O.C. visited REZUVAL and examined premises of bath with Town Major and saw as to water for Billets. Inspected drainage and conservancy systems at E. Lep. Rest Station and interviewed O.C. Visited BARTON and inspected cavalry & 27 Howitzer A 139 Heavy Battery R.G.A. and 1/1 Welsh Heavy Battery R.G.A. visited Town Major and advised as to improvement of sanitation & attached to moperator latrine and conservation. O.C. 8/ Brigade R.F.A. visited and advised as to construction and latrines. Capt. 7.9 G.S.Wen, R.A.m.C. 57 Field Ambulance reported for few days training with Section. Two sanitary inspectors with 87 & 87 Brigades present camp. 119 Divisional Ambulance either two

WAR DIARY or INTELLIGENCE SUMMARY

Army Form C. 2118.

Place	Date	Hour	Summary of Events and Information	Remarks and references to Appendices
DOULLENS			Staying at DOULLENS. The following Units marched - 7 Loyal North Lancashire Regiment Transport, No 3 (Divisional Train) Supply Column, Farms of Royal Field Artillery, Left Transport and Depots 8th Royal Marston Battery, 7/D and A B and D Britain's 59th Brigade R.F.A. Also 1/5, 1/6, 1/7 and one attached 9th Div. enjoyed a sanitary station at BERNAVILLE. Arrived of attached men under direction of A.D.M.S. section engaged in sanitary work at BERNAVILLE. U.S. began cycles in removal of refuse & materials employed 12 W.H. and erecting latrines at BERNAVILLE. Accommodation for officers prepared and supplies to troops. Indicated distance Into tunnel for the above C.U.T.	
BERNAVILLE	31st Dec		Arrived at 19 Brancourt Depot at SCHIMETZ area extended from a to found on the lock with entrance from case of Bridge of road leaving from m… A short DUTRESOIS above Solten content of the arms are from been sent and arrived in New Transport TREAUNICTS for patrols with the contacts arranged to Monday of Inset-etc. mainland NEUZECOURT and Experience with 1/10, 9/1/15.	

Army Form C. 2118

WAR DIARY
— or —
INTELLIGENCE SUMMARY
(Erase heading not required.)

Instructions regarding War Diaries and Intelligence Summaries are contained in F. S. Regs., Part II. and the Staff Manual respectively. Title Pages will be prepared in manuscript.

Place	Date	Hour	Summary of Events and Information	Remarks and references to Appendices
			regarding isolation of contacts in case of Measles; visited FIENVILLERS and made arrangements with MOR for isolation of contacts of case of Cerebro Spinal Meningitis which had occurred in No 2 Co 19" Divisional Train. Two sanitary inspectors with 58" Brigade, one with 57" Brigade, two with 58" Brigade, two with 19" Divisional Artillery and two stationed at DOULLENS. The following were inspected 5" Ammunition Sub Park Headquarters & North Staffordshire Regt and transport, No 6 Divisional Train, "Y" Trench Mortar Battery and 9 Cheshire Regt, the M.G.B. and S.A.A. attached were engaged in sanitary duties at BEZAINCOURT. Inspected of attached men under direction of 128 & Section engaged in sanitary duties at BERNAVILLE. B/S wagon supplied for removal of refuse the Corporals constructing latrines. Notes written prepared and supplied ADMS. Marks cards issued for free chlorine.	

C. V. Kilroton Col. A.D.M.S.

COMMITTEE FOR THE
MEDICAL HISTORY OF THE WAR
Date **13 MAR. 1917**

36th Casualty Station

WAR DIARY
or
INTELLIGENCE SUMMARY.

Army Form C. 2118.

36 Sanitary Se 1/9

War Diary
of
36th Sanitary Section
R.A.M.C (T.F.)

From 1st to 31st January 1917

Vol 19

WAR DIARY
INTELLIGENCE SUMMARY.

Army Form C. 2118.

Place	Date	Hour	Summary of Events and Information	Remarks and references to Appendices
BERNAVILLE	1st January 1917		Two evening inspections with 36th Brigade, two with 57th Brigade, two with 58th Brigade, two with 19th Divisional Artillery and two obtained at DOULLENS. The following units of the 19th Division inspected – 10th Royal Warwickshire Regt, 57th Trench Mortar Battery, 8th Wiltshire Regt Hors and Repr, 58th Brigade HQ, 58th Trench Mortar Battery, HQ R.F.C. FIENVILLERS and 19 and 27 Squadrons of R.F.C. Ammunition Dump at FIENVILLERS inspected. The 1st 6th and one attached men engaged in sanitary duties at BEZAINCOURT. Squads of attached men engaged in sanitary duties at BERNAVILLE under direction of 1st 6th of Section. U.S. wagon supplied for removal of refuse to incinerator. Attached carpenter constructing latrines. Main dishes prepared and supplied K.R.M.B. Water carts inspected and tested for use by chlorine. 6 O. engaged on office routine etc. C.O.	
BERNAVILLE	2nd January		6 O inspected 8th Wiltshire Regt at BOIS BERSUES and H.Q. interviewed as to latrine and completion of incinerator, inspected Divisional Baths at OUTREBOIS, inspected latrines at BRETEL; inspected baths, latrines and incinerator at BEZAINCOURT; interviewed Staff Capt 57 Infantry Brigade as to sanitary improvements at	

WAR DIARY
INTELLIGENCE SUMMARY.
(Erase heading not required.)

Army Form C. 2118.

Place	Date	Hour	Summary of Events and Information	Remarks and references to Appendices
			Brigade H.Q. inspected baths at CANDAS and interviewed Town Mayor as to sanitation and hospice of same. Two platoons with 57 Brigade, two with 57 Brigade two with 58 Brigade, two with 19 Divisional Artillery and the remainder at DOULLENS. The I.T.O. was also asked over engaged in sanitary duties at GEZAINCOURT was in employed on removal of refuse from huts. Squad of attached men under direction of N.C.O. of section, engaged in sanitary duties at BERNAVILLE. O.C. was inspected his several ?? offices to incinerators. Attached conducting conducting latrines with Indian labour with latrine supplied 18 R.F.A. Naturcous inspected and latine for use obtained. The following Units inspected – 9 Nick Regt 58 Brigade Machine Gun Co 57 Brigade Machine Gun Co. 8" Gloucestershire Regt and Transport 57 Brigade 19 Divisional Salvage Co. Planet. Farm & Wiltshire Regt and 52 Field Ambulance inspected. CCJ.	
BERNAVILLE	3rd Jany		L.B. attended conference at office of D.D.M.S. 3rd Corps DOULLENS. interviewed O.C. 38 Mt. K.S. Division as to baths and sanitation at Divisional School; visited OUTREBOIS and sanitary inspection made; visited ?? visited LE MEILLARD and interviewed H.Q. 9"	

A 5834. Wt. W4973/M687. 750,000. 8/16. D D. & L. Ltd. Forms/C.2118/13.

WAR DIARY
INTELLIGENCE SUMMARY.

Army Form C. 2118.

(Erase heading not required.)

Place	Date	Hour	Summary of Events and Information	Remarks and references to Appendices
			9 Royal Welch Fusiliers Regt. moved MONT RENAULT FARM reference water supply etc. and ambulance and consulted Staff O/C 19 Division as to sanitation at new Divisional Cowl. Two sanitary inspectors with 56th Brigade, two with 57th Brigade, two with 58th Brigade, two with our Unit lately vacated by 19 Divisional Artillery and two stations at DOULLENS. Blankets from 82nd Field 6°R.E. and Field Ambulance disinfected. Six at 6.0. and six attached men engaged in sanitary duties at GEZAINCOURT. O.S. began employed on removal of refuse or horse troughs at GEZAINCOURT. O.S. began employed in removal of refuse at + incinerate. Carpenter fixing new latrine seat mitres supplied to R N.D. Netheath inspected and held for fire distance. The following Units inspected. 7 Kings Own Royal Lancaster Reg. 9 Royal Welch Fusiliers Regt. 58 French Mortar Battery and 57 Brigade H.Q. Billets of BRETEL inspected. C.V.J.	
BERNAVILLE 4 Jany			C.O. travelled to LONGUEVILLETTE and inspected sanitation and proceeded thence to came to an 8and. 19 Bruain inspected 8th North Staffordshire Regt. moved HARDINVAL and inspected Public latrine. proceeded to BOUCHES and inspected sanitation Bath. Inspected T.A. Conductor Newcastle	

WAR DIARY
or
INTELLIGENCE SUMMARY.

Army Form C. 2118.

(Erase heading not required.)

Place	Date	Hour	Summary of Events and Information	Remarks and references to Appendices
			O Bonen attached to 57 Field Ambulance after completion of preceding training. Two sanitary inspection with 58 Brigade. Two with 57 Brigade, two with 58 Brigade. Two in area lately occupied by 19 Divisional Area and two detained at DOULLENS. The following Units inspected:- 7 Field Evacuation Bearer transport, of Shelter Reg. transport and supply attached to 7 Field Ambulance. Rep. on transport halts, horses, bivouacs and supplies to R.H.S. Motoriets inspected and noted for his attention. Sa. M.D. and was attached over engaged in sanitary duties at GEZAINCOURT; 18 mag. emergers in general of refuse from huts. Reports of Employment attached men engaged in sanitary duties under instruction of S.S.O. J. Received BERNAVILLE. 18 mag. engaged in removal of refuse to his huts. Blankets from 6 Offices & Reg. examined Ambulances inspected in areas Major Mongkol from POMMERALEHE NOMERD and HEDIECOURT prior to departure. No new cases coming in from 3 regiments at ASTHIEBLE.	
			C.C.T.	
BERNAVILLE 5ᵗʰ Jany			C.O. inspected sanitation of HARDINVAL DOS CANES, NEZEROLLES and OUTREBOIS and proceeded afterwards on some to BOMIS & troops. Two sanitary inspection with 56ᵗʰ Brigade, two with 57 Brigade, two with 58 Brigade, two in area lately occupied by 19 Divisional Artillery and two detained at DOULLENS. The	

Army Form C. 2118.

WAR DIARY
or
INTELLIGENCE SUMMARY.
(Erase heading not required.)

Place	Date	Hour	Summary of Events and Information	Remarks and references to Appendices
			Following Units inspected. 7 South Lancashire Regt and bivouac, 56th Machine Gun Co, 19th Section 6th Field Co R.E. 57th Machine Gun Co and bivouac, 57 French Mortar Battery, 315 Battery R.F.A. 6th Wiltshire Regt bivouac and sport. 6th & 8th of Section and one attached man engaged in sanitary fatigues at GEZAINCOURT. N.C.Os, men employed running refuse from trench. Squads of attached men under direction of N.C.O. of Section engaged in sanitary duties at BERNAVILLE; N.C.Os, men employed in removal of refuse from trench. Water troughs inspected and traced for two schemes. Branches from 6th Wiltshire Regt transferred to Green Wood Bivouacs. De-lousing arrangements machine of Pulex Insecticide at AUTHIEULE.	
BERNAVILLE	6th Jany		C.O. arranged with 19th D.H.Q. as to transfer of attached men to 17/19th Divisional Baths. Fortnightly inspecting routes arranged as arranged for Sections. Officers from town and cooks. Others were laundry. Two sanitary inspectors with 57th Brigade, two with 58th Brigade. Two on an emergency work received by 19th Divisional Artillery and one Coy stationed at DOULLENS.	C.C.D.

WAR DIARY
INTELLIGENCE SUMMARY.
(Erase heading not required.)

Army Form C. 2118.

Instructions regarding War Diaries and Intelligence Summaries are contained in F. S. Regs., Part II. and the Staff Manual respectively. Title pages will be prepared in manuscript.

Place	Date	Hour	Summary of Events and Information	Remarks and references to Appendices
			The following Units inspected: Section 21 Field Coy RE, 231st Manch Pioneers, Section 7 Loyal North Lancashire Regt and transport, 55th Machine Gun Coy, B.V.M.R. Staffordshire Regt, 57th trench Mortar Battery, 7 Cheynd Welch Fusilier Regt and 58th Trench Mortar Battery, 81 1.8 of Action and six attacked men engaged in sanitary duties at BEZAINCOURT. N.C.O's & men employed removing refuse from trench. N.C.O. & 9 men of Action engaged in sanitary duties at BEFINVILLERS. N.C.O. & 9 men employed for removal of refuse from trench. Plate parties inspected and handed to R.M.B. Inclements inspected also Baker's trench latrines. Newly Sanitary and water carts and refuse removed. Platoon 9 14 Division. Blankets from 5th Welsh Regt inspected. No sign of 14 Division. OUTHIEULE supervising construction of public urinals.	
BERNAVILLE	7th Army		M.O. visited AUTHEUX. reviewed cases of Rubella at 9 Cheshire Regt and arranged suitable measures. BUSSEROUES and arrived M.O.8 Wiltshire Regt as to outbreak of Rubella. visited OUTREBOIS and inspected new cooking kitchens & baths. Inspected first cooking Baths at BEZAINCOURT. Baths. Went anterroomer. Army Major on sanitary matters inspected La Forte	C.C.T.

WAR DIARY or INTELLIGENCE SUMMARY

Army Form C. 2118.

Place	Date	Hour	Summary of Events and Information	Remarks and references to Appendices
			At CANDAS two men selling tarts at Ration. Arrested with arms of Brownie & outbreak of Rubella and failed official accommodation. Inspected 101 B.H.Q. advance details reliving 1st men. Two sanitary inspectors with 57th Brigade. Two with 57th Brigade. Two on area recces by 19 Divisional Artillery and by Adjutant at DOULLENS. Manufacture Base and tipping point 2 M.T.A.S.C. inspected. Six with 89 Return and one attached men engaged in sanitary duties at GEZAINCOURT. Six men employed removing refuse from trench. Six men of Engineers attached men engaged in sanitary duties at BERNAVILLE. Under direction of T.C.B of Return. R.E. men employed in removing refuse from trench & encampments. Worked carpenter preparing nail notice. Notice cards inspected and looked for the chlorine. Inspection of greases and other rubbish removed.	C.C.T.
BERNAVILLE	8 May		A.C. arranged with Town Major, BERNAVILLE as to continuity of evacuation of attached men working with 19 Division. Engaged in routine office work and anonymous matters. Running of attached men etc. Two sanitary inspection with 56th Brigade, two with 57th Brigade, two with 58th Brigade, two on area recces by 19 Divisional Artillery and two adjutant at DOULLENS. The following units inspected - Royal Flying Corps and	

WAR DIARY or INTELLIGENCE SUMMARY

Army Form C. 2118.

Place	Date	Hour	Summary of Events and Information	Remarks and references to Appendices
			Visited Divisional HQrs at CANDAS, M.T. Reserve Park A.S.C., H.T. 6th Division Regt. No 1 & 2 A.S.C. and 255 Brigade R.F.A. The M 60 of Division Train are attaching men engaged in sanitary fatigue at BEZINCOURT. (Two parks unthinking army to move of 1st Division) Hogard of Employment attached men engaged in sanitary fatigue at BERNAVILLE under direction of MO of Division. MO urges employment of unaccompanied from trench to increase attacks who have been on duty in trenches last few days. Plan of Area prepared. Waincourt inspected and lists for his scheme. Blocks of infected houses and areas condemns to demol. of Bernard. C.C.F.	
BERNAVILLE	9th May		D.D. returned from Paris and conferred with Capt. Sinclair as to march. Two sanitary inspectors stationed at DOULLENS. The following Units inspected as to sanitary conditions:— 61st Divisional Ammunition Column at OUTREBOIS and OCCOCHES, 167 Divisional Salvage Coy. Bivouac nearly vacated by the following units inspected — 7th East Lancashire Regt. 56 Trench Mortar Battery, 56 Brigade HQ 56 Machine Gun Co, 10 Worcestershire Regt. 10 Royal Warwickshire Regt., 57 Trench Mortar Battery, N.I 6th A.S.C., 8 North Staffordshire Regt., 8 Gloucestershire Regt and	

WAR DIARY
OF
INTELLIGENCE SUMMARY.
(Erase heading not required.)

Army Form C. 2118.

Instructions regarding War Diaries and Intelligence Summaries are contained in F. S. Regs., Part II. and the Staff Manual respectively. Title pages will be prepared in manuscript.

Place	Date	Hour	Summary of Events and Information	Remarks and references to Appendices
			53rd Machine Gun Co. train fitted forward trotinier inspection horses for free chosens. Further movement of attached men forward over to P.O. 19 Divisional Baths Laundry. GMcC.	
BERNAVILLE	10th Jany	6.C	marched to STOMP. Troops at DOULLENS. Junks entrained with keep trembles as to mazzes on hand. Two sanitary inspectors observed at DOULLENS. The following Units inspected as to sanitary arrangements – A & C even II Battn 3/1 Brigade R.F.A.(62=Division) Ward & Bathing Trench tenders (19 Division) 223 Action Batt. Field R.E. Billets at BERNAVILLE inspected and reported to Town Major. Billets vacated by 7 Kings two Royal Lancaster Regt and 7 South Lancashire Regt inspected. Three forces at BEAUVAL Marcia but billets also this forms at LONGUEVILLETTE. Holiwash inspected and used for the chlorine. Billets of 6 Brigade HQ Middlesex Regt and Essex Regt 2nd Division inspected. GMcC.	

Army Form C. 2118.

WAR DIARY
or
INTELLIGENCE SUMMARY.
(Erase heading not required.)

Place	Date	Hour	Summary of Events and Information	Remarks and references to Appendices
BERNAVILLE	11 Jany		10.0 interviewed Town Major. BERNAVILLE inspection latrine occupied by Corporal 1 and 7 Battalion, rooms which most inspection carried out. Horse carts inspected and noted for fine schedule. Out of Bounds notices placed at farms in LONGUEVILLETTE, farms at MATOINVAL and Beer Author at HEM. Billets and general sanitation of BERNAVILLE inspected. The following french at BERNAVAL examined - N° 7, 8, 9 and 12. Billets N° 1, 8, 15, 16, 22 and 2.) at BOIS BERGUES examined. Two sanitary inspectors examined at DOULLENS. Brigade HQ of 2nd Division (MONDICOURT) inspected also 17 Middlesex Regt at AUTIEUX and 13th Essex Regt at BUSBERGUES. 18th Durham Light Inf. Regt and units of 30th Brigade RFA (62nd Division) inspected. [sig]	
BERNAVILLE	12 Jany		During Lt back at Transport arrive no inspection service in service out by C.O. interval visit in office work. HQ and N° 1, 2 and 3 Sections of 19th Divisional Ammunition Column inspected. Sanitary Inspection inhabitants over area. Notes prepared and instructions inspected. [sig]	

WAR DIARY
or
INTELLIGENCE SUMMARY.
(Erase heading not required.)

Army Form C. 2118.

Place	Date	Hour	Summary of Events and Information	Remarks and references to Appendices
BERNAVILLE	13th Jany		Owing to lack of transport the CO could not carry out inspection of area. Sanitary Inspector further disliked our area. Sanitation of BERNAVILLE inspected by CO. Capt Z Knot-Muhr Bellevue inspected at OUTREBOIS and W Bailey at OCCOCHES. (19 Durham Light Infantry inspected FROHEN-LE-PETIT. MEZEROLLES, OUTREBOIS and OCCOCHES noted and firing latrines AUTHIEULE and TERRAMESNIL inspected.	
BERNAVILLE	14 Jany		CO inspected farms and camps at AMPLIER and SARTON and reported fully on condition to XXth Corps XIII Corps and also upon provision to form new AMPLIER. The following units inspected as to sanitary conditions :- 7 R N Kent Regt 55 Field Ambulance, 8 East Surrey Regt (18 Division) 18 Durham Light Infantry Regt (31st Division) Brench at GEZAINCOURT inspected. Billets of 15 West York Regt at SARTON inspected, also billet of 112 Battery R.F.A.	
BERNAVILLE	15 Jany		CO inspected 31st Divisional Bayonet School at BEAUMETZ also sanitation of farm and reported on conditions to XXth Corps XIII Corps. CO inspected CANDAS and AUTHIEUX and reported on sanitary arrangements at Corps XIII Corps farm thence TERRAMESNIL.	

WAR DIARY
INTELLIGENCE SUMMARY
(Erase heading not required.)

Army Form C. 2118

Place	Date	Hour	Summary of Events and Information	Remarks and references to Appendices
			Conferred with a.d. Kitchener of Sanitation for village. Sanitation at AMPLIER inspected. Also BERNAVILLE, GORGES and BERNEUIL. EPECAMPS inspected. Billets of X Battery, Durel Morton (9th Division) and 1st Durham Light Inf. Regt (3rd Division) at FROHEN-LE-PETIT inspected. Billets at MEZEROLLES and BOISBERGUES inspected. Billets and sanitation of AUTHEUX and MACPER Fm inspected. 19 Divisional Ammunition Column billets at HEM and HARDINVAL inspected. Latrines inspected and noted for the Chlorine. Five ponds at BERNEUIL and OUTREBOIS placed "Out of Bounds."	
BERNAVILLE	16th Jany		C.O. visited COCOCHES and interviewed Town Major, referred to D.D.M.L. XIII Corps at DOULLENS, made necessary arrangements for moving technical Re 10.a.m. Inspection proceeded to AMPLIER on return duty. Latrines inspected and noted for the Chlorine. Billets at MACQUERIE of 189th MG machine Gun Co., 63rd Division and 9th Field Ambulance, 3rd Division inspected. Billets at Aijul Nasal Brown at GORGES and BERNEUIL inspected. Also billets at CANDAS and GRIMONT. Billets of 15th West Yorks Regt, 9th Division, at OUTREBOIS inspected. Billets vacated by 5th Argyll Sutherland Highlanders at LE	

WAR DIARY
or
INTELLIGENCE SUMMARY
(Erase heading not required.)

Army Form C. 2118

Place	Date	Hour	Summary of Events and Information	Remarks and references to Appendices
BERNAVILLE	17 Jany		MEILLARD inspected. Sanitation of BEAUVAL inspected good. A.D.M.S. visited TERRAMESNIL and inspected hirse-water troughs. CO visited HEUZECOURT refresher cros. of Carpentry. On instruction from DDMS XIII Corps, 12 men of section sent to area church to be taken over by section and 12 men from 7½ Sanitary Section reported to this Unit and distributed over area. Water supplies at AMPLIER, MARIEUX, SARTON, AUTHIEULE and TERRAMESNIL investigated and labelled where necessary. Sanitation of HEUZECOURT inspected also HULEUX. G.N.a.	
BERNAVILLE	18 Jany		A.D.M.S. visited AUTHIEULE and inspected sanitation of camps and village; proceeded to SARTON and inspected camp, reticulants inspected and tested for free chlorine. Sanitation of MARIEUX inspected. Billets at LE MEILLARD inspected and wire traps notified as to construction. 12 men	

WAR DIARY
or
INTELLIGENCE SUMMARY
(Erase heading not required.)

Army Form C. 2118

Place	Date	Hour	Summary of Events and Information	Remarks and references to Appendices
BERNAVILLE	19th Jany		Section in forward area. Sanitation of GEZAINCOURT inspected. Billets at TERRAMESNIL inspected, also SARTON. GMc.	
BERNAVILLE	19th Jany		C.O. visited MARIEUX and investigated complaints as to latrines and refuse pits at BONNEVILLE. C.M.P's conferred with Town Major MARIEUX and AMPLIER hut at AMPLIER disinfected. CO conferred with Town Major TERRAMESNIL. Billets at BONNEVILLE after DOULLENS visited 2/O.@ Divisional Gunners. ORVILLE. Conferred with OC 71st Sanitary Section as to arrangements on changing over area. Sanitation of FIENVILLERS. VACOGERIE and DOMESMONT inspected. Billets at FROHEN-LE-PETIT inspected. Sanitation of BRETEL inspected. Railheads inspected and tested for fire scheme. 12 men in forward area. 12 men from 71st Sanitary Section instructed in system of inspection of area. Billets at MARIEUX inspected. GMc.	
BERNAVILLE	20th Jany		C.O. visited GEZAINCOURT, LONGUEVILLETTE and BRETEL and inspected sanitation of these villages. Refuse and instructions furnished to Town Major GEZAINCOURT.	

WAR DIARY
or
INTELLIGENCE SUMMARY
(Erase heading not required.)

Army Form C. 2118

Place	Date	Hour	Summary of Events and Information	Remarks and references to Appendices
BERNAVILLE	21st Jan'y		Sanitation of CANDAS and LONGUEVILLETTE inspected. Inspection made of huts and farm sanitation at BERNAVILLE and GRIMONT. Latrines prepared and disinfectants in use inspected and tested for free chlorine. 12 men of section in forward area and 12 men of 71st sanitary section shown normal siftings in this division area. Two men stationed at DOULLENS.	GWA
BERNAVILLE	21st Jan'y		D.D.M.S. visited DOULLENS and informed K.D.M.S. XIII Corps. Two men of section stationed at DOULLENS. 12 men of section in forward area; 12 men of 71st Sanitary Section with section. Billets of 185th Brigade R.F.A. at BEAUCHEL inspected. Sanitation of GORGES inspected. Billets No. 1 at OUTREBUIS inspected (occupied area of Electro-Pneumatic Workshop) Latrines and area inspected and tested for free chlorine.	GWA
BERNAVILLE to COUIN	22nd Jan'y		H.Q. proceeded from BERNAVILLE to COUIN. Remaining men of section together with stores and equipment moved to new billets at COUIN. 12 men of section in forward area making arrangements. Water supplies in new area inspected.	

Army Form C. 2118

WAR DIARY
or
INTELLIGENCE SUMMARY
(Erase heading not required.)

Instructions regarding War Diaries and Intelligence Summaries are contained in F. S. Regs., Part II. and the Staff Manual respectively. Title Pages will be prepared in manuscript.

Place	Date	Hour	Summary of Events and Information	Remarks and references to Appendices
COUIN	23rd Jany		Area investigated. Two men stationed at DOULLENS. GMcA. M.O. visited COIGNEUX, AUTHIE and ST LEGER: visited DOUINS I Corps at ACHEUX. Bath options at COIGNEUX and SAILLY DELL investigated. Sanitation of the following districts inspected - FAMECHON, AUTHIE, ST LEGER, BAYENCOURT, SAILLY, SAILLY DELL and COUIN. GMcA.	
COUIN	24 Jany		I.O. inspected camp on AUTHIE ROAD occupied by 1/5th West Yorkshire Regt. Latrines inspected and holes for use chlorine. Six men suspecting enteritis (sanitary apparatus at 17 Heavy Artillery Group). Six men instructed to two men of Field Ambulance in work as an A.D.S. HEBUTERNE. Sanitation of the following districts inspected - COUIN, COIGNEUX, ST LEGER, AUTHIE, FAMECHON, SAILLY, SAILLY DELL and BAYENCOURT. The following units inspected at COUIN - 19 Bde Salvage Co, Mounted Military Police, 19 Bde Workshop Co. and Church Army Hut. GMcA.	

WAR DIARY or INTELLIGENCE SUMMARY.

Army Form C. 2118.

Place	Date	Hour	Summary of Events and Information	Remarks and references to Appendices
COUIN	25th Jany		A.D.M.S. accompanied A.D.V.S. 19 Division to SAILLY, inspected 19 Divn Ammn Bavard with stores, overhouse of 113th Battery R.G.A.; proceeded to FAMECHON accompanied by inspects and examined fully the latrines, incinerators at THIEVRES and interviewed Town Major and made necessary recommendation to him. Construction of sanitary appliances at St Henry Rutelling Room supervised. Instruction in water order given to Field Ambulance personnel at A.D.S. HEBUTERNE. Intricants inspected and holes for fire showers. The Sanitation of the following districts inspected. COUIN, COIGNEUX, ST LEGER, AUTHIE, FAMECHON, SAILLY, SAILLY DELL and BAYENCOURT. The following Units at FAMECHON inspected. 9th Yorks Lancs Regt, 4/6th and 7/ Ammunition Columns. Units at COUIN inspected. 19 Bnd Salvage Co, 19 Bnd Unit Jas School Band. Mounted Military Police. Units at COIGNEUX inspected. 57 and 58 Brigade Rutelling Bomb camps at J 9.c.2.4 (sheet 57D) A, D Howitzers of 1st R.F.A., 4/6 and B Howitzers of 157 R.F.A., B Howitzers of 58 R.F.A. Units at ST LEGER inspected 4/23 & 19 Divl Train, 6 Labour Batt, R.E. 47 New Yorks Luen Rifles.	

G.M.A.

Army Form C. 2118.

WAR DIARY
or
INTELLIGENCE SUMMARY.
(Erase heading not required.)

Instructions regarding War Diaries and Intelligence Summaries are contained in F.S. Regs. Part II and the Staff Manual respectively. Title pages will be prepared in manuscript.

Place	Date	Hour	Summary of Events and Information	Remarks and references to Appendices
COUIN	26th July		A.D.M.S. accompanied by A.D.M.S. 19 Brown marcou HEBUTERNE and inspected sanitation and water supply of village. Given instruction of sanitary organisation. Supervised at 17 Heavy Artillery Group. Instruction in water duties given to Field Ambulances. Proceeded to A.D.S. HEBUTERNE. Relieved inspected and noted to/we chlorine. Instruction in following matters inspected. COUIN, COIGNEUX ST LEGER, AUTHIE, FAMECHON, SAILLY, SAILLY DELL and BAYENCOURT, also following units:- 36 Brigade A.D., 82 Field Co. R.E. 19th Column, 19 Brig Ammunition Column, 79 Ammunition Column, 198 Siege Battery R.G.A. 96 Siege Battery R.G.A. 19 Div Sub Park Gas School, 62 Brig Ammunition Column, 6 Labour Battn R.E., 2/6 West Yorkshire Regt. M.T.O. 69/9 Div Train, 30 M.A.C. Workshop, 19 Div Mobile Veterinary Section 48 Heavy Battery R.G.A. + 65 Siege Battery R.G.A. 6.O. engaged in inspection of Mounts and Necks Sanitary Patrols. E.R.C.	
COUIN	27th July		C.O. inspected Sanitary lines of 7 Sherwood Forester Regt, 5 Sherwood Forest Regt, 2/6 West Yorkshire Regt at ROSSENDOL FARM, 2/5 West Yorkshire Regt near COUIN. Weekly Chlorination returns prepared. Inspections inspected and tested for Free Chlorine. Sanitary areas inspected COUIN, COIGNEUX,	

A 5934. Wt. W4973/M687. 750,000. 8/16. D.D. & L. Ltd. Form C/2118/13.

WAR DIARY
or
INTELLIGENCE SUMMARY.
(Erase heading not required.)

Army Form C. 2118.

Place	Date	Hour	Summary of Events and Information	Remarks and references to Appendices
			ST LEGER AUTHIE, FAMECHON, SAILLY, SAILLY DELL and BAYENCOURT also following units :- 62nd Divn Ammunition Column, 19 Div Artillery Park, 58th Brigade Transport Lines, B. & H/Johns Bau, R.E. B. Bailey 86th Brigade R.F.A. 18" and 113th Ammunition Column 3/2nd West Riding R.E. AUTHIE following 58th Lunch Mortar Battery, 5th Machine Gun Co. 58 and 72nd Heavy Artillery Groups 81st Field A.R.E. 238th Siege Battery R.G.A. 9th West. Regt. 36th Brigade H.Q. 7th South Lancashire Regimental Transport and 56 Brigade H.Q.	A.M.A
COUIN	28 Jany		G.O. visited SAILLY DELL and inspected Divisional camp occupied by 2/5 West Yorkshire Regt. and again on inspection forwarded to CROWN 62nd Divn: 58th and 72nd Heavy Artillery Groups inspected and other subunits NISSENS & Carts. Male outfits in area noted and inspected. Network inspected and tested for free chlorine. Visited SOUIN, COIGNEUX, ST LEGER, AUTHIE, FAMECHON, SAILLY, SAILLY DELL and BAYENCOURT, also following Bivvy. Q1st and 2nd DID Ammunition Columns, 7 West Lancashire Regt, Y.M.C.A. Hut at BAYENCOURT, 5/3d	

WAR DIARY
INTELLIGENCE SUMMARY
Army Form C. 2118.

Place	Date	Hour	Summary of Events and Information	Remarks and references to Appendices
			Trench Mortar Battery, Personnel of 87th Field Co. R.E. Personnel of 1 MB 28th Brigade R.F.A. 6 Wiltshire Regt. 1/R War Yorkshire Regt. 1st Ammunition Column 2nd Light mortar Workshop, 19 Divn M.G. 19 Div. Train H.Q. 1/4 York Para Regt. 1/4 King Own Yorkshire Light Inf., 3/R Machine Gun Coys, 1/1 Devon R.E. 1/9 Div R.E. Dump at J.3.c.4.6 (Sheet 57 D)	WR
COVIN	29th January		16 C. visited COIGNEUX and inspected 88 and B Battery 87 Brigade R.F.A. and B Battery 88 Brigade R.F.A. and report on inspection ABDMS 19-D1-5. Personnel of A and D Batteries 87th Brigade R.F.A., 14 Divn A.T.Co R.E. and 6 Yukon Det R.E. inspected and report on attached. 4 Devons I Cys. Malvoirs inspected and tested for fire discharge. Main station in area inspected. Inoculation in following districts inspected: COIGNEUX, ST LEGER, AUTHIE, FAMECHON, SAILLY, SAILLY-DELL and BAYENCOURT also following units 7th Loyal North Lancashire Regt. 5 South Wales Borders Regt. Transport 27th King Own Royal Lancaster Regt. Transport, 1 2/5 York Lanes Regt, 231 Siege Battery, R.G.A. 7 Saw Sanitation Regt. Report 2nd R.A.R.E. 62 Div Ammunition Columns 24 Yorkshire Light Inf. Regt. 18 Squadron R.F.C., Um3 & 19 Div Train. 19 Div Ammunition Column, 9 Clearing Regt. Transport.	WR

WAR DIARY
INTELLIGENCE SUMMARY.
(Erase heading not required.)

Army Form C. 2118.

Place	Date	Hour	Summary of Events and Information	Remarks and references to Appendices
COIGN	30 Jany.		ADMS 19 Divn. referred carriers of area proposed BAUTHIE and interviewed Town Major respecting housing of H.Q. & Bn. 19 Bn. & Ammunition Column. The manner at these times is used as a screen for obstructing the troops. Town Major recommended that it be removed. Medical Station visited. Particulars inspected and taken for use ahead. The sanitation in following villages inspected:- COIGN, COIGNEUX, ST LEGER, FUTILE, FAMECHON SADLE, SAILLY DELL, BAYENCOURT and HEBUTERNE, also following units - 58 Divnl. Motor Battery, 58 Machine Gun Co. 56 + 17 Heavy Artillery Groups, Br. Field Co. R.E. 72nd Heavy Artillery Group, 7 and 15 Siege Batty. R.G.A. 2/5 York & Lancs. Regt. 58 Brigade H.Q. L.A.D. Section, Ammunition Sub-Section, A.S.C. and D. Section 87 R.F.A. 58 Artillery Brigade Ammunition Column. No. 2 and Co. 19 Divl. Ammunition Column. 9 Welch Regt. 183 Infantry Brigade. Brev. H.Q. at ST LEGER also inspected. From conversation it was found Gas attached to Section for purpose of labour & organization. Y.M.B.	
COIGN	31st Jany.		A.D. Works BAYENCOURT area and conferred of inspection of village & premises & FAMECHON. Inspected sanitation of village. Water station no seen visited. Particulars inspected and taken for the Villene. Sanitation of following districts	

WAR DIARY
or
INTELLIGENCE SUMMARY.
(Erase heading not required.)

Army Form C. 2118.

Place	Date	Hour	Summary of Events and Information	Remarks and references to Appendices
			Inspected COLIN, COIGNEUX, ST.LEGER, AUTHIE, FAMECHON, SAILLY, SAILLY DELL and BAVENCOURT, also following units:- 6th Wiltshire Regt, 7th Royal North Lancashire Regt, 19 Bde Amm Col School, Condual J.F. & g/c (Noel 57 D), 3/2, 16, 19, Divn. Train, 3rd Mobile Veterinary Section, 3/5 York Lancs Regt, 9 Welsh Regt. Sickcomm Present in extra weakened	

A. M. Anderson

140/1991

19th Div.

No. 36. Sanitary Section.

Feb 19"

COMMITTEE FOR THE
MEDICAL HISTORY OF THE WAR
Date 4 APR 1917

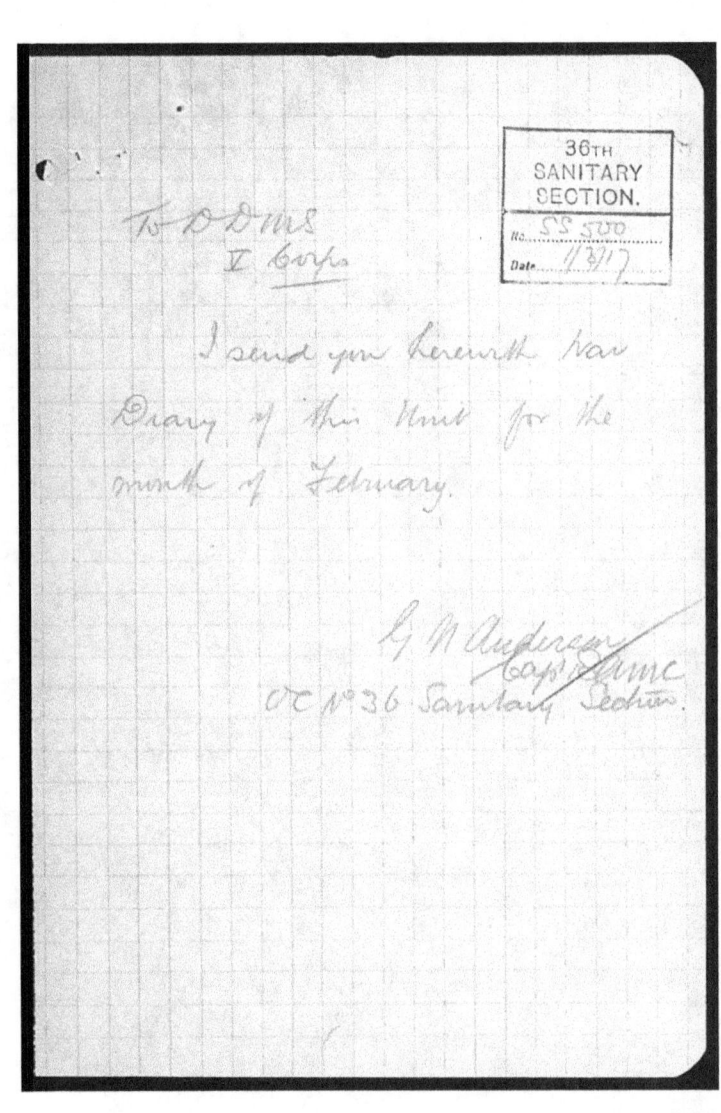

To DDMS
I Corps

36TH SANITARY SECTION.
No. SS 500
Date 1/3/17

I send you herewith War Diary of this Unit for the month of February.

G N Anderson
Capt AMC
OC No 36 Sanitary Section.

Army Form C. 2118.

WAR DIARY
or
INTELLIGENCE SUMMARY.
(Erase heading not required.)

Vol 20

War Diary

of

36th Sanitary Section

From 1st to 21st February 1917

Vol 20

WAR DIARY
INTELLIGENCE SUMMARY.

Army Form C. 2118.

Place	Date	Hour	Summary of Events and Information	Remarks and references to Appendices
COUIN	1st February		Water Stations in area visited, and Water Carts inspected and tested for free chlorine. Sanitation of the following districts inspected :- COUIN, COIGNEUX, St LEGER, la AUTHIE, AUTHIE, FAMECHON, SAILLY au BOIS, SAILLY DELL and BAYENCOURT, also the following units 79th Ammunition Column, 46th Ammunition Column and 77th Ammunition Column 15 cry 2/4th Yorks & Lancaster Regt, 7th East Lancs Regt, 9th Welsh Regt, 223rd Field Coy R.E., 7th East Lancs Regt. Depot, 5th South Wales Borderers Depot & Q.M.S. Stores, 58th Trench Mortar Bty, 58th Machine Gun Co., A Coy 9th Welsh Regt Horse Lines. A" & B" BSPS 86th R.F.A., 62nd D.A.C., 2/4th West Yorks Regt (Camps on AUTHIE Rd.) Transport of 5th Co. 11th Batn Sherwood Foresters, 57th & 58th Bde Refilling Points 2/4th K.O. Yorkshire Light Infantry No 15 Pharmacie of New Company H.Q. Refilling Point (9th Bde). Sole Leclerc the Marine Queue at Authie. B.O. engaged on Officer Routine work. 86th Bde R.F.A HQ, 113th Hy BS, R.F.A.	SMA
COUIN	2nd February		B.O. visits SAILLY au BOIS and inspects billets of 7th East Lancs Regt. Herewith Town Major inspects the general sanitation of the village. Manure Queues were collected and the Public Lavatories + etc of 58th Inf. Bde H.Q. The camps of 5th South Wales Borderers were also inspected, and a site for manure dump was selected. C.O. engages on other + Routine work and preparation for weekly Sanitary Reports. Water stations in area inspected and water Cart materials tested for fire chlorine. Sanitation of following area inspected :- COUIN, COIGNEUX, St LEGER la AUTHIE, AUTHIE, FAMECHON, SAILLY au BOIS, SAILLY DELL and BAYENCOURT; also the following units 2/7th W.Yorks Regt, No 2 Sec., 62nd D.A.C., 19th Bde H.Q. camp, 45th Heavy Bty. Amm Col R.G.A., 65th Siege Bty, R.G.A., 75th Bty, 86th Bde R.F.A attack of 16th + 115th Amm Col. R.G.A., 58th Bde Tramway, 22nd Batt Reserve Sec. R.F.C., No 2 Coy 19th Div. Train, 2/4th K.O.Y.L.I. Regt, 303rd M.A.C. Workshop, 7th East Lancs Regt, 9th Welsh Regt, 220th Siege Bty, R.G.A., A Bty R.F.A, 82nd Field Co. R.E., 2/5th West Yorks R, 19th D.A.C. 2/4th Yorks & Lancaster Regt, 2/6th West Yorks Regt C.O. visited D.D.M.S., I. Echelon at ACHEUX	SMA

WAR DIARY
or
INTELLIGENCE SUMMARY.
(Erase heading not required.)

Army Form C. 2118.

Place	Date	Hour	Summary of Events and Information	Remarks and references to Appendices
COUIN.	3rd February		(A)Visited and Inspected sanitation of No 15 Prisoners of War Coy camp at AUTHIE. Visited Town Major and Inspected Hall &c. 19th B.A.C. horse lines. C.O accompanied by Lieut Hale. W.S, RAMC who is attached to his section from No 59 Field Ambulance for five days instruction in Field Sanitation. C.O. attended conference of 5th Army Medical Society at No 11 C.C.S&., with Capt Hale, on VARRENES Water Stn, on Area unaspected and Water & Baths trails for Div Reserve Bns on AUTHIE – FAMECHON – ST-LÉGER – SAILLY DELL and BAYENCOURT. Reports seen to ADMS. 19, ADMS 2, and 62 Sqdn. Sanitation of following distracts inspected :– COUIN, COIGNEUX, & LÉGER, AUTHIE, 9th Amn (b&), 250th Amn Col, 2/5th West York'rs Regt supplies fatigue party to clean nullah left by last unit. 112th Siege Bty RGA, 58th M.G.C, T.M.B's, 11th R.E.S, 4th Welch Regt, 5, 6 & 7th A Anchors, 2/5th K.O.Y.L.I, 201st Siege Bty R.G.A, 7 K.O.R'fusn hammock, 1, 2/5 S.W.B's, 1st E Lancers, 161st Hvy Bty RGA, 19th Bn's (Inf) (for school) and 62nd D.A.C.	
COUIN.	4th February		C.O. indorsement Reinfer Area Officer as to methods of Sanitation in Area, also S.M.B'n S.Sanitary Officer 46th Division. Inspected RESIGNOL F.A and Camps. COUIN, St.LÉGER Road with B.D.M.S. & Colonel investigating civilian outbreak of measles at COIGNEUX and cannot bact Sanitation of following areas inspected :– COUIN, St LÉGER Area inspected and Water Carts routes for the Chlorine. Sanitation of following units :– COIGNEUX. St-LÉGER, AUTHIE, BAYENCOURT, SAILLY, SAILLY DELL FAMECHON, also following units :– 12th Durham R&MR R.E., 885th R.G.A, 220 Siege Bty R.G.A, 13th Durham 80th Bde (army) R.F.A, 3rd Bde Pontoon R.E, 6th Labour BA&R.F, HQ 885th Bde R.F.A, 2/5 York Lancashire Regt. C.O engages an Officer and 5 O.R's Wetoh Regt, 7 S Lancs Regt, 2/5th West Yorks Regt. Routine Work	GMQ
COUIN	5 February		E.O. proceeded to SPILLY DELL with Lieut HALE RAMC and Major Pattee (I.M.S.) and inspected the sanitation of 151st Siege Bry R.G.A, 177th Siege Bty R.G.A, 6th Wills Regt, Public latrines SAILLY-au-BOIS, and offr-men latrines at No 1574 SAILLY. 150th Siege Bty R.G.A, 717th Siege Bty No 150 Aeroplane, Case of German measles at COUIN Streets, drains, etc, inspected Billets and billets of Certain Bat at N.o 1C° Bde 88th Bde R.F.A and cookhouse R.A.H.Q. M., Bde's, Ma'r' & Shelters. Inere men inspected, COUIN, St LÉGER, three trains of 4 1C° Bde 88th Bde R.F.A, also the following district's inspected – COUIN, St LÉGER, AUTHIE, BAYENCOURT, FAMECHON, COIGNEUX, and SAILLY DELL and SAILLY-au-Bois; also the following units:– 1st R.N. Lancs Regt 154th, 1st Siege Bde and 72nd H.A.G, 1/8th Welch Regt, A coy, 6th Wells Regt, 2/5 York and Lancs Regt, HQ 58th Inf Bde, 12 Sec Water Divroaft Btln, HQ 57 Inf Bde, Y.M.C.A Hut BAYENCOURT, ROSSIGNOL FARM.)	GMQ

WAR DIARY
or
INTELLIGENCE SUMMARY.

Army Form C. 2118.

(Erase heading not required.)

Place	Date	Hour	Summary of Events and Information	Remarks and references to Appendices
COUIN	6th February		C.O. proceeded to HEBUTERNE accompanied by the DADMS 19th Bde. and inspected the general sanitation of that place; also the 7th Somer. Regt. the Water Supplies and system of disinfection were investigated. Water Supplies in area inspected and water carts examined. Arrived for tea Ellonie Sanitation of the following districts inspected:- COUIN, St LEGER, FAMECHON, AUTHIE, BAYENCOURT, SAILLY DELL, SAILLY au BOIS, and COIGNEUX, also the following units:- D.A.C., 2nd West Yorks Regt, 19th Bde D.A.C., 2/5th K.O.R. Lanc Regt, 2/6th York + Lancs Regt, 7th N. Lancs Regt, 19th Sussex Regt, 11th Sussex Regt, 9th + 10th Army, 7th R.O.R. Lanc Regt, 5th T.M. Brig, Siege Transport Regt, 40, 56th M.G. Coy, 13th Sussex Regt, Wilmore Ambulance Hse, 187th R.A. and Y.M.C.A. BAYENCOURT 2nd R.A.R.E., 1st Sussex Bakers, 3rd Sussex Bas. depot, 1/5th Leichshire Regt.	Sna
COUIN	7th February		C.O. arranged for posting of New Water Guards from 19th Division. Four parties at SAILLY DELL and five at COIGNEUX water stations. Inspected billets on COUIN and Compendant 19th Division suggests means for improving existing camp for Water Guards. Visited and inspected sanitation of 2/5 York + Lancs Regt, COIGNEUX, Examined proposals site for manure dump on COIGNEUX - SAILLY DELL Rd. and visited Canteens of Sanitary officers at DDMS Office Z Corps ACHEUX. The following districts and units inspected: COUIN, COIGNEUX, ST LEGER, BAYENCOURT and FAMECHON, AUTHIE, following districts and units inspected. 51st Suss Regt, R.G.A., 1st Suss Regt, R.G.A., 56 M.G. Coy, 1st K.O.R. Lanc Regt, 187th R.A., B.IR. Siege Bty, R.G.A., 220 Siege Bty, R.G.A., 15/66th (Army) R.F. Bde, Ammel. 2/5 K.O. K.H. R.B., Reg Reg T.M. B.S., 77th Amm. Column, 19th Sussex Regt, 2/7th West Yorks Rgt, 13/66 (Army) R.F. Bde, Ammel. 2/5 H.H. KIBG, Ren. 1st Duff. Trench, Pot. Board, 1st Sussex Regt, 57th + 58th R.H. Bdes Canteen, 5th + 7th Pion, 8th Seaforth Saunalees, 5th Souhi Waltes, Ren 3.	Sna

A 8831. Wt. W4973/M657. 750,000 8/16 D.D.&L., Ltd. Forms/C.2118/13

WAR DIARY
or
INTELLIGENCE SUMMARY.
(Erase heading not required.)

Army Form C. 2118.

Instructions regarding War Diaries and Intelligence
Summaries are contained in F. S. Regs. Part II.
and the Staff Manual respectively. Title pages
will be prepared in manuscript.

Place	Date	Hour	Summary of Events and Information	Remarks and references to Appendices
COUIN	8th February		(O) Sanitary details for manure dumps for 59 Field Ambulance ant T.M.B. Area were in hand with inspections. 59 Field Ambulance received in SAILLY DELL inspected and indicated contact of Case of Measles in 6" A/115 Rgt., also a case of Diphtheria in WALDS STEGER to AUTHIE and made investigation in a case of stooping cough, also of 7 miles Fox which however was found to be chicken Pox. C.O. engaged in Office ant Routine Work. Water Station and Baths inspected, bad water for use. Sanitation of following Areas inspected:— COUIN, ST LEGER, BAYENCOURT, COIGNEUX, FAMECHON, SAILLY and BOIS and The DELL and AUTHIE also the following units:- 16th AW. T.M.B. 258th Siege Batt., R.G.A., 235th Siege Bat. R.G.A. 16" Heavy Bat. R.G.A. 14th D.A.C., 2/4 Yorks Lancs Rgt, 154 B6 R.G.A. 2ⁿᵈ (e) R.E., 1/6 (e) W.R. Rgt, 12 Sec Amb, Amm Bn, 56th, 72" H.A.Coombs, 58 Divl. Amb., 1/5th MVE Batloon SC, R.F.C., 19th D.W. Signal Coy to Labour Bn R.E., 85 R.F.A., 87 R.F.A., Heavy By. of 15th Trans. R.E.	HA.
COUIN	9th February		C.O. engaged on Office ant Routine Work, out Preparation of Weekly Sanitary Report. Visits SAILLY DELL Water Stations in the Area inspected ant Water Carts inspected and Laden for the Chlorine. Sanitation of following Ant.C.C. inspected:- COUIN, COIGNEUX, AUTHIE, ST LEGER, FAMECHON, BAYENCOURT, SAILLY and BOIS ant The DELL also the following units:- 1st (M.G.?) 220th Amm Column, 7 Sect Armm Rgt, 6 Welsh 'A' Coy, 14 D.H.Q., 19th Indians Coy, 72 ant 88 R.F.A, 11th Hy B.P., R.P.A 2/4 Royl Lr Bn ant 2/4 York Lans Am 241 S.	HA.
COUIN	10th February		C.O. visits BERTRANCOURT and interviewed OC 1st 10 Sanitary Section. Recover to AUTHIE, visit Town Major ant inspects the 15 Rooms of War Log camb 7 hospitan which was commands. 3 days course on Sanitation. Ideas were sent from Regimental Sanitary Squads. C.O. gave lecture on Service. After which they were engaged on practical work. C.O. engaged Office.	

A 831 ² Wt W4973 M687. 750,000 8/16 D. D. & L. Ltd. Forms/C.2118/13.

WAR DIARY
or
INTELLIGENCE SUMMARY.

Army Form C. 2118.

(Erase heading not required.)

Place	Date	Hour	Summary of Events and Information	Remarks and references to Appendices
			COIGNEUX, BAYENCOURT, ST LEGER, AUTHIE, COUIN, PAMBECHON, SAILLY au BOIS, IVY BELL also the following units:- 2/8th West Yorks R[T], ROSSIGNOL FARM, K.N. (Comm. Pop 18), 2nd T.M.B, 46th & 7th Ammn Columns, 2/7 West Yorks R.T., H.Q. 195th Bde, Transport 9th R. Welsh Lncs, 3rd (?) Mobile Vetinary Section, 2/4 Yorks Lanc R, 5th S.R. M.G., 5th R.W. T.M. B.W, 8th R.E.s, 5th Lancs Regt., 231st R.A., 119th D.A.C., 2/4 Yorks Lancs R[T], 15 May 8.	
COUIN	11 February		C.O. visits AUTHIE and investigates case of infection Disease. Finds case to be a self inflicted wound. Town Major could not give account of either Billets pass. Only 2 Bombs with as. 57 Infantry Regt. Sanitary Squad charged to clean up after training in distance for this Instructions given by C.O. Well Sentries shown no signs as much at the office Dragoons, Samaritains of following Units:- 21/8 West Yorks Regt = COUIN, COIGNEUX, ST LEGER, PAMBECHON, BAYENCOURT, SAILLY au BOIS, and ROSSIGNOL FARM, 19 Bde Anti Gas School, 119 D.T.M.B., 65 Sup Bn, R.F.A., Transport coys of 5 SWBs, 7th E.Lancs Regt, 7 KORL Regt, 2/4 Yorks Lancs Regt., 7 KOR Lancs Regt.	Encl.
COUIN	12 February		CO accompanied ADMS 19th Div to BAYENCOURT and inspected Sanitation of the Village, and duties of 7th E. Norf Regt. Sanitation Squad. K.M. Brown MinorM suggested, and advice to visit staff for instruction to man of Regt Sanitary Squad of present when Sector of Sanitary Unit Section and a number (C.C.) and of the Baths impress an taking for the Chlorine Sanitation of the Drinking Water inspectability. COUIN, ST LEGER, PAMBECHON, AUTHIE, BAYENCOURT, SAILLY au BOIS, COIGNEUX, and the DELL 96 (Pam.t Section), 4th H.Q. Bde, Park G, R.F.A, 58 Bn Tunneling Coys, 5th May Art. Gmps, 19 Bde Sup Pk Tk R.E, 159 Bde R.F.A., 211th Coys R.E, 58 M.G. Coy, 69 Wilts Regt, 72 H. Artillerie, 1/8 West Yorks Regt, 17 KN Fusans R[T], 2 KO Lancs Regt, 70th — 220th Ammunition Column,	Encl.

WAR DIARY / INTELLIGENCE SUMMARY

Army Form C. 2118.

Place	Date	Hour	Summary of Events and Information	Remarks and references to Appendices
COUIN	13th February		C.O. visited ST LEGER and inspected sanitation of the following units:- 11th & 113th Heavy Bty RGA Ammunition Columns, No 3 Coy 19th Div Train, also P's 169th K.O.Y.L.I. in Corps HQ. Water Station in area inspected and water carts fitted for the attachment of lachrymose gas or fly screens, and sanitation of the following units:- COUIN, COIGNEUX, ST LEGER, BAYENCOURT, PAMMECTON, AUTHIE, SAILLY & SAILLY-DELL dealing with following units:- 187th Field Stn Am Col, 7/L + 1/9 Ammunition Column, 55th Bde R.F.A., 113th Hvy Bty RGA, 315th Siege Bty R.G.A., 18th Bde (R.H.A. + R.F.A.), Next Issue Road, 1st X.O.Y.L.I. Regt (no Pipers) 3rd A Echn Div an ROCLINCOURT (Farm) and 6th Rifle Bde Regt.	Sria
COUIN	14th February		C.O. visited PAMMECTON and inspected 2/4th York and Lanc Regt, 19th Div Amm Sol, 1st & 4th Section, 187th Field T.M. Bty, 187th Bde Stokes Mortar Bty, visited AUTHIE to investigate Suspected case of Scarlet Fever. Visited ACHEUX to attend conference of Sanitary Officers of DDMS Ist Corps. Visited Sanitary Section of Sanitation Sections (COUIN, COIGNEUX, BAYENCOURT, ST LEGER) by 6 men of Regt. Sanitary Section Sanitation of (Received Medical Inspection for Reg't Arrangements AUTHIE PAMMECTON, SAILLY and SAILLY-DELL done. Sent Sgt — belief of report & impec, your Report sent to T.Ruis sidelm) Sanitation of the following units inspected:- 8th Y.R & A Transport Lines of & Mobile Vet'y Sec 19th D.A.C. 2/4 York & Lancs Regt, 7034th & 220th Amm Sub Pk Colomn, 119th & 216th Bdes, 19th RFA, 55th T.M. Battery, 7 Provincial & 23rd T.M.Bde, 64th 5th South Staffs Bandsmen, a 23rd L Bty R.G.A. & 7th K.O.Rifleman Regt, 5th and Lance Regt, 215th 9th Yorkshire, 5th South Staffs.	Sria
COUIN	15th February		C.O. inspected Burial works near COUIN, 12th Burnt Buildrs + Armoury, 22nd Rifle Brde Sectn Collimpsel? ER.E 19th Divs and 19th Divs Band do gave lectures to men of Regt. Sanitary Dept on Anatomy, the duties, importance, inhale strain blends and how can be treated for the chlorine Sanitation of following dealt with. COUIN, BAYENCOURT, COIGNEUX, ST LEGER, PAMMECTON, AUTHIE, ST LEGER, SAILLY & SAILLY-DELL, also the following units:- 9 Welsh Regt, 5th + 6th Bn R.O.Y.L.I.Regt, Pipeline Repairs 116th + 115th Hvy Bty R.G.A. Amm Col, 3 Canadian Fld Amb, RE Dep (2nd Line, 1st Corps) 4/6 Scottish Rfls, B.M. (Army) Field Artillery Robin, 87, 5/5 S. Staffs, Y.M.C.A. Houses Bayonworth, 7 S. Lancs Regt., 47 Siege Bty R.G.A., 157 Bde RGA, 1/4 Northants, 2/4 S.R.E. 16 York & Lance Regt.	Sria

A5834 Wt W4973/M687 750,000 8/16 D.D. & L. Ltd. Forms/C2118/13

Army Form C. 2118.

WAR DIARY
or
INTELLIGENCE SUMMARY.
(Erase heading not required.)

Instructions regarding War Diaries and Intelligence Summaries are contained in F.S. Regs., Part II. and the Staff Manual respectively. Title pages will be prepared in manuscript.

Place	Date	Hour	Summary of Events and Information	Remarks and references to Appendices
COUIN	16 Feby		C.O. inspected 17th Reserve Park A.S.C., D/155 R.F.A Brigade, 48th, 77th and 79th Ammunition Columns. C.O. gave lecture to Regimental Sanitary personnel attending lecture school of instruction. Notes taken in own words. Naticants inspected and tested for free chlorine. Sanitation of following districts inspected – COUIN COIGNEUX, ST LEGER, BAYENCOURT, FAMECHON, AUTHIE, SAILLY and SAILLY-DELL, also the following units – B.C. 2/4th North Lancs Regt. 48.19 Div Trench Mortars, 3rd Siege Battery R.G.A. also 29th and 235 Batteries, 58 Signal M.C. 91st Field & R.E. N°12 Section Anti Aircraft Battery, A.B. + B. Cos 6th Wiltshire Regt. Bath erected by units at AUTHIE emphasized. Men from Regimental sanitary squads instructed in practical sanitation. GWA.	
COUIN	17th Feby		C.O. visited Town Major COUIN and arranged for removal of refuse behind 59 Field Ambulance at COIGNEUX; in conjunction with Town Major and O.C. 59 Field Ambulance arranged for the posting of men as incinerators for burning of this refuse. C.O. gave lecture to Regimental Sanitary personnel attending school of instruction + men instructed in practical sanitation. Noted latrines inspected. Watercarts	

WAR DIARY or INTELLIGENCE SUMMARY

Army Form C. 2118.

Place	Date	Hour	Summary of Events and Information	Remarks and references to Appendices
			Inspected and tested for free chlorine, sanitation of following districts inspected. COUIN, COIGNEUX, ST LEGER, BAYENCOURT, FAMECHON, AUTHIE, SAILLY and SAILLY DELL also following Units – 7" Royal North Lancashire Regt, B/170th/line Reg, 72" HQU 5t" Machine Gun Co, 7 East Lancashire Regt (Bgars) 38th Brigade HQ Transport, ATC Batterie 85" RFA, 302 Road Construction Co. RE. C Co 1/4 Yorks Yeoman Regt 1/4 Kings Own Yorkshire Light Inf. A.D. Rations 88" RFA, HQ and 'B' Battery 87" RFA 85" RFA 19 Div Ammunition Sump. COIGNEUX Camp and ROSSIGNOL FARM inspected. Tpts at 6" Wiltshire Regt Mainfield (cases of Measles). G.McQ	
COUIN	15 July		G.O. visited ST LEGER and inspected huts and sanitation of 6 Lincoln Regt 11" Division 65" and 48" Siege Batteries R.G.A. 302" Road Construction Co R.E. and 19" D.A.C. at COUIN. G.O. gave lecture to Regimental Sanitary Personnel attending School of Sanitation and men instructed in practical sanitation, hutch station, mares and inspected. Plans of water supplies in area inspected. The sanitation of the following districts inspected – COUIN, COIGNEUX, ST LEGER, BAYENCOURT, FAMECHON, AUTHIE, SAILLY and SAILLY DELL also following Units – 7" Kings	

WAR DIARY
or
INTELLIGENCE SUMMARY.

Army Form C. 2118.

Place	Date	Hour	Summary of Events and Information	Remarks and references to Appendices
			Own Royal Lancaster Regt. 7 Kings Own Lancashire Regt. 8th Brigade RFA. New Action 19 SAC. 3/B Bann D Coy of Norts & Derby Regt. Ammo Pack Ani 19 SB. 8 Brigade RFA (HR) 113 Heavy Battery RGA. 148 9th Brigade RFA Transport 7 Kings Own Royal Lancaster Regt Transport of Border Regt. Transport 7 Kings Lancashire Regt 58 MGC Transport 231 Heavy Battery RGA 12 MAC and 19 Brigade ARE.	
			S.N.O.	
COUIN	19th Feb.		C.O. inspected billets of 19 Div Amb Pers Cyclist Salvage Co. 3/NBUS. billets and workshops. C.O. visited ROSSIGNOL FARM and inspected sanitation; also "C" Battery 88 FA Brigade; investigated scabies case of truants at COIGNEUX. C.O. gave lecture to Regimental Sanitary Personnel attending School of Sanitation and men enrolled on practical Sanitation. Water Station in area visited. Maps showing water supplies in area prepared. Sanitation of following visited & inspected. COUIN, COIGNEUX, ST LEGER, BAYENCOURT, FAMECHON, AUTHIE, SAILLY and SAILLY DELL. also following units. J Bertin Regt. VIII Corps Sunday 118.19. As Refilling Point 147 Reserve Pk ASC 155 Battery AFA 58 Brigade HQ. 82nd Field Coy R.E. 7 Kings Own Royal Lancaster Regt. 17.58, 72 and 112 MACs 152 Battery R.G.A. 6 Border Regt. D section Anti Aircraft Battery 8 Field CRE 57 Brigade HQ. A/87/14th R.F.A. 7 Field Regt D Coy 58 Brigade Refilling Point.	

MDR

WAR DIARY of INTELLIGENCE SUMMARY.

Army Form C. 2118.

Place	Date	Hour	Summary of Events and Information	Remarks and references to Appendices
COUIN	20th Feby.		10 AM inspected 157th Battery R.G.A. 211 Field Co. R.E. "D" Co. 9 Cheshire Regt. 448 & 449 HAC. 55 MAC. CO gave lecture to Regimental Sanitary personnel attending School of Instruction in Sanitation and min gave practical instruction in area visited. Maps showing latrine supplies in area prepared. Sanitation in following Places inspected:- COUIN, COIGNEUX, ST LEGER, BAYENCOURT, FONCHON, AUTHIE, SAILLY and SAILLY DELTABE following Units - No 1 and 4 of 19 Divisional Train, Nos 1 and 2 Sections 19 Div Ammunition Column, Co. M. S. H. Q. Veterinary Section, 83 Bde R.F.A., 7 Loyal North Lancashire Regt, 448 and 449 Siege Batteries Ammunition Column, 2nd G.R.A., R.E., 7 Lancashire Fusiliers Regt, 58 Brigade 23r Battery R.G.A., 58 Brigade Transport, 19 Div Signals Co, 111th R.G.A., 8th Heavy Artillery Wireless transport, 9 Machine Regt transport, 9 R.Welsh Fus Regt transport, 14 Wilshire Regt transport, 112 & 3rd Bn Ramcourt and 55 Siege Battery R.G.A.	G M A
COUIN	21st Feby.		6 P.M. proceeded to AUTHIE and inspected 7 Div Laundry and interviewed 2nd CMS 5th Bde. Observed conference at Mme DUBOIS' s'café. Regimental Sanitary personnel of Sanitary School of Instruction Neles Clarkin and supplies visited. Sanitation in following details inspected:- COUIN, COIGNEUX, ST LEGER, BAYENCOURT, FONCHON, AUTHIE, SAILLY and SAILLY DELL, also following Units No 4 & 6 19 Div Train, 19 Div Ammunition Column, 6 Lancashire Regt, 19 Div Tunnel Workers, 17 H.L.I. 3rd Siege Battery R.G.A. 235 112 and 29 Siege Batteries R.G.A. 58 Bde HQ 7 Loyal North Lancashire Regt, 5 North Lancs Machine Gun Co. 7 King Own Lancashire Regt, 5 Border Regt 448, 58 Bde R.F.A. D Battery 83 Bde R.F.A., Transport of Wiltshire Regt, 9 R.Welsh Fus Regt, 58 Machine Gun Co, Q.M. Stores Lancashire Regt, 9 RWF, 301 Road Construction O.R.E. 118 squadron R.F.C.	G M A

WAR DIARY
INTELLIGENCE SUMMARY
(Erase heading not required.)

Army Form C. 2118.

Place	Date	Hour	Summary of Events and Information	Remarks and references to Appendices
COUIN	22nd July		G.O. visited FAMECHON and inspected general sanitation of village, also accompanied M.O. of Notts Batt. Regt. around his tents, inspected lines of 19 DivnAmmunition Column. Notts. Battn. men were visited and inspected. Regimental Sanitary personnel attended labout / Sanitation and the sanitation of the following claimed inspected:— COUIN, COIGNEUX, St. LEGER, BAYENCOURT, FAMECHON, AUTHIE, SAILLY and SAILLY DELL also following Units: 15th Battn. R.F.A. 47th Reserve Park. A.S.C., XIII Corps Cavalry, H.Q. 19 Divn. Train, 3rd Div. Ammunition Column, 1st East Yorkshire Regt., 11th Durham Light Inf. C 88 F.A. Brigade, 13 East machine Gun Coy., 7 Durh. Jones Regt. 42nd 78th M.A.C., 1 East Lancashire Fd. Depot, 12 Fd. Gen. Hospt., 93 Machine Gun Coy., 12 Field B.C. R.F.A., 9th Machine Gun Co., 1st East Lancs. Transport, 1st East Yorks. Transport, 87th R.F.A. and 19 Batt. Depot Co.	G.H.A.
COUIN	23rd July		G.O. visited SAILLY and inspected cookhouses and latrines of 1st Durham Light Inf., also inspected 11th Heavy Battn. R.G.A., H.Q. 88 Siege Battn. R.G.A., 231st Siege Battn. R.G.A. and lines of 2nd Anzac Battn. visited AUTHIE and interviewed Brooms 3rd Dn. amn. Co. visited Regimental Sanitary personnel attending Platt of Instruction and men given practical instruction. Notts. Battn. visited and rations issued for her exhum. Sanitation in Funmn. visited, inspected:— COUIN, COIGNEUX, St. LEGER, BAYENCOURT, FAMECHON, AUTHIE, SPILLY and SAILLY DELL also following Units: 93rd Machine Gun Co., 93 Inf. Bde H.Q. 62 Siege Battery Posn., 9th Siege Battn. R.GA. 37 Mobile Veterinary section, 10 Yorks. Lancs. Regt. Transport, 1st East Jones Regt. 19 D.A.C., Dn. R.E., B' Battery 2nd Brigade R.F.A., 6 Brdn Regt., 48 Heavy Battn. Ammunition Col., B' Battery 80 Brigade R.F.A., 18 Lancashire Light Inf. 10 West Yorks Transport, 13 East Yorks Transport, 93 Infantry Brigade H.Q.	G.H.A.

WAR DIARY
or
INTELLIGENCE SUMMARY.
(Erase heading not required.)

Army Form C. 2118.

Place	Date	Hour	Summary of Events and Information	Remarks and references to Appendices
COUIN	24 Feb		C.O. visited COIGNEUX and inspected general sanitation of village, also camp occupied by 6 Border Regt. C.O. engaged on monthly Sanitary Report. Regimental Sanitary personnel attached for instruction in sanitation. Water Machine visits and verificants issued for five chlorine. The sanitation in the following districts inspected COUIN, COIGNEUX, ST LEGER, BAYENCOURT, FAMECHON, AUTHIE, SAILLY and SAILLY DELL also following units - 9 tents Liberty Regt, 70 siege Batty Amm Col, 3rd Army Workshop, No 4 Co 3rd Div Train, 6 Labour Batln R.E., 30 M.A.C., 10 Lacy Yorks Regt, 1st East Yorks Regt, 7 North Staff Regt 6 Border Regt, 221 MC Beatson Section 30th Divl Sanitation Co R.E., 5 and 30 Engine Repairing Parks, 92 Fde M.G.C Lenoard and 112 Co 3rd Div. Train.	GNA
COUIN	25 Feb		H.O. engaged on monthly Sanitary Report and routine office work. Water stations in area visited. Manuals inspected and tested for five chlorine. Sanitation in following districts inspected - COUIN, COIGNEUX, ST LEGER, BAYENCOURT, FAMECHON, AUTHIE, SAILLY, THE DELL and HEBUTERNE also following units - 6 Leicester Regt, 1st East Lancashire Regt, 7 North Lancs Regt, 92 Trench Mortar Battery, 15 West Yorkshire Regt, No 2 Section 10 Div Ammunition Column, Trailing Co II Corps, 31st Div Signals, 31st Divl Workshops, 31st Divl Workshop and Post Office, 30th 94th & 126 31st Div Train.	GNA
COUIN	26 Feb		C.O. visited COIGNEUX with regard to certain case of measles; inspected billets and compston of 1 West Yorkshire Regt. Visited AUTHIE and interviewed A.D.M.S. 31st Division. Water Stations...	GNA

Army Form C. 2118.

WAR DIARY
or
INTELLIGENCE SUMMARY.
(Erase heading not required.)

Instructions regarding War Diaries and Intelligence Summaries are contained in F. S. Regs., Part II. and the Staff Manual respectively. Title pages will be prepared in manuscript.

Place	Date	Hour	Summary of Events and Information	Remarks and references to Appendices
			No area noted. Sanitation in following districts inspected:- COUIN, CORNEUX, St LEGER, BAYENCOURT, FAMECHON, AUTHIE, SAILLY and THE DELL also following Units:- 10 East Yorkshire Regt, 17 East Yorkshire Regt, 10th East Yorkshire Regt, 13th East Yorkshire Regt, 12 Yorks Lancs Regt, 231st Battery RGA, 72nd HAY, 42nd HAY, 17 HAY, 151st Battery RGA, 7 South Lancs Regt, 58 HAY, 6 Lincoln Regt, 9th Machine Gun Co, 11 East Lancashire Regt, 19 Div Ammunition Col, 19 Sig Signal Co, 19 DAC Mobile and workshop, 9th Military Police RAHQ, 8th Border Regt, "A" Dane C Battario 105th RFA, 9th Machine Gun Co, 93 Trench HQ, 15 and 31 Div Ammunition Column, 47th Reserve Park ASC, 155th Battery RFA, W.3.G. 87th Div Train. G.N.H.	
COUIN	27 Feb	6.0	Engaged in office routine work. Visited OC 62 Div Sanitary Section with regard to transport, care of sanitation of 19 Div Area, how this section and B 62 Div Sanitary Section are arranged of relief or newly occupied sanitary. Huts. Batham visited. Sanitation in following districts inspected COUIN, CORNEUX, St LEGER, BAYENCOURT, FAMECHON, AUTHIE, SAILLY and THE DELL also following Units, 7th Ammunition Col. 19 and 31 Div Ammunition Cols. 33rd Brigade RFA, 18 Durham Light Inf, 12 East York Regt, 16 West York Regt, 17 th Branch Machine, 170 Suc R.FA, A+C Batt Machine, 85 Dur RFA, 93rd Ste Spelling Park 92, Bee Spelling Point B.C, W Cheshire Regt C.R.E. 35th Division, HQ of 31 Div Train R.A. DA. G.N.H.	

WAR DIARY or INTELLIGENCE SUMMARY

Army Form C. 2118.

Place	Date	Hour	Summary of Events and Information	Remarks and references to Appendices
COUIN	28th Feb		3rd Bss, 302 Perm Constructn Coy R.E. 42nd and 72nd H.A.Gs, 11 East Yorks Regt (148 & 13 Cos), Visitors R.E. and 91st Siege Batt. R.G.A. G.N.A.	
			6 Oxfield A. and C. Machine 170 Battery R.F.A. 19th Div Signal Coy instructors and 9th Yorkshire Regt attended conference of Sanitary Officers at 9a.m. of P.O.M.S.I. info Water Supplies on the former area investigated and samples forwarded to Laboratory. Tonnetables to following Districts inspected — COUIN, COIGNEUX, ST LEGER, BAYENCOURT, FAMECHON, AUTHIE, SAILLY and SAILLY DELL also following Units:– A/81, 19th Brigade R.F.A., M.M. P.19 Division 9th Machine Gun Co. 12 Stab. 48 Heavy Batt. Ammunitn Col. R.G.A. B/81 Brigade R.F.A. 31st Div Ammunitn Col. I Corps Cyclists. A/B 92 Brigade. 231 Battery R.G.A. 10 West Yorkshire Regt. 93 Machine Gun Co. 93 Trench Mortar Batery, 31st Div Mobile Veterinary Section. 19 D.H.Q. Deloviens Point and 31st Div Signal Co.	

G.N. Audram

140/2043

109th to 31st Div. ?
5th Army

36th Sanitary Section

Mar. 1917

COMMITTEE FOR THE
MEDICAL HISTORY OF THE WAR
Date 11 MAY 1917

Army Form C. 2118.

WAR DIARY
INTELLIGENCE SUMMARY

(Erase heading not required.)

Vol 21

War Diary
of
N° 36 Sanitary Section.

From 1st to 31st March 1917

Vol 21

Army Form C. 2118.

WAR DIARY
or
INTELLIGENCE SUMMARY.

(Erase heading not required.)

Instructions regarding War Diaries and Intelligence Summaries are contained in F.S. Regs., Part II. and the Staff Manual respectively. Title pages will be prepared in manuscript.

Place	Date	Hour	Summary of Events and Information	Remarks and references to Appendices
COUIN	1st March		A.C.O. inspected further latrines and billets at COUIN and 10th East Yorkshire Regt at FIR CAMP. Visited A.D.M.S. 3rd Division and proceeded to FAMECHON and inspected HURTBISE FARM with sanitation. 1 FAMECHON, interviewed Town Mayor THIEVRES. Made observations and visited and made and inspected and tested Mr Lee's chlorine Vanulakim; and also inspected COUIN, COIGNEUX, BAYENCOURT, FAMECHON, AUTHIE, ST LEGER, SAILLY and THE DELL, also following units:— Bde R.F.A. H.Q. 93rd Bde Ammunition Dump, 12 New Yorkshire Regt, YMCA, BAYENCOURT, No 3 Bn A.S.C. M.T. Div, 148 Bty R.F.A, 227 Siege Batty, R.G.A, 91st and 220 Ammunition Cols, 33rd Bde signals, 93rd Bde H.Q. 93rd Brigade Trench Mortar, 16th Sudan Light Infantry, 11/16 Heavy Bty Ammunition Col, 13 Bde R.G.A. 58th B.A.C. RE, Transport, 11th York Lancs Regt Transport, 1st W. Yorks Regt, 9th Medium trench M.T. Leicester Batt'y R.E, 17 Med & 12 York Lancs Regt, 152 Aux Bde R.G.A. 112 Brig R.G.A. 11 East Yorks Regt, 10th Hann B.A.C. B. Subsection 23rd Battery R.G.A. and transport lines stand on THE DELL. Buses at SAILLY disinfected. g.m.g.
COUIN	2nd March		A.C.O. inspected sanitation of 1 Bde Brigade R.F.A. engaged in their ambulance work. Moreover 19th Division proceed to visit and inspected and instructed on their duties. Sanitation in training and inspected COUIN, COIGNEUX, BAYENCOURT, FAMECHON, AUTHIE, ST LEGER, SAILLY and THE DELL also following units — 92nd Brigade Pioneers, 504 Remounted R.E, H.Q. 3rd Divn Tran, 111 Battery R.G.A, 10 Field A.R.E, 223 Field A.R.E, 3rd Brigade R.F.A 13th Yorkshire Regt. 93 Brigade H.Q. 211 Field A.R.E. Builts disinfected. g.m.g.

WAR DIARY
INTELLIGENCE SUMMARY.

Army Form C. 2118.

Place	Date	Hour	Summary of Events and Information	Remarks and references to Appendices
COUIN	3rd March		S.O. engaged in preparation of weekly sanitary Report. Inspected BROSSIGNOL FARM and inspected sanitation. Inspected 170th Spare R.F.A. in their Bivouacs at ROSSIGNOL FARM and W. Down. C.R.E. Fatiguemen re-arranging and posted at latrines in area. Sanitation of following districts inspected: COUIN, COIGNEUX, BAYENCOURT, FAMECHON, AUTHIE, ST LEGER SAILLY and THE DELL. Also the following Units: B.13 West York Regt, 10 Battn 17th Bn. R.F.A., 155 Battery R.F.A. H.T. Reserve Brigade 18 Corps Cavalry, 3rd Prov. Brigade 11 East Yorks. Transport, 3rd Bn. East Cape N.4 C.3rd D.A.C. 1/32 and 1/11 Fusrs. 11 West Yorkshire Regt. 77 Light Sign. R.E.A. M.2 Sectn. Ambulance Battn 11 East Yorks Regt 161 Div Signal & 95 Sec. Refilling Point. 97 Div. Refilling Point. 12 K.O.Y.L.I. 92 Inf. Pioneer Bn. 957 C.Q.M.S. R.E. A.D.C. District 165 Bde. R.F.A. 113 Heavy Batt. 20th Ammunition Col. and 220 Battery R.G.A.	
			G.M.R.	
COUIN	4th March		S.O. inspected sanitation of BAYENCOURT and interviewed Town Mayor, inspected cable received by C 6th Border Regt and camp of 1 B.C. 20th Cheshire Regt. also for the latrine at COIGNEUX Ammunition Dump. Water Mahine in area visited and materials inspected for free chlorine. Sanitation of following districts inspected: COUIN, COIGNEUX, BATENCOURT, FAMECHON, AUTHIE, ST LEGER, SAILLY and THE DELL. Also following Units: 1st/3rd and 4th Co. A.S.C. 3rd Divisional Train, Trench To V Corps. 11 East Lancs Regt. 1/2 & 1/1/6 North Lancs. Ordnance Workshop (Right) 97th Machine Gun Co.	

Army Form C. 2118.

WAR DIARY
—OF—
INTELLIGENCE SUMMARY.
(Erase heading not required.)

Instructions regarding War Diaries and Intelligence Summaries are contained in F. S. Regs. Part II. and the Staff Manual respectively. Title pages will be prepared in manuscript.

Place	Date	Hour	Summary of Events and Information	Remarks and references to Appendices
COUIN			H.Q. and 1/73 to 31st Div. Train. 65 Siege Battery R.G.A. 151 West Yorkshire Reg. 12 Yorks Lance Reg. 114 Yorks Lance Regt. and Advanced H.Q. Army 31st Division. G.R.R.	
COUIN	5 March		C.O. inspected sanitation of 17, 32, 41, 42 and 72 Heavy Casualty Units, 152 Siege Battery R.G.A. and 151 West Yorkshire Regt. Nalu Shelves are over-used. Samples of water from ROSSIGNOL WOOD forwarded by O.C. 223 Field C.E. found to be pure in one were Amm. fill encamped. Sanitation in following districts inspected: COUIN, COIGNEUX, BAYENCOURT, FAMECHON, AUTHIE, St LEGER, SAILLY and THE DELL also following Units: 23rd Siege Battery R.G.A. 170 Brigade R.F.A. 118, 9th Light Infantry Brigade B., 2A Signal Co., 92nd Divisional 31st Div. H.Q. 31st Div Workshops, R.Div. 31st Mounted Military Police. R.P. 1/61 31st Div. 88 Div R.F.A. Ammunition Column, 118 31st Div. Train, 118, 169 Siege R.G.A. B Battery 170 Brigade R.F.A. 5 hifs Cyclists, P.C. + D. Battrie. 185 Brigade A.T.C. 118, 71 and 72 Ammunition Columns and P/191 SSE. MSM employed. G.R.R.	
COUIN	6 March		C.O. visited St LEGER and inspected Huts and Latrines of 31st Div Ammunition Column. 65 Siege Battery R.G.A. and 304 Road Construction Co R.E., visited AUTHIE and inspected sanitation of Huts visited FAMECHON and inspected huts of 9 Note Sentry Regt. Nalu Shelves in over-used and notework looked for her children. Sanitation on following districts inspected COUIN, COIGNEUX, BAYENCOURT, FAMECHON, AUTHIE, St LEGER, SAILLY and THE DELL also following Units: H.Q. 165 Brigade R.F.A. and B, D, D & T.I. d. B.S. & T., 13 Yorks Run Pass Regt. 1/1 Scon (ATS) R.E. 18 Durham Light Inf.	

Wt. W.4973/M687 1,500,000 8/16 D'D & L't'd Forms/C.2118/22 A 9434

Army Form C. 2118.

WAR DIARY
or
INTELLIGENCE SUMMARY.
(Erase heading not required.)

Instructions regarding War Diaries and Intelligence Summaries are contained in F. S. Regs., Part II and the Staff Manual respectively. Title pages will be prepared in manuscript.

Place	Date	Hour	Summary of Events and Information	Remarks and references to Appendices
COUIN	7th March		7th Divisional Cavalry, 118 Bde Bde Signal RFA, 3rd DAC, B Battery 86 RFA, 16th Heavy Battery AC, RGA, 111th Battery RGA, 223rd Field Coy RE and 210 Field Coy RE. G.N.A.	
			T.O. visited BAYENCOURT and SAILLY and inspected Waterguards at COIGNEUX near Slashin; visited A.D.M.S. 19th Division at BUS and attended weekly conference at Offices POTONIS II Corps. Held Stables in area visited and ordinances inspected. See below, Sanitation in the following districts inspected. COUIN, COIGNEUX, AUTHIE ST LEGER BAYENCOURT, FAMECHON, SAILLY and THE DELL also the following Units - 377 Road Construction Coy R.E. A Battery 165 Brigade RFA, Transport of 14th Yorks Lancs Regt., Transport of 13th Yorks Lancs Regt. transport of 12 Yorks Lancs Regt. Transport of 11 East Lancs Regt. 1st West Yorks Regt. 93rd Machine Gun Co. D Battery 170th Brigade RFA. 47 Reserve Park A.S.C. 15th Corps Laundry. 30th M.A.C. 6th Base Labour Corps, Br Bocage, G' Nets v Lents Regt 3rd DAC. A Battery 170 Brigade RFA also C Battery. G.N.A.	
COUIN	8th March		T.O. visited BAYENCOURT and inspected 17 West Yorkshire Regt, Incr., Waterguards at SAILLY DELL. Arranged for booking of new waterguards supplied by 31st Division near Stations visited and new guards posted, guards from 19 Division returned to their Division. Sanitation in following districts inspected - COUIN, COIGNEUX, AUTHIE ST LEGER, BAYENCOURT, FAMECHON, SAILLY and THE DELL also following Units.	

WAR DIARY

INTELLIGENCE SUMMARY

Army Form C. 2118.

(Erase heading not required.)

Instructions regarding War Diaries and Intelligence Summaries are contained in F.S. Regs., Part II and the Staff Manual respectively. Title pages will be prepared in manuscript.

Place	Date	Hour	Summary of Events and Information	Remarks and references to Appendices
			6" Lincoln Regt and transfer. 9" Machine Gun Co. 77 and 15th Regt Batter R.G.A. 113 Heavy Battery R.G.A. 181 West Yorks Regt, D Co 11 East Yorks Regt, H.Q. 92 Brigade 28 Battery R.F.A. No 2 Section Anti Aircraft Battery HQ 170 Brigade RFA No 2 Section 37 CMC D Battery 115 Brigade RFA, Pioneer Co 92 Brigade 12 K.O.Y.L.I. 92 and 95 Brigade Signalling Sects. HQ 93 Brigade 93 Machine Gun Co & MCA (BAYENCOURT) 9/Notts & Derby Regt. 46 93rd and 270 Ammunition Column.	E.N.C.
COUIN	9 March		I.O. interviewed Town Major COUIN regarding sanitation of COIGNEUX and conferred with him as to drafts notice for Town Major's weekly conference of district inspectors, invited A.D.M.S. 19 Division and handed in an correspondence relating to reference Sickness concerning Meat Ration. visited A.D.M.S. 3rd Division engaged in preparation of weekly Sanitary Report. Main Station in area visited and materials issued for use chlorine translation in Mayors authorinchemed. COUIN, COIGNEUX, AUTHIE, ST LEGER, BAYENCOURT, FRMECHON, SAILLY and THIEVRES. Also following Units :- H.R. 3 and D Co 11 East Yorks Regt 22 Battery RFA, 170 Brigade RFA, HQ 18 R.F.A. 42 T.M.B. B Battery C/17 FA. HQ 4th SAC, 18 West Yorks Regt 18 West Yorks Regt Machine & SAC and 7 North Lancashire Regt	E.N.C.

WAR DIARY
INTELLIGENCE SUMMARY.
(Erase heading not required.)

Army Form C. 2118.

Place	Date	Hour	Summary of Events and Information	Remarks and references to Appendices
COUIN	10th March		G.O. visited AUTHIE and inspected 7 Bn. Laundry and 6/ador. Bath, and general sanitation. Portage visited FAMECHON and inspected Baths, sanitation and Latrines of 9 N.F. and N.F. Regt. Main Clothes washed in area Sanitation & Showers, Clothes Inspected. COUIN, COIGNEUX, AUTHIE, SOUASTRE, FAMECHON, BAYENCOURT, SAILLY and THE DELL also following units – 6/Lincoln Regt. and Transport lines, 94th Co. 31st Divn. Train, B Battery 170th Brigade R.F.A., R.B.O.S. 72 Siege 13th East Yorks Regt. H.Q. 170 Brigade R.F.A. 6/adour. Bearers R.E. 93rd Ammunition Col. 11 Divn. (A.T.C.) R.E. 3rd Divl. Ammunition Column. 9/N.F., N.F.R. Dept. 31st/59th DADOS 7 East Lancs Regt. and 18 War Machine Regt.	T.N.A.
COUIN	11th March		G.O. investigated water supply at advanced H.Q. 92nd Infantry Brigade at ROSSIGNOL WOOD, and sample boiled for known etc. Sanitation of following districts inspected – COUIN, COIGNEUX, AUTHIE, SOUASTRE, FAMECHON, BAYENCOURT, SAILLY and THE DELL also the following units, Hnsd. 91st Siege Batt. R.G.A. 3rd Div. Goal Bump. 15 West Yorks Regt. 94th Co. A.S.C. 31st Divn. 46th 77th and 79th Ammunition Columns 93rd Brigade H.Q., 211 Field Co. R.E. 18 West Yorks Regt. D 170 Brigade R.F.A. 93rd Machine Gun Co. 93rd Brigade Hd. Qtrs. No 3 Co. A.S.C. 31st Divn. 171st 32nd and 58th Army Artillery Groups. 154 Siege Battery R.G.A., Hand C Batteries 170th Brigade PR.F.A., H.Q. 31st Divn. and 31st Div. H.Q.	T.N.A.

WAR DIARY
of
INTELLIGENCE-SUMMARY

Army Form C. 2118.

Place	Date	Hour	Summary of Events and Information	Remarks and references to Appendices
COUIN	12th March		G.O.C. visited Sanctuary Officer 46th Division at HENU and interviewed Acting A.D.M.S. 46th Division. Proceeded to SOUASTRE and inspected camps with Sanitary Officer 46th Division; interviewed A.D.M.S. 3rd Division; inspected line of 1st West Yorks Regt and lines vacated by D Battery 170 Brigade R.F.A. Proceeded to St LEGER transport lines of D Battery 165 Brigade R.F.A. but times had moved again. Motor transport an area visited and inspected; return for the chlorine fountain in following districts — COUIN, COIGNEUX, AUTHIE, St LEGER, BAYENCOURT, FAMECHON, SAILLY and THE DELL also following units — 91st, 139th, 202nd and 270th Ammunition Column. 11 Divl Signal Co. 47 Reserve Park A.S.C. XIII Corps Cavalry, B Battery 81 R.F.A. Brigade, 6 North Staffs Regt, Nos 136, 137 Machine Gun & Nos 136, 137 Brigade 3rd Divl Ammunition Sump, XIII Corps Cyclists, No 2 Section, 3rd Divl Ammunition Column, 97 Siege Battery R.G.A, 1st Durham Light Inf, 13 East Yorks Regt, H.Q. 92 Brigade Howitzer 170 Brigade R.F.A. H.Q. 81 Section Anti-Aircraft Battery. 3rd Divl Anti Gas Cohort, Annex Army Inst.

E.P.A. |
| COUIN | 13th March | | G.O.C. visited SAILLY DELL and COIGNEUX; interviewed O.C. S.B.J./A.T.(3.) R.E. regarding constructor. | latrine, interviewed O.C. 95 Field Ambulance; inspected billet portion with man accompanied by O.C. 15 West Yorks Regt; inspected 18 Durham Light Inf at SAILLY DELL also 1 ½ HALL and O.C.A.O.H Camp, bodyguards in area withdrawn arms; took guards supplied by 4th Inf Brigade. Station |

WAR DIARY
INTELLIGENCE SUMMARY
(Erase heading not required.)

Army Form C. 2118.

Place	Date	Hour	Summary of Events and Information	Remarks and references to Appendices
			posted and guards posted. Visitation in following districts inspected – COUIN, COIGNEUX, AUTHIE, ST LEGER, BAYENCOURT, PAMECHON, SAILLY and THE DELL also the following Units – 4/8", 7/7", 7/9" and 23rd Ammunition Columns. 30th Motor Ambulance Convoy, 6 Labour Batt. R.E. X Corps Troops Coy, 13, 18 RFA Brigade and Ammunition Column. H.Q. 3rd D.A.C. 14th Yorks & Lancs Regt. 12th Yorks & Lancs Regt, 13th East Lancs Regt 15th West Yorks Regt. 14th & 6th A.S.C. 3rd & 5th 3rd Divl Signal Co. 6th, 3rd Divl Train 11th West Yorks Regt Transport, 11th East Yorks Regt Transport, 12th East Yorks Regt Transport, 92nd Machine Gun Co. Transport. G.N.A.	
COUIN	14th March		6.0 inspected ACACIA CAMP, SAILLY DELL also Gas tanks in command of B. Johnston M. H. Sgt Ammunition Columns on STLEGER, attended weekly conference at Offices of 3 D.M.S. X Corps. ACHEUX. Works carefully at ROSSIGNOL WOOD selected and supplies investigated. Sanitation in following districts inspected – COUIN, COIGNEUX, AUTHIE, ST LEGER, PAMECHON, BAYENCOURT, SAILLY, THE DELL and HEBUTERNE also following Units – #8, 3rd Divl Train, 6th Lincoln Regt, 113th Heavy Battery R.G.A. A'Down E Battery 23rd Brigade R.F.A. 111 Heavy Battery R.G.A. 223 Field C. R.E. 3rd Divl R.E. Store Transport & 15 West Yorks Regt. HQ R.E. 11th Brown. 77 Siege Battery R.G.A. 18 West Yorks Regt. G.N.A.	

WAR DIARY
INTELLIGENCE SUMMARY.

Army Form C. 2118.

Place	Date	Hour	Summary of Events and Information	Remarks and references to Appendices
COUIN	15th March		C.O. inspected sanitation of SAILLY also examined site for new manure dump. Interviewed Town Mayor regarding provision of latrines and fatigue parties. Inspected 92nd Brigade HB. Interviewed Town Mayor BAYENCOURT also Staff Capt. 173 Brigade and inspected parties taken in cmn [common] / sanatation at COIGNEUX. Nath Station moved and sanitical inspected and tested for buckthorne. Sanatation / Latrines. districts inspected - COUIN. COIGNEUX. AUTHIE. ST LEGER. FAMECHON. BAYENCOURT. SAILLY and THE DELL also following Units:- 16 West Yorks Regt. 6 South Staff Regt. 137 Brigade HB. S. Frak Staff Regt. H.B. 4th D.Y.L.I. 92 Brigade Runners, 30 Division Signallers, 1st Cheshire Labour Batt. D.H.Q. & C.R.E. 137 Machine Gun Co. Canadian Railway Engineers. 192 Tech. Co. and B Sections 3rd Sect. B. Battery 88 A.F.A. Brigade. A Ammunition Column. 31st Kite Balloon Section. H.Q. 170 Brigade R.F.A. 88 Section Auth Aircraft Battery. Transport / M.T. 12", 18" and 13" East Yorks Regt.	G.R.A.
COUIN	16 March		C.O. visited SAILLY DELL and inspected 231 May Battery R.G.A. and Auth Aircraft Battery & H.B. 173 Brigade. Interviewed Town Mayor BAYENCOURT. Engaged in weekly sanitary report. Rath. Station marks and cart stores tr / fri chlorine. Sanatation / Latrines districts inspected - COUIN. COIGNEUX. AUTHIE. ST LEGER. FAMECHON. BAYENCOURT. SAILLY and THE DELL also following Units:- 137 Brigade HB. 6 Lincoln Regt. 17, 72 and 42 MGC's 170 Brigade R.F.A. H.B. 92 Brigade H.B. 113 Heavy Battery R.G.A.	

WAR DIARY
INTELLIGENCE SUMMARY

Army Form C. 2118.

Place	Date	Hour	Summary of Events and Information	Remarks and references to Appendices
COUIN	17ᵗʰ March		C.O. inspected camp of Nalignard at COUIN also FIR TREE Camp; enquired in ordinary report that water approved. Water Station visited and cart water for free chlorine. Examination of following units inspected: COUIN, COIGNEUX, AUTHIE, SAILEGER, PAMECHON, BAYENCOURT, SAILLY and THE DELL also following Units, 169 Divison M.D., A.C. & D. Batiene 81 A.F.A. Brigade, 117 Ammunition Column & South Staff Regt, Unit Regt, 5 South Staff Regt, 137 Brigade H.Q., 16 West York Regt, 148, 3ʳᵈ D.A.C., 3ʳᵈ North Midland Field Ambulance, C.R.E., 65 Siege Battery R.G.A. 46 Ammunition Column, 7 Ny & KSLI Regt, 62 Trench Mortar Battery, 47 Reserve Park A.D.C. 31ˢᵗ D.A.B., R.A.M.C., 93 Squadron Transport, 16ᵗʰ Lancers Regt 17 and 32 M.H. 111 Heavy Battery R.G.A., 77 Siege Battery R.G.A. 111 Heavy Battery A.C. 13 West York Regt, 251 Siege Battery R.G.A. and 92 Brigade H.Q. L.M.O.	
COUIN	18ᵗʰ March		C.O. inspected 17 and 32 M.H., 77 Siege Battery R.G.A. magazine, 111 Heavy Battery R.G.A. Transport lines of 10/11/12 and 13 West York Regt, 12 K.O.Y.L.I. and 92 Machine Gun Co; visited AUTHIE and inspected 30 Motor Ambulance Convoy, visited PAMECHON and inspected Ammunition Column. Water Station visited and cart water tested for free chlorine. Sanitation in following Units inspected: COUIN, COIGNEUX, AUTHIE, SAILEGER, BAYENCOURT, PAMECHON, SAILLY and THE DELL also following Units - 16 West York Regt, 18 Durham Light Inf., 5 South Staff Regt.	

WAR DIARY
INTELLIGENCE-SUMMARY.
(Erase heading not required.)

Army Form C. 2118.

Place	Date	Hour	Summary of Events and Information	Remarks and references to Appendices
COVIN	19 March		137 Lincs Motor Battery. 6" Lincoln Regt. 4/8 3rd DAC 58 7 Devon (A.T.C.) R.E. 6" Labour Batt" R.E. N° 4 & 31st Div. Train and 15" East Yorks Regt. G.R.A.	
COVIN	19 March		A.D.M.S. inspected transport lines of 6" Lincoln Regt in COVIN-STEGER Road also 13 Battery 86 A.F.A. Brigade. STEGER, Canadian Railway Co and 70 Cheshire Labour Batt" went to Labour Batt" Water Station and cart holes for hucktorns. Sanitation in following checked COVIN. COIGNEUX, AUTHIE. STEGER. BAYENCOURT, FAMECHON, S'AILLY. THE DELL and HEBUTERNE also following Units. 11" East Lancs Regt, 94" Brigade H.Q. 93" Brigade H.Q. 31st Div. Mobile Veterinary Section, No Section 31st DAC. B" Echelon 31st DAC. B" 8th Brigade. A.F.A. 12 K.O.Y.L.I. Regt 12" East Yorkshire Regt 92" Brigade Reserve Co 12,13" and 14" Yorks — Lancs Regt transport 11" East Lancs Regt transport. G.M.A.	
COVIN	20" March		G.O.C. inspected 16 HEBUTERNE and inspected general sanitation of village existing vats for erection of manure also interviewed M.O. 1" Monmouth Regt and inspected Baths occupied by this Unit. Inspected temporary bath erected in mot mobile station and made arrangement for the station of N.C.O and two men and stalls infront of HEBUTERNE. Water supplement [illegible]. Sanitation in following orchards inspected.	

WAR DIARY
INTELLIGENCE SUMMARY

Army Form C. 2118.

Place	Date	Hour	Summary of Events and Information	Remarks and references to Appendices
			COUIN, COIGNEUX, AUTHIE, ST LEGER, BAYENCOURT, FAMECHON, SAILLY, THE DELL, and HEBUTERNE also following Units - 3rd A.A. Rest Office H.Q. 91st B.G.C., H.Q. C. 91st Div Train, 5th Army Workshop Co., 231st Brigade R.F.A. 113 Battery R.G.A. 12 K.O.Y.L.I. Regt. 77th + 79 Ammunition Columns. 91st and 220th Ammunition Columns, 92 Brigade H.Q. 47 Reserve Park A.S.C. 223 Field C.R.E. 111th Battery C.R.A. 31st Div Ammunition Repairing Point & Corps Eyebath M.C. Section 91st R.G.C. 169 Brigade H.Q. C1 Battery R.F.A. Brigade	
COUIN	21st March		C.D. inspected 92nd Brigade H.Q. and ROSSIGNOL FARM; attended conference of Sanitary Officers at 1/2 Divn. & Corps. Water station in area visited and inspected. Sanitation in following stations inspected - COUIN, COIGNEUX, AUTHIE, ST LEGER, FAMECHON, BAYENCOURT, SAILLY. THE DELL and HEBUTERNE also following Units - 3rd Bart Veterinary Section, 23rd Div Refilling Point, and Dump. Water Square R.E. 1/1st Cheshire Fatigue Rests. Canadian Railway Engineers. A.D. and H.Q. 86 A.F.A. Brigade. 92nd Brigade Pioneers. D. Battery, 231st Brigade R.F.A. b'Ivine Rests Regt. S. Manure Trade Rest. 113 Battery R. 91. 220th and 91st Ammunition Columns	G.M.
COUIN	22nd March		C.D. conferred 15 billets with Influenza. Water supplies in found are investigated. Sanitation in following stations inspected - COUIN, COIGNEUX, AUTHIE, ST LEGER, BAYENCOURT, FAMECHON, SAILLY	

WAR DIARY
INTELLIGENCE SUMMARY.
(Erase heading not required.)

Army Form C. 2118.

Place	Date	Hour	Summary of Events and Information	Remarks and references to Appendices
			THE DELL and HEBUTERNE also following Units:- 6" Border Regt Transport, 117 Ammunition Column B Battery 230 Brigade R.F.A. 220 Ammunition Column 468 C/R.E. 466 C/R.E. Transport, H.Q. 129 Infantry Brigade, S. Sherwood Forest Regt 113 Battery R.G.A. 4.6 C/H.B. Machine Police 4.6 Div. 4.6 Div. Signals. H.Q. 4.6 Div R.A. [signed]	
COUIN	23rd March		C.O. engaged with district inspection as to sanitation in area. Water supplies in forward area noted and main stations visited. Sanitation in following district inspected:- COUIN, COIGNEUX, AUTHIE, ST LEGER, BAYENCOURT, FAMECHON, SAILLY, THE DELL and HEBUTERNE also following Units:- B Battery 23rd Brigade R.F.A. 8" MTR Heavy Regt, 189 Machine Gun Co. 4.6 Div Training School, H.Q. 139 Brigade, 468 C/R.E. 466 C/R.E. 6" Inch Staffs Regt Transport Train B. Battery 230 Brigade R.F.A. Transport 139 Trench Mortar Co. Transport 1.5 Mortar [signed]	
COUIN	24th March		C.O. engaged in office routine and preparation of Weekly and Monthly Sanitary Report. Water stations in area visited and inspected. Water supplies in forward area investigated. Sanitation in following districts inspected:- COUIN, COIGNEUX, AUTHIE, ST LEGER, BAYENCOURT, FAMECHON, SAILLY, THE DELL, HEBUTERNE and BUCQUOY also Units in occupation of these districts. The districts of COUIN, ST LEGER, and AUTHIE taken over from the Units by 7th Sanitary Section. Water supplies - D Battery 230 Brigade R.F.A. 6" Border Regt 4.6 Div Artillery. [signed]	

WAR DIARY
or
INTELLIGENCE SUMMARY.
(Erase heading not required.)

Army Form C. 2118.

Instructions regarding War Diaries and Intelligence Summaries are contained in F. S. Regs., Part II. and the Staff Manual respectively. Title pages will be prepared in manuscript.

Place	Date	Hour	Summary of Events and Information	Remarks and references to Appendices
COUIN	25th March		C.O. inspected Field Ambulance site on SOUASTRE ROAD and reported on same 10-30 a.m. E Enfr. Main Shelters in area visited. Main supplies in forward area investigated. Sanitation of following districts inspected - COIGNEUX, BAYENCOURT, FAMECHON, SAILLY, THE DELL, HEBUTERNE and BUCQUOY also names work in reciprocation / area - 567 (?) Berm (A.T.Co) R.E., A.B.C.D. Batteries 156, 86 A.F.A. Brigade, 230 Siege Battery, R.G.A. 370 Siege Battery R.G.A. The FAMECHON district taken over from section by 71st Sanitary Section. G.R.R.	
COUIN	26th March		C.O. inspected camps vacated by E. Battery 86th A.F.A. Brigade and camps at BAYENCOURT and COIGNEUX evacuated by troops inspected by John Ross R.E. Main Shelters in area visited and inspected. Main supplies in forward area investigated. Sanitation in the following districts inspected - COIGNEUX, BAYENCOURT, SAILLY, THE DELL, HEBUTERNE, BUCQUOY and ABLAINZEVELLE Also names work in reciprocation / area - 1st (A Barrel D) Battery - 30th Brigade R.F.A. and Kinetons, Canadian Railway Engineer, 4-6 Div. Ammunition Refilling Point, 111 Heavy Battery R.G.A. C.O. attended sick men of 317th Field Ambulance. C.R.E. were being in M.B. vicinity. G.R.R.	
COUIN	27th March		C.O. inspected sanitation of COUIN and superintended cleaning up of Shelters and billets	

WAR DIARY
INTELLIGENCE SUMMARY
(Erase heading not required.)

Army Form C. 2118.

Instructions regarding War Diaries and Intelligence Summaries are contained in F. S. Regs., Part II. and the Staff Manual respectively. Title pages will be prepared in manuscript.

Place	Date	Hour	Summary of Events and Information	Remarks and references to Appendices
			Fatigue parties engaged in wire work. M.O. also supervised cleaning up of Field Ambulance Rest Station. Water stations in area visited and inspected. Water supplies in forward area investigated. Sanitation of following districts inspected. COUIN, COIGNEUX, BAYENCOURT, SAILLY, THE DELL, HEBUTERNE, BUCQUOY and ABLAINZEVELLE also following units - 233rd Siege Battery R.G.A., 77' Siege Battery R.G.A., 198 Siege Battery R.G.A., D Battery 86" A.F.A. Brigade. 70" Chester Labour Batt. 42nd Batt. 17 Heavy Battery R.G.A., 72° Batty, 2nd Queens Regt, 58, 25, 12 and 81st Brigades R.F.A. G.M.L	
COUIN	28 March		M.O. visited COIGNEUX and gave certificate to O.C. B. Co. 6 Labour Batt R.E. that camp has been left in satisfactory condition; superintended cleaning up of Chateau at COUIN and Field Ambulance site on SOUASTRE ROAD; attended sick of Local Units no other M.O. being in the locality. Fatigue parties at COUIN superintended. Water supplies in forward area investigated. Water Stations in area visited and inspected. Sanitation in following districts inspected. COUIN, COIGNEUX, BAYENCOURT, SAILLY, THE DELL, HEBUTERNE, BUCQUOY and ABLAINZEVELLE also Units in occupation of area. G.M.L	

WAR DIARY
INTELLIGENCE SUMMARY.
(Erase heading not required.)

Army Form C. 2118.

Place	Date	Hour	Summary of Events and Information	Remarks and references to Appendices
COUIN	29th March		C.O. superintended clearing up of Field Ambulance area at COUIN and general sanitation of village. Interviewed D.D.M.S. V Corps and made arrangements for move forward to BUCQUOY. Attended sick of local Units as there M.O. being on the locality. Water supplies in forward area investigated. Water stations visited and inspected. Sanitation of following districts inspected, COIGNEUX, BAYENCOURT, SAILLY, THE DELL, HEBUTERNE, BUCQUOY and A-B LAINZEVELLE also the various Units in occupation. Fatigue parties at COUIN superintendent. G.W.	
COUIN	30th March		C.O. visited BUCQUOY and arranged as to billets for Section. Part of Sections equipment and stores moved to BUCQUOY together with escort of personnel. Water supplies in new area investigated and tabulated. Sanitation of following districts inspected – COIGNEUX, BAYENCOURT, SAILLY, THE DELL, HEBUTERNE, BUCQUOY and A-BLAINZEVELLE also the Units in occupation of area. G.W.	
COUIN BUCQUOY	31st March		Move of Unit from COUIN to BUCQUOY completed. C.O. arranged for distribution of personnel in new area and for sanitary measures to be adopted. Water supplies investigated in new area and tabulated. Sanitation in following districts inspected – COIGNEUX, BAYENCOURT, SAILLY, THE DELL, HEBUTERNE and BUCQUOY also Units in occupation. Waterparties supplied by 31st Division returned to Parthenope for dispatch to Rennes. A.W. Anderson Capt. R.A.M.C.	

www.ingramcontent.com/pod-product-compliance
Lightning Source LLC
Chambersburg PA
CBHW080634010526
44108CB00054B/2361